Third World Politics

Third World Politics

A Concise Introduction

Jeff Haynes

BLACKWELL
Oxford UK & Cambridge USA

First published 1996

2 4 6 8 10 9 7 5 3 1

Blackwell Publishers Ltd
108 Cowley Road
Oxford OX4 1JF, UK

Blackwell Publishers Inc
238 Main Street
Cambridge, Massachusetts 02142,
USA

British Library Cataloguing in Publication Data

A CIP catalogue record for this book is available from the British Library.

Library of Congress Cataloging-in-Publication Data

Library of Congress data is available.

ISBN 0–631–19777–X
ISBN 0–631–19778–8 (pbk)

Typeset in 10½ on 12½pt Souvenir
by Photoprint, Torquay, Devon
Printed in Great Britain by Hartnolls Limited, Bodmin, Cornwall

This book is printed on acid-free paper.

Contents

Contents

Tables

1

Introduction

The aim of *Third World Politics: A Concise Introduction* is to present an analysis of politics in the contemporary Third World, with particular emphasis on the post-Cold War 1990s. 'Politics' is a term with a great deal of resonance and with wider connotations, I believe, than a 'standard' comparative politics approach would allow. A 'standard' comparative politics approach to Third World politics would be primarily concerned with such issues as the political effects of 'the heritage of the past' (i.e. the colonial era), the relationship between state and society, legislatures and political parties, citizens' formal participation in politics, the role of the military in politics, and, perhaps, revolution.

Where I diverge from such an approach is in seeing politics in the contemporary Third World as the result of the interaction of both *internal* and *external* factors, rather than as the result of domestic developments alone. The influence of external factors is pronounced in the 1990s, as a result of the startling changes that have taken place in world politics in recent years, especially the end of the Cold War in 1989 and the demise of the Soviet Union two years later.

I seek to provide an examination and analysis of what seem to me to be the most important political issues in the Third World at the present time: the striving for democracy, the political consequences of economic growth and development (or the lack of them), the struggle for religious and ethnic minorities', women's and human rights, and the politics of the protection of the natural environment (Beck 1994: 16–23).

These topics have been selected for three reasons. First, after 15 years of study of Third World politics, they appear to me to be crucial to understanding the situation in the 1990s. Second, most of the main topics of the book were the focus of international conferences in the 1990s under the auspices of the United Nations, including: the natural environment (Rio de Janeiro, 1992), human rights (Vienna, 1992), social and economic development (Copenhagen, 1995) and women's rights (Beijing, 1995). These conferences were the result, in part, of pressure on national governments and the United Nations from citizens' groups and non-governmental organizations. In other words, the subject-matter of the conferences reflect what people and organizations around the globe – including the Third World – believe are important to them in the 1990s. Finally, the topics chosen for analysis in this book reflect what many other students of Third World politics believe are important at the current time, as a perusal of the Bibliography will indicate. In order to illustrate the importance of these issues throughout the Third World, and to compare and contrast political developments on a regional basis, chapters will focus on five Third World regions: Latin America and the Caribbean, South Asia, East and South-east Asia, the Middle East and North Africa, and sub-Saharan Africa.[1]

I do not attempt to develop a new explanatory paradigm in respect of contemporary Third World politics, beyond emphasizing the interaction of domestic and external factors – which is hardly novel! Despite my own temerity in failing to present an explanatory paradigm not all have been so reticent. From the late 1950s until quite recently, theorizing about Third World politics was dominated by two broad schools of analysis: developmental and dependency theory. While this book's analysis is not overburdened with theory,[2] it is, however, important for the reader to be aware of how these traditionally influential explanatory paradigms sought to explain politics in the Third World. Comparing, contrasting and criticizing the paradigms will provide us with an adequate theoretical framework for the book's concerns. A focus on issues under-analysed in the traditional approaches – such as human and women's rights and the politics of the natural environment – will enable us to appreciate how the subject-matter of Third World politics has developed in recent years.

Having explained what we will be concerned with in the book and why, the remainder of this introductory chapter focuses on a number of issues which are important to give the necessary background and historical knowledge to understand politics in the Third World in the 1990s. First, I define what I mean by the term 'Third World'. Second, I introduce the assumptions of developmental and dependency theory, in order to highlight the differences between them. Finally, in setting out the book's structure, I briefly introduce the concepts and issues addressed in later chapters.

What is the Third World?

One fundamental aspect of what might be called 'Third World-ness' is that virtually all countries which are conventionally placed in this category were, at one historical period or another, a colonial possession of a foreign power. Beginning in Latin America[3] in the early nineteenth century, the decolonization trend quickened after World War II. Dozens of former colonies in Africa, Asia, the Caribbean and the Middle East gained political independence after 1945. Alfred Sauvy, a French economist and demographer, was probably the first to use the term 'Third World', in an article published in 1952. By the late 1950s it was beginning to be widely recognized that there was a need for a term to describe the emerging states regarded by many as qualitatively different from the older countries of Europe and North America. As Randall and Theobald (1985: vii) note, 'Western political scientists found themselves increasingly challenged to develop frameworks for understanding and predicting the politics of [the] new . . . states.'

'Third World' is a useful shorthand term to refer to what is now a group of more than 120 countries, i.e. at least two-thirds of the world's total. It should be noted, however, that the term 'Third World' has only limited uses analytically. Certainly, the vast majority of Third World countries were at one time or another colonies of a few countries, including Belgium, Britain, France, Japan, the Netherlands, Portugal, Spain and the United States. Yet, there are important economic and political differences between them. For example, economically diverse states such as the United Arab Emirates (gross national product (GNP) per capita, $21,430[4] in 1993), South Korea ($7,660) and Mozambique ($90), politically singular countries such as Cuba (Communist one-party rule), Nigeria (military dictatorship), India (multi-party democracy) and Iran and Saudi Arabia, both theocracies,[5] are uniformly perceived as belonging to the Third World. In short, there are significant political, economic and religious differences between Third World countries. What, then, do they have in common apart from the fact that nearly all are former colonies?

The term 'Third World' has both political and socio-economic connotations. In a political sense it refers to countries which have generally played only a relatively minor role in international relations over the last few decades, especially during the Cold War (1945–89), when international politics was dominated by the superpowers, the United States and the Soviet Union. During this time, Third World states were defined essentially by their position in the situation of superpower rivalry, implying for some a 'positive neutralism' in the context of the superpower imbroglio. In a second, *socio-economic* sense the Third World category refers to countries which generally, although not uniformly, failed fully to develop economically after independence.

If the countries of the Third World were partly defined by their relations with the superpowers during the Cold War, then it should follow that in the *post*-Cold War era their status would change. In this regard, Bayart (1991) asserts that the Third World no longer exists: he argues that it is a 'fantasy' with no analytical and conceptual utility. Berger (1994) agrees that we should no longer use the term, as the concept of the 'Third World', he argues, has become meaningless. He makes the point that because many Western industrialized countries feature so-called underclasses who live in what are essentially Third World conditions, and because Third World political and economic elites are increasingly integrated into an international class structure, then the term is without validity, because it does not signify anything; in a sense we are all Third – or First – World now. While having sympathy for Bayart's and Berger's views, I do not believe that the term 'Third World' has outlived its analytical usefulness, for two main reasons: one to do with *economic development*, the other to do with the construction of *nation*-states.

All Third World countries share two basic problems: one is essentially socio-political, the other intrinsically economic. From a socio-political perspective, the vast majority of 'third world' governments are faced with the difficult problem of needing to *create*, often from scratch, a *nation*-state from often diverse congeries of peoples. A second, economic problem is the need to build up national income, often from comparatively low levels at the time of independence, in order to develop a country's productive capacities (Hawthorn 1991). In short, the fact that all Third World states face two similar problems, how to develop economically and how to build nation-states, sets them apart from the former Communist countries of Eastern Europe as well as the industrial democracies of the West.

While the blanket term 'Third World' obscures often considerable cultural, economic, social and political differences in individual states, it has advantages over common alternatives like 'the South' or 'developing countries'. The expression 'the South' is essentially a geographic expression, which ignores the fact that some 'Western' countries – Japan, Australia, New Zealand – are in the geographical south. The idea of the 'South' does, however, have the advantage of getting away from the connotation of developing towards some pre-ordained end state or goal which is explicit in the idea of '*developing* countries'. It is by no means clear, however, what the idea of a 'developed' state looks like. Does it connote only a certain (high) degree of economic growth, or is there an element of redistribution of the fruits of growth involved? What of widely divergent social conditions in a 'developed' country? Because of the problems linked to alternatives, I will use the term 'Third World' in this book.

What characterizes the contemporary Third World is what many of its states *lack*: satisfactory, sustained levels of economic growth; real, as opposed to cosmetic, governmental concern with redistribution of wealth to allay poverty; democratic politics characterized by the regular election of representative governments; satisfactory standards of human rights; an equal position for women with men in politics and development; sustained concern with protection of the natural environment; and, finally, adequate standards of education and literacy.

This is *not* to assert that *no* Third World peoples and states enjoy democracy, care about the environment, have acceptable levels of human rights and literacy, and so on. It is rather to make the point that what links the vast majority of Third World countries is an absence of one or more of these attributes, characteristics which Western industrial democracies (albeit imperfectly) and former Eastern European Communist countries (more imperfectly still) share. The embedding of these issues in Third World political agendas in the 1990s, however, impels a rethinking of what the important issues of politics are. The concerns of the traditional approaches to analysing Third World politics – developmentalism and development theory – are rather limited, focusing upon general issues of political and economic development. We need to be aware of the concerns – and drawbacks – of the traditional approaches to understanding Third World politics, so that we can appreciate the importance of the new issues which have emerged.

Developmental and Dependency Theories

The natural environment, human rights, gender, democracy, economic development and the problems of identity during modernization are all high on the global political agenda in the 1990s. Traditional analyses of Third World politics focus, rather narrowly, on why most Third World countries are economically underdeveloped and/or not democratic.

Developmental theory

Decolonization and the resulting dozens of new countries introduced a qualitatively new concern – 'development' – to the study of politics after World War II. Before then there had been a handful of colonial countries and a large number of colonized areas. The colonizers were not especially interested in the nature and characteristics of the areas that they ruled, despite the diversity of cultures; what they wanted was as far as possible acquiescence to their rule from the indigenous people of their colonies and the maximization of economic gains.

After the war, everything changed. The rise of the United States as a superpower after 1945 resulted in a much greater official American interest in the emerging Third World. American social scientists were encouraged, often through direct government funding, to develop an interest in the new countries, increasingly a target of US foreign policy concerns, as a result of the Cold War with the Soviet Union. Yet, as Randall and Theobald (1985: 12–13) explain, there was probably less urgency on political scientists than on 'sociologists and economists because of the early prevailing assumption . . . of a relatively unproblematic chain of causation from cultural modernization to economic development to democracy'. Perceived shared characteristics, including poverty, technological backwardness, and a preponderance of 'tradition' over 'modernity', combined in a general state of what would now be called 'underdevelopment' in Third World countries; assumed similarities between them were thought to be of far greater analytical salience than were any differences.

For some, it was a simple task to trace the development of societies in an undifferentiated chain of cause and effect towards a state of 'modernization' thought to have reached its apogee in the liberal democracies of Western Europe and the United States. The concerns of developmentalism encompass two main emphases. The first is that governments of Third World states are interested in increasing their countries' wealth by enlarging their productive capacities. A second emphasis, related to the first, involves increasing differentiation and complexity in available roles in developing societies. One of the most influential accounts of the problems and probability of Third World development, written from a developmentalism perspective, was *The Stages of Economic Growth: A Non-Communist Manifesto*, published in 1959 by the American economic historian Walt Rostow. Because of the importance of Rostow's work to developmentalism theory, I shall examine his approach and assumptions.

Rostow helped to popularize the idea of a 'take-off' into self-sustaining economic growth as the key stage of the development process. His theory of economic growth is based upon the concept of a five-stage process through which, he argued, all developing societies *must* pass, in order to attain the 'promised land' of a stable liberal democratic system along the lines of those of the United States or Britain. The first is the *traditional stage*. At this point it is very difficult to expand production beyond a limited ceiling, because of the existence of a pre-Newtonian science and technology, a fundamentally agricultural economy, and a rigid, hierarchical social structure.

The second stage, *pre-conditions for take-off*, is triggered by some kind of external impulse (although Rostow is vague about specifying precisely which), manifested in changes which begin across a whole range of institutions. The appropriate pre-conditions emerged in Western Europe 'when the insights of modern science began to be translated into both agricultural and industrial production' (Randall and Theobald 1985: 19–20). At this juncture the economy becomes less self-sufficient and localized, as trade and improved communications facilitate the growth of both national and international economies. These processes are socially and politically related to the emergence of an elite group, able and willing to invest wealth, rather than use it solely for immediate personal consumption. These developments gradually proceed until the threshold of the third stage, *take-off*, is attained. Two characteristics of this stage are crucial. First, investment as a proportion of national income rises to at least 10 per cent, thus ensuring both that increases in per capita output outstrip population growth and that industrial output increases appreciably. Second, as a result, political and social institutions are reshaped in order to permit the pursuit of growth to take root. The take-off stage lasts, typically, about 20 years. Rostow attempted to date the take-off of the countries which, when he was writing, had reached that stage: Britain (1783–1803), the United States (1843–60), Japan (1878–1900), Russia (1890–1914), and India and China (from 1950).

The last two stages of Rostow's putative scenario can be dealt with briefly. By definition, any society that reaches such a position is no longer underdeveloped. Stage four is the *drive to maturity*, a period of consolidation. By this time, modern science and technology are extended to most if not all branches of the economy, thus acquiring a wide range of leading sectors. The rate of investment remains high, at between 10 and 20 per cent of national income. Political reform continues, and the economy is able to compete internationally. The conclusion of the five-stage development process is reached in the age of mass consumption, which involves further consolidation and advance. Such is the productive power of the society by this stage that three broad strategic choices of orientation are available. Wealth can be concentrated in individual consumption, as in the United States; channelled into a welfare state, as in Western Europe; or used to build up global power and influence, as in the former Soviet Union (Foster-Carter 1985: 104).

An important feature of Rostow's development scenario is that, whereas for the agriculturally based societies of the Third World the initial stimulus to modernization arrives from outside, through the example set by the industrialized countries, the basic problem for them of taking off is totally *internal* to the economies concerned (Randall and Theobald 1985: 21). Essentially the problem is to produce enough individuals with entrepreneurial abilities. This is in line with, and inspired by, Max Weber's analysis that there was something unique about the development of Protestantism in north-west Europe which led to the evolution of capitalism.

Rostow's five-stage programme for development, and the

developmentalism approach more generally, has been criticized on a number of grounds. First, it fails to stress the political and economic diversity of Third World countries, a diversity which makes comparative analysis of development along a single trajectory highly problematic. Second, it fails to emphasize inter- as well as intra-societal connections – i.e. relationships *between* as well as *within* societies – especially those between the industrially developed countries and the Third World. Third, there is a general failure to analyse the role of cultural factors in the development process, an astounding omission given the cultural diversity of the Third World.

Dependency theory: explanation for the failure of 'take-off'

Dependency theory[6] emerged in the late 1960s to question developmentalism's assumptions about Third World development. It suggested that the *nature of the structure* of the international state and economic systems would preclude Third World development along the lines Rostow predicted. Dependency theory has at its core the denial of both the possibility of development and of the salience of developmentalism. Leading scholars of the dependency tradition, such as André Gunder Frank (1971), writing about Latin America, and Samir Amin (1987) and the late Walter Rodney (1972), concerned with Africa, argue that Western development was possible *only* as a result of the creation of a capitalist world economy, the central mechanism for exploiting non-Western areas and preventing them from developing, thus ensuring they remained economically 'underdeveloped'.

Dependency theory starts from the assumption that the world economy has been capitalist since the sixteenth century. The world economy is divided into 'core' (industrially developed) states and 'periphery' countries – i.e. under-industrialized Third World states relying on the production and export of primary products. Between them lie a residual category of 'semi-periphery' states. Such countries interact economically with both the core and the periphery, occupying 'a kind of half-way house position in terms of such features as profit margins and wage levels' (Randall and Theobald 1985: 123–4). Economic 'surplus' flows from periphery to core maintaining the division between the wealthy and non-wealthy states. Europeans took possession of non-European colonies in the nineteenth century, especially in Africa and Asia, for the primary purpose of economic gain. As a result, an 'interdependent but unequal relationship was established between coloniser and colonised' (Spybey 1992: 225).

One of the most influential dependency analyses is *Capitalism and Underdevelopment in Latin America*, written by the Chicago-educated German, André Gunder Frank, and published in 1971. His key term, 'the development of underdevelopment', was the radical counterpoint of Rostow's 'take-off'. Like Rostow and others writing within the developmentalism framework, Frank virtually ignored the interaction of cultures and politics in his essentially class-based treatment of Latin America's history of failure to develop, whether economically or politically. This is an astounding omission when one bears in mind the role, historically, of Roman Catholicism in the region. It is understandable, however, when we understand that Frank's analytical focus was the international capitalist system.

Both methodologically and politically, Frank's starting-point is radically different from Rostow's. Frank perceives national economies as structural elements in a global capitalist system, rather than taking individual societies as the unit of analysis. This is so because the whole global system, according to Frank, is unevenly structured in a whole chain of 'metropolis–satellite' relations. This chain links the entire system. As a result, for Frank, the developmental scenario is to be wholly rejected, because it does not correspond to historical or contemporary reality; it is impossible to find anywhere in the world today a society which exhibits the characteristics of Rostow's 'traditional' stage. The reason, Frank asserts, is that such 'traditional' societies have long since disintegrated because of their incorporation into the global capitalist economy. Such a view necessarily highlights the asymmetrically interdependent nature of the metropolis–satellite relationship, a relationship which Rostow does not investigate.

Frank argues that the development of the industrialized countries from the sixteenth century was a direct result of their economic, and later political, dominance of today's underdeveloped countries, a huge majority of which were colonies. The process sucked the latter into a long-term, structurally disadvantageous relationship which resulted in the development of some countries and the current underdevelopment of Latin America, and by extension other Third World regions. This is the main foundation of Frank's argument: that the development of the industrialized countries was possible only because of the underdevelopment of the Third World.

Frank argues that satellites can only develop when their ties with the metropolis are weakened, citing, *inter alia*, Brazil (in the 1930s) and Japan (before 1939) as examples (Foster-Carter 1985: 108). Self-sufficiency and inward-orientated development strategies are appropriate, indeed essential. Such a situation, whether coming about through economic recession and/or war, reduces the chain of metropolis control. When the period of disequilibrium is passed, however, the metropolis reasserts control, in contemporary times through the penetration of multinational business corporations. Frank asserts that regions which are most severely underdeveloped today are those which had the closest links with the metropolis in the past. He cites the example of Brazil's impoverished north-east, which was formally a major sugar cane-growing area. Its current poverty and accompanying backwardness are not the least 'traditional', as formerly the area was one of the most flourishing parts of Brazil. Its economic decline is explained in terms of its agricultural monoculture: the demand for sugar was filled elsewhere; as a result, the region lapsed into the poverty which it continues to exhibit.

In sum, Frank's model is externalist, bilinear and stagnationist; his approach is on the macro-economic level of the global capitalist system, in complete contrast to that of the developmentalism approach. To Frank and other dependency analysts, decisive politico-economic change comes from *outside* the Third World. Metropolis and satellite pursue different structural roles. The Third World's role is unchanging as supplier of (under-priced) raw materials to the metropolis. The route out of economic stagnation lies in disengagement from the global capitalist system via self-sufficiency, socialism and increased trade with 'progressive' – i.e. until recently, the former Eastern European socialist – states.

Dependency analysis has been extensively criticized, not least because it failed to predict – much less explain – the economic rise of the East Asian newly industrializing countries, such as South Korea and Taiwan, in the 1970s. In addition, the dependency focus upon the 'international capitalist system' leads it to neglect domestic factors which affect the development chances of Third World countries.

In conclusion, each paradigm emphasizes an important aspect of politics and economics in the Third World to the neglect of others.

Developmental analysis marginalizes the effects of the international economic system, while dependency theory focuses on little else than the latter's allegedly baleful effects. Developmentalism is preoccupied with issues such as institutional transformation and the impact of 'agents of modernization' on indigenous Third World communities, highlighting the necessary marginalization of 'tradition' by modern state structures necessary to transform political, social and economic realities. Dependency analysis, on the other hand, emphasizes the negative effects of imperialism and the international economic system, while downplaying or ignoring cultural factors, such as religion and ethnicity. As Smith (1985: 559) notes: 'The problem with developmentalism was that it was too fragmented; with [dependency theory], that it is too holistic.'

Despite their drawbacks, each paradigm enjoyed prolonged periods of intellectual predominance: modernization theory from the late 1950s to the beginning of the 1970s; dependency theory in the 1970s and into the 1980s. By the mid-1980s, however, a growing lack of satisfaction with their insights was exacerbated by developments which went directly against their core assumptions. For dependency theory it was the rise of the (mostly Middle Eastern) oil-producing states and of the East Asian newly industrializing countries from the 1970s: economically successful Third World countries could, even if only temporarily, escape from the con-strictions of an international system dominated by the economically developed countries of the West. For developmentalism, on the other hand, the triumph of the Iranian revolution in 1979, reversing the country's apparent trajectory towards Western-style modernization, and the plethora of religious and ethnic conflicts in the Third World in the 1980s served to cast serious doubts on its core assumptions.

What developed into a crisis of Third World political analysis was reflected in the opening sentence of James Manor's 1991 book: 'The study of Third World politics is in disarray.' Part of the problem was that there was *too much information*: from the 1960s a great deal became known about politics in many Third World countries; yet, paradoxically, generalizing insights across the Third World became increasingly difficult as the amount of knowledge grew. As Manor (1991: 1) explains, 'the task of those who would bring coherence to the field and generate broad theoretical insights [became] enormously difficult ... since the cultural and other complexities that arise are so daunting.'

As a result of the complexities Manor refers to, it is, I feel, virtually impossible to come up with precise hypotheses with *universal* resonance across the Third World. My own approach, to restate it, is to stress (a) the interaction of domestic and international factors affecting many aspects of Third World politics; and (b) that a new, qualitatively different, set of concerns of Third World politics resulted from recent international changes, especially the end of the Cold War and the demise of the Soviet bloc, and general concern with human rights, democracy, pollution and environmental degradation. The most important effect of these developments was to embed firmly in the political agenda of the Third World issues which had previously been understated.

Structure and Concerns of the Book

Because of their centrality to the analysis of this book, the remainder of the current chapter identifies and briefly discusses the key concepts examined in chapters 2–8: state and society, democracy, economic growth and development, ethnic and religious identity and conflict, human and women's rights, and environmental concerns.

State and society

At the root of politics in the Third World, as everywhere, is the relationship of the state to its people and vice versa. At independence, most citizens of Third World countries envisaged that freedom from colonial rule would lead to greater political and economic justice. Over time, however, the optimism of independence often waned. Many people in Third World countries do not see their state as a champion of their interests at home and abroad, but rather as a group of men and women who strive primarily to 'feather their own nests' and those of their families and ethnic or religious group at the expense of others. In other words, the state is often regarded as a vehicle for the benefit and self-interest of a usually small political elite, using control of state power for their own ends. The state in the Third World often cannot protect people from crime, terrorism, job loss, inflation, natural disasters and so on (if it could, many people might be able to put up with the corruption of its servants);

why, then, should they respect those in power? The diminution of respect in turn led to vociferous demands – encouraged by international developments – for democracy, i.e. the right to choose one's government rather than put up with one which has been imposed.

Democracy

Until quite recently very few – no more than a dozen – Third World states were democratic. From the mid-1970s, however, democracy spread from Latin America to Asia and Africa. Only the Middle East seems virtually immune from the democratic trend. We can best understand the spread of democracy as a symptom of both domestic and international developments, with the extinguishing of East European Communist dictatorships in the late 1980s important as both catalyst and symbol. A significant number of civilian dictatorships, one-party states and military regimes do, however, remain in the Third World. When states are governed by non-democratic means, this does not simply connote that citizens do not get the chance to choose their rulers. It also very often means that a number of other rights and benefits are denied: basic human rights are often flouted, women's demands are belittled, environmental safeguards – if they exist – are ignored, and ethnic and religious minorities are denied autonomy or freedom of expression. When a state is democratic, such issues are at least contested ground: they can *appear* on the political agenda. Democracy, then, is the key to the improvement of conditions in many other areas; it is a first step, a stepping-stone to wider social, political and economic reforms.

Economic growth and development

Third World states are often referred to as 'developing' or 'underdeveloped' countries. But what is development? 'Development' has two broad meanings: it can refer simply to sustained economic growth over time until a certain stage is reached, or it may imply something more: a combination of cultural, political, economic and technical change from which society generally benefits.

Until recently, the lack of democracy in the Third World was matched by a general shortfall in economic growth – and hence development – for many countries. This was due not only to the fact that many government officials were busy extracting funds from the state's resources for their own ends. Third World countries were faced with the prospect of dealing with an international economic system which was not of their making and which they could not control. Many people believe that the best way for Third World countries to develop is for them to industrialize after developing the export of raw materials and using resulting profits to sustain emergent industrial sectors.

The building up of the export sector is judged necessary because few, if any, Third World countries have the natural resources and technical expertise to thrive through a policy of *autarchy*, i.e. economic self-sufficiency. The only alternative is to trade with others. This strongly implies that for a nation to be economically prosperous, it will, of necessity, cultivate a strong export sector. Yet, a serious problem for many Third World countries over the last 15 years or so has been generally declining world prices for raw materials exports in relation to manufactured goods imported, for the most part, from the industrial democracies of the West, which generally rose steadily in price.

A result of widespread trade imbalances was that many Third World countries, especially in Latin America and sub-Saharan Africa, experienced a steady rise in international indebtedness. Debt service – i.e. the percentage of export earnings devoted to repaying the interest on debts – rose swiftly. Economic downturn coincided with and enhanced demands for democracy. The disturbances caused by political and economic upheavals had another result: increased tension and conflict between groups striving for their own identity within the confines of an often putative nation-state.

Religion, ethnicity and identity

Having explored the issues of democracy and economic development, we move on to a further area of state–society conflict in the Third World: the striving by various groups for ethnic and/or religious identity in the context of attempts by governments to build nation-states. Many Third World governments are challenged by ethnic, racial, religious, cultural or class-based groups which have their own notions of solidarity and development. Yet, as Bangura (1994: 1) explains, 'The subject of identity is very complex as it encompasses the totality of social experience, much of which is influenced by history.' What makes a group's collective identity is often difficult to determine, because individuals are socialized in a variety of ways, simultaneously, during their lives; as a result, one's identity may well change over time. Apart from religious, ethnic or cultural affiliation, individuals are also members of a range of social institutions, such as families, clans, small communities, villages, larger population centres, professions, trade unions and other social interest groups. Because of multiple membership of a variety of social institutions, a person's *identity* is often a contested issue. Yet, if judged by the types of state–society conflicts common in the Third World, many people's core values seem to be based on religion, ethnicity, or an assumed common culture or class. The point is that such conflicts are themselves a result of wider strains in the fabric of state–society relations. It is no coincidence that demands for ethnic autonomy or religious independence have emerged during a time of serious political upheaval in the Third World.

Human rights

The question of identity is closely linked to the issue of human rights. Demands for greater choice in what kind of government one has, what kind of economic policy is pursued within a state, or what freedoms a minority ethnic or religious group may have are all human rights issues. Virtually every Third World state is a signatory of the Universal Declaration of Human Rights (UDHR) of 1948, as well as other human rights agreements. The UDHR proclaims, *inter alia*, that 'Everyone has the right to life, liberty and security of person . . . the right to freedom of thought, conscience and religion . . . the right to seek, receive and impart information and ideas through any media and regardless of frontiers' (quoted in Thomas et al. 1994: 22). The issue of human rights is a controversial area, however, some governments claiming that because of their society's cultural singularities not all articles of the UDHR apply. This raises the question of the *universality* of human rights: does the UDHR apply in all countries of the Third World? *Which* human rights can properly be regarded as *universal* rights? Like issues explored in earlier chapters, the question of human rights is also an important area of conflict between states and societies in the Third World.

Women and power

Nearly half a century after the UDHR declared that males and females have identical rights, serious gender inequalities remain in many Third World countries. The generally scandalous position of females was reflected in the concerns discussed at the Fourth United Nations Conference on Women held in Beijing in September 1995: women's physical well-being, women and work, women and education. In many Third World countries, like other countries elsewhere, women are less healthy than men, live shorter lives than men, get less education than men, and have less skilled jobs, with lower rates of pay, than men.

While cultural factors do in some cases play a part in the treatment of women in the Third World, they are insufficient to explain the very widespread situation of women's inferior social and economic position in relation to men. In chapter 7 I explore the causes and consequences of women's subordination, before examining what they are doing about it.

The politics of the natural environment

Many of the issues examined in earlier chapters are high on the political agenda of most Third World countries. In chapter 8 I examine one which is also emerging as central: the degradation of the natural environment. A series of environmental catastrophes in the 1980s – including the burning of the Amazonian rain forest, the Union Carbide disaster at Bhopal, India, the nuclear accident at Chernobyl, acid rain and holes in the ozone layer – provided the catalyst for the 'politicization' of the environment. Following the 1992 Earth Summit at Rio de Janeiro, the extent of public concern at damage to the environment was further demonstrated by the unprecedented worldwide protests at the French nuclear weapons testing at Muroroa Atoll in late 1995.

In some respects, however, environmental degradation is not (yet) a Third World problem. Industrialized countries, with only 20 per cent of the earth's population, produce more than 65 per cent of the gases which contribute to global warming, and pump out over 80 per cent of the chlorofluorocarbon (CFC) gases which cause depletion of the precious ozone layer. Most of the sulphur dioxide and nitrogen oxide emissions causing 'acid rain' also emanate from the industrialized countries. While a few Third World countries in East and South-east Asia and Latin America recorded rapid economic growth rates in the 1980s and 1990s, the most currently significant forms of environmental degradation in the Third World are a result of primary commodity production. One of the consequences of contemporary economic reform programmes in the Third World is to speed up the destruction of the natural environment, as a consequence of over-exploitation of natural resources, often leading to desertification and deforestation.

Analysis of Third World politics in the contemporary era must take into account a wide array of both domestic and global concerns and developments. Transcending the rather narrow concerns of the traditional paradigms, my chief concern in this book is to provide an exploration and analysis of what I believe are the most important contemporary political issues in the Third World. In order to locate the contemporary period in historical perspective, in the next chapter we turn, first, to a discussion of the decolonization process after 1945 and, second, to an examination of characteristics of the state–society relationship.

Notes

1 This is a conventional regional division derived from World Bank usage. Latin America and the Caribbean is made up of the countries of South America plus the islands of the West Indies. South Asia is the Indian sub-continent plus Pakistan. East and South-east Asia embraces the countries of Asia – apart from Japan – between the Indian sub-continent and the Pacific. The Middle East and North Africa region comprises the predominantly Muslim countries of West Asia and Africa north of the Sahara, while sub-Saharan Africa comprises the African countries south of the Sahara desert.

2 For assessments of theoretical approaches to understanding Third World politics, see Randall and Theobald 1985 and So 1990.

3 Many Latin American states became independent from colonial rule in the 15 years after 1811. The term 'Latin America' was invented in the nineteenth century by French writers anxious to promote French influence in the Roman Catholic world. It now refers to all of the Western hemisphere south of the Mexico–United States frontier, particularly those states where French, Spanish or Portuguese is widely spoken.

4 'Dollars' in this book refers to US dollars.

5 A theocracy is a state where God is regarded as the sole sovereign.
6 Dependency theory is sometimes referred to as 'underdevelopment
   theory'. A variant of dependency theory, 'world system theory', covers
   essentially the same ground, and will not, as a result, be examined
   separately (Gills 1995: 142). A refinement of dependency theory, neo-
   Marxist analysis, begins from the chief premiss of dependency: that the
   possibilities of autonomous capitalist development in Third World
   societies are severely limited by relations of economic dependency.
   Neo-Marxism emphasizes indigenous developments: the need to
   examine local social structures, the nature and extent of social class
   formations, and the goals of different classes (Randall and Theobald
   1985: 137).

2

State and Society

This chapter is concerned with (a) an examination of the post-World War II decolonization process and (b) an exploration of the characteristics of post-colonial states and the relationship with their societies. The first part is concerned with decolonization and the emergence of a great number of Third World states after 1945. Soon after World War II, due to a changing international climate, the post-war weakness of colonial powers and domestic pressure from within colonies, retention of colonies by imperial countries was no longer acceptable. The result was a decolonization process which began slowly in the 1940s and 1950s and gained pace in the 1960s. By the 1980s there were very few colonies remaining.

The second part of the chapter focuses on the characteristics of Third World states, and considers their relationship with their citizens. States which emerged from the colonial period in the Third World were often qualitatively different from those created in an earlier epoch in Europe. In the latter the nation created the state, whereas in the Third World it was necessary for the state to try to create the nation. Because of extant social and cultural divisions in many Third World societies, this was by no means an easy task. Over time, many Third World governments became increasingly more authoritarian in their attempts to build nation-states. Many of their citizens came to believe that the main goal for politicians of achieving political power was to advance their personal interests rather than those of society.

One result of a growing division between rulers and ruled was the development of a modern form of *clientelism*, i.e. where 'patrons' and 'clients' find each other mutually useful for various purposes (Hadjor 1993: 65–6). Another was that in some countries increasing societal opposition led to the emergence of strong *civil societies*, i.e. citizens organized into interest groups to check the power of the state. Civil society, if sufficiently strong and organized, can put a great deal of pressure on governments to democratize and economically reform. As we shall see in chapter 3, the reformist efforts of civil societies were augmented in the 1980s and 1990s by international demands for non-democratic governments in the Third World to democratize.

The End of Colonial Rule in the Third World

Beginning in the early nineteenth century, each successive period of international upheaval and conflict has resulted in a significant net accretion of states. The decolonization process began in the early nineteenth century with the independence of former Spanish and Portuguese colonies in Latin America. The emergence of more than 20 countries in Latin America and the Caribbean in the first half of the nineteenth century came not only in the wake of two successful revolutions, the American (1776) and the French (1789), but also after a major international conflict, the Napoleonic wars (Jackson 1990: 64). The independence of Latin American and Caribbean countries was facilitated by their isolation from the Spanish and Portuguese empires as a result of Napoleon's successes in the Peninsular War (1807–14).

A century later, after World War I (1914–18), the demise of the Turkish Ottoman Empire was the catalyst for the independence of a number of countries in the Middle East and North Africa, including North Yemen (1919), Egypt (1922), and Iraq and Oman (both 1932).

The greatest agent for the creation of new countries in the Third World was, however, World War II (1939–45). As a result of weakness caused by years of war, the colonial powers – including Britain, Japan and France – relinquished nearly all their colonies in the 20 years after 1945. As a result, dozens of new countries, mostly in Africa, Asia and the Middle East, were created.

A fourth wave of creation of new states came at the end of the Cold War, after 1989. Yugoslavia fell apart, and several new countries struggled to be born, including Croatia, Serbia, Slovenia, Bosnia-Hercegovina and the Serb Republic of Srpsa. The demise of the Soviet Union in 1991 also saw the founding or re-establishing of many new states, including Estonia, Lithuania, Latvia, Armenia, Estonia, Georgia, Tadjikistan, Uzbekistan and several others. In sub-Saharan Africa, Namibia, Eritrea and Somaliland also emerged as new states following the Cold War.

In sum, the four waves of new state creation which followed the Napoleonic wars (Latin America and the Caribbean), World War I (the Middle East), World War II (Asia, Africa, the Middle East), and the Cold War (Africa, the Balkans, the former Soviet Union) were the result of the effects of international conflict. We will focus on the post-World War II period of state creation in the Third World in the current chapter, because the great majority of existing Third World countries achieved independence after 1945. From less than 50 in 1945, the numbers of states in the world rose to more than 180 by 1995; at least two-thirds of that total are Third World countries. There was an especially concentrated period of decolonization during the 1950s and 1960s, when more than 40 Third World countries, mostly in sub-Saharan Africa and Asia, gained their independence from colonial rule.

Following World War II, initial determination to retain colonies by the European powers was quite soon followed by an understanding that such a course of action was not tenable because of three factors: an international climate that no longer regarded colonialism as appropriate; the post-war weakness of the leading colonial powers, such as Britain and France; and the increasingly confident demands for decolonization expressed by nationalist politicians. Independence during 1945–50 for a large number of countries, predominantly in Asia, including India, Bhutan, Ceylon (Sri Lanka), Burma (Myanmar), Korea, Laos, Lebanon, Nepal, Israel (Palestine), the Philippines, West Pakistan, East Pakistan (Bangladesh),[1] and Indonesia signified that, for the colonial powers, the game was up: the imperial dream was over. The greater the number of states gaining their independence, the swifter and more vociferous the demands for freedom from colonial rule from remaining colonies became.

The Anti-Colonialism Lobbies

There were both local and international anti-colonialism lobbies which combined to exert pressure on the colonial administrations to withdraw.

The local dimension: challenges from below

Propelled by anxiety as to whether nationalist leaders like Gandhi in India, Nkrumah in the Gold Coast (Ghana), Azikiwe in Nigeria and Kenyatta in Kenya would be willing, or able, to defuse growing urban protests or at least keep them peaceful – was a significant factor in the European regimes' decision to decolonize after 1945 (Hargreaves 1979; Hopkins 1973; Cooper 1993). The pressure on nationalist leaders to head the fight to oust colonial administrations was led by troops returning home from the war. Thousands of soldiers from British and French colonies fought against the Nazis or the Japanese, and, having lived with European troops, went home with the myth of their invulnerability destroyed. After the war, such people emerged in the forefront of demands for political autonomy and self-expression (Furedi 1994).

The anti-colonial position in Africa was generally marked by the growing self-assurance and certainty of success of its nationalist politicians as it became increasingly clear that the colonialist powers were looking for a way out with dignity. There was little international surprise when the decolonization floodgates in Africa broke in 1956 with the independence of Sudan, followed over the next decade by the freedom from colonial rule of another 30 states, many of them former French colonies.

In South and South-east Asia, the post-war weakness of the colonial powers and the determination of local people to oust their colonial masters were exemplified by the defeat of the British at the hands of the Japanese, by the stiff resistance to French colonialism by the northern Vietnamese, and by the Indonesian resolve to force the Dutch to quit (Potter 1993: 360–1). The latter, who had controlled Indonesia for 350 years, left the country in 1950 after a bitter civil war. Regarding the British, their hold on their South-east Asian colonies was weakened by the events during World War II. Japan took over much of British-run South-east Asia (i.e. Hong Kong, Malaya, Singapore, Burma) in a few weeks in late 1941 and early 1942, and seriously threatened India, though without conquering it. Although the Japanese were swiftly ousted from South-east Asia following the dropping of atomic bombs on Hiroshima and Nagasaki in August 1945, neither the British nor the French powers were able to reinstate their control after the war. Whereas the British handed over control of their South Asian colonies almost immediately after World War II, the French sought for a while to resume control of their South-east Asian possessions, but without ultimate success. Independence for the French colony of Laos in 1949 was followed by liberty for Cambodia (Kampuchea) and Vietnam in 1954. In the latter, the French found themselves fighting a savage war. Following a serious military defeat at Dien Bien Phu in 1954, however, the French quit the country – although this was not to be the end of Vietnam's travails, as serious conflict was to wrack the country until the 1980s.

In sum, World War II was an important catalyst for the end of colonial rule, especially in Africa and Asia. In South Asia nationalist politicians succeeded in driving out the British by the late 1940s, while the French were persuaded to leave Vietnam as a result of civil war. In Africa, nationalist politicians were increasingly influential, gaining widespread popular support for a policy of decolonization. By the mid-1960s Africa's freedom from colonial rule was well advanced. It was not, however, solely domestic pressures which persuaded the colonial powers to quit. There was also an influential international anti-colonial lobby which played a major role.

Decolonization: the international dimension

As we have already seen, it was a series of international conflicts which helped to lead to the emergence of Third World states in Latin America in the early nineteenth century and a number of others in the Middle East after World War I. After World War II, it was the growth of an international climate of anti-colonialism which served, in tandem with the nationalist struggles, to open the flood-gates of decolonization in the 1950s and 1960s. The emergent superpowers, despite their ideological differences, which would shortly lead to the Cold War, were nevertheless united after the war in their opposition to colonization. The main argument was that because World War II had been fought by the Allies against both racism and totalitarianism, it was quite inappropriate to return to the situation which had prevailed before the war, when large portions of the globe were ruled by Europeans. Another reason for the anti-colonial stance of the United States government was that it was anxious to remove the colonial powers' economic control of their colonies so as to facilitate access for the country's emergent transnational business corporations anxious to expand their trade links (Cooper 1993: 141).

The international environment was, in several ways, conducive to anti-colonial ideologies, augmented by domestic concerns promoting enfranchisement of racial and ethnic minorities in Western states. One of the leading ideas, self-determination, was institutionalized as a primary international value in the Charter of the United Nations (UN), the leading international security organization which emerged immediately after World War II. The General Assembly of the UN, comprising nearly all the world's states, was often to articulate this doctrine in later years, applying it in various declarations and resolutions.

In sum, as a result of a combination of domestic and international ideological, moral and economic pressures, the European colonial powers were unable to shore up the belief in the legitimacy of colonialism, and, as a result, failed to maintain their colonial empires in the Third World for long after World War II.

State and Society in the Third World

The net result of these international and domestic developments was to usher in a growing number of new countries after 1945. At the outset there was considerable optimism about their economic and political prospects, which, with hindsight, seems somewhat misplaced. Many, especially in Africa, were small, economically underdeveloped and beset by existing or potential societal schisms: it would take skilful governments to overcome existing and potential economic and societal problems. It was usually a prerequisite for a colonial handover of power that Third World nationalist politicians adopt the trappings and outward forms of democracy. Yet, many did not necessarily feel a close affinity with a form of politics which was alien, which had never been encouraged to develop during authoritarian colonial rule; to them the acquisition of power itself was by far the most significant reward. For Huntington (1968), cultural mistrust between peoples who feel no affinity with each other, yet are forced to coexist in states with inflexible boundaries, leads nearly always to an incapacity to build strong, durable political structures. As Mouzelis (1986) notes, however, *some* Third World states – the Communist countries of Asia: North Korea, Vietnam, Laos, China – were apparently able to overcome cultural mistrust between different sections of society and to develop strong national political institutions.[2]

Decolonization constituted a momentous break in Third World political development. For the first time local politicians were running the local and international affairs of their country; yet very often the only model they had to go on to establish their rule was that created by their colonial predecessors. Colonial administrations, wherever they were located, always had a high degree of autonomy with respect to indigenous society, much more than did governments with their citizens in the long-established states of Western Europe and North America. In other words, whatever the validity of claims regarding European colonialists' 'civilizing imperative', colonial states were invariably *imposed* systems, vehicles of the victorious over the vanquished (Engels and Marks 1994). The main point is that colonial state precedents, especially those relating to the high degree of autonomy with respect to local society, and this is as true of the most recently decolonized region – sub-Saharan Africa – as it is of the oldest, Latin America, are of great significance when seeking to understand the nature of the contemporary relationship between Third World states and societies.

The usual mode of ruling in the Third World is not simply a function of politicians' desire for power and an imperative to retain it, once achieved, a trait common to politicians the world over. In addition, governments of Third World states face two unique problems, the first is social and political, the second economic. First, there is the problem of how to establish and then maintain control over their citizens – i.e. how to build *nation*-states from often disparate congeries of people, thrown together through the whims of imperial administrators.[3] Second, it is probably easier for citizens to be satisfied with their governments if the latter are perceived as presiding over satisfactory, sustained economic growth than when they are not. The fact is that the vast majority of Third World countries emerged at a time when the global economic system was already established. How could they hope to prosper in this economic system not of their making, whose 'rules' they could not change? The answer is that many have not been able to; this has significantly affected their ability to gain the loyalty and acquiescence of their people.

Third World governments have not only to deal with an often hostile, or at least uncertain, international environment, but also to persuade, cajole, threaten or force their citizens to do their bidding in the 'national interest'. It is not wholly surprising that many governments have found these two tasks beyond their capacities.

Over time, initial loyalty and belief in government's efficacy on the part of newly liberated populations have given way to cynicism and despair regarding their competence and probity. Many ordinary people in the Third World do not see their state as a reasonably coherent champion of society's collective interests at home and abroad, a set of institutions whose personnel work for the common good. Instead, the state is often regarded as the vehicle for the self-interest of an often tiny political elite.

The state in the Third World

I follow Skocpol (1985: 7) and Migdal (1988: 4) in using a definition of the state popularized by Max Weber. The state is a 'compulsory association claiming control over territories and the people within them. Administrative, legal, extractive, and coercive organizations are the core of any state'. The state has two distinctive functions, one internally orientated, the other externally focused. The first is to maintain political order, the second to deal with states and other external actors, such as international organizations like the United Nations.

States everywhere are made up of sets of institutions employing large numbers of people – often thousands – to run their affairs. The state, theoretically, has six attributes: (a) it commands – or at least aspires to command – *a monopoly of the legitimate use of force* within its domain; (b) it has *territoriality* – i.e. it rules over a discrete geographic area; (c) it is *administratively and politically centralized* – i.e. national control is co-ordinated and exercised from a national centre, almost invariably the country's capital; (d) it seeks, or strives to retain, a *monopoly of sovereignty* – i.e. no alternative centres of power will be allowed to challenge the state's centralized predominance; (e) it tries to extend or to maintain *the rule of law* over the entire area of its jurisdiction; (f) it desires to *regulate and oversee economic development,* both within its boundaries and in relation to the international economy.

It is simpler to discuss the 'state' as though it were a homogeneous entity with a common purpose at all times and under all circumstances. Yet we need to bear in mind that it is often an entity riven by internal tensions which serve to reduce its capacity for presenting a united front to outside forces both at home and abroad. In other words, most states, particularly in the Third World, do not have a coherent set of clear-cut, rational goals which they pursue with vigour and application. This is in part because, as already noted, nearly all Third World states are artificial constructions. Whereas in Western Europe and North America the nation nearly always created the state, in the Third World the reverse is more usually true: state formation precedes nation building.

The state's capacity to govern is dependent on the extent to which its authority and the legitimacy of those who run the state are perceived by the various social groups and classes which make up its society. A state's successful imposition of its will on its citizens depends on the means of social control and on the relative effectiveness of those means in achieving state goals (Migdal 1988: 22) The ability of state leaders to put their policies into practice will range widely. It can be often especially difficult for a state to establish its authority when it presides, as in many African and Asian countries, over a population made up of a large number of groups with separate cultures.

Outside of the West[4] *nation-states* – i.e. where the state and nation more or less coincide – are rare. Third World countries often include within their borders a variety of culturally separate peoples who often find it difficult to regard the state as their primary source of political allegiance. A result is that political interactions between, on the one hand, different ethnic or religious groups and, on the other, between various groups and the state, are often characterized by tensions and conflict, as we shall see in chapter 5. Sometimes the domination of those in power is facilitated by these societal divisions. Huntington (1968) argued that the fragility and frequent breakdown of democratic political systems in the Third World was due to weak institutionalization of political controls during a period of growth of a mass politics as a result of societal tensions and divisions. According to him, the military – as we shall see in chapter 3 – then feels duty bound to use force to take power to reimpose order. The likelihood of political and societal fragmentation is probably enhanced by the fact that few Third World states in modern times gained their independence from colonial control by way of a unifying liberation war unlike, for example, the United States' fight for freedom from Britain in the late eighteenth century or Latin American states' struggle for independence from Spanish or Portuguese control in the early nineteenth century.[5]

One result of political and societal fragmentation is that states in the Third World are often weak. While some states *are* strong, e.g. Communist China and North Korea, others are quite impotent. In

Angola, Mozambique, Sierra Leone and Zaire, e.g., the state's capacity has more or less collapsed as a result of extreme institutional weakness (Bayart 1993; Haynes 1993b). The most common type of state in the Third World, however, is that which is neither strong nor collapsed. In other words, the most common state is that with limited, but still significant, capacity in relation to society. It follows, then, that we should not overestimate its power. Sanneh (1991: 212) claims that the state in Africa is 'omnipotent', gaining for itself 'a wide channel of power, being not merely content to restrain and arbitrate but seeking to prescribe faith of a fundamental kind and conformity of an absolute form'. This overstates the African state's capacity. As Hyden (1983) argues, African society's ability to deflect the power of the state is shown in a number of ways, including the ability of many people to avoid paying taxes. In sum, as Migdal (1988) explains, in the Third World, as elsewhere, a state's capability for governing is a function of the relations that exist between it and civil society. The ability of the state to impose its will can be estimated through 'its capacities to penetrate society, regulate social relationships, extract resources, and appropriate or use resources in determined ways' (Migdal 1988: 4).

In conclusion, given that the post-colonial state was the inheritor of the colonial entity's framework of rule, it is not surprising that it would attempt to govern in the same authoritarian fashion. Yet, over time it appeared that many states in the Third World had only limited capacity to enforce their will on their citizens; there was frequently a failure to build a societal consensus or a widespread sense of national unity and direction. State leaders sought a comprehensive penetration of society to enhance their control, yet success was decidedly patchy: the state in the Third World is usually unable to gain either omnipotence or absolute conformity from its citizens.

Clientelism and the state

The common failure to build nation-states means that Third World politicians have to find other ways of expanding their constituencies and to staying in power; one of the most common is to develop patron–client relations. For example, local brokers in India have been responsible in part for the predominance of the Congress Party in national elections since the 1940s (Sisson 1993). Clientelism is the relationship which engages the attentions of 'patrons' and 'clients' in many parts of the Third World so that each party benefits from a mutually advantageous relationship (Roniger and Günes-Ayata 1994; Clapham 1985: 54–9).

Clientelism comes into its own when kinship arrangements can no longer sustain the necessities of life. As a result, individuals ('clients') must step outside the existing system of kinship relations and arrange relations with other patrons instead. Many political scientists see the development of patron–client relations as an important facet of political mobilization in the Third World; some draw a parallel between Third World patron–client links and American 'machine politics' (Clark 1994). The point is that patron–client ties, whether in the Third World, the USA or elsewhere, are by nature non-ideological and non-class-based. The aim for both parties is to gain access to resources: the patron will gain the allegiance and the vote of the client; the latter will receive fungible resources – money, employment, protection – in return.

Developmental and dependency scholars differ in their interpretations of clientelism. Hadjor, writing in the latter vein, argues that the widespread existence of patron–client relations in the Third World is a result of the character of politics there: 'politics in certain Third World societies is very much the product of the inability of the capitalist class to act as a class' (Hadjor 1993: 66). In much of the Third World, Hadjor argues, access to the state is necessary for the well-being of individual capitalists. Patronage is, as a result, an inescapable aspect of the nature of the post-colonial or 'neo-colonial' state.[6] Clientelism, in Hadjor's (1993: 66) view, endures because 'the masses are excluded from politics'; power is monopolized 'by a small group of political patrons' who will fight 'any attempt to democratize society. Behind the façade of the patron–client relation lies the usurpation of political power by the neo-colonial political bosses'.

There are at least three problems with the dependency view of clientelism. The first is that many democratic societies in the West – not only the United States, as already noted, but also, among others, Portugal, Italy, Russia, Canada and Israel – have systems where patron–client relations are politically, socially and economically important (Roniger and Gunes-Ayata 1994). Second, the dependency view assumes the existence of states led by a tight knit coterie of 'political bosses' sharing similar objectives and goals; as we have already noted, this assumed unity of purpose is problematic. Third, the notion of 'neo-colonial political bosses' implies that leaders of

Third World states work primarily for the benefit of foreign interests. It seems quite clear, however, that for many Third World political leaders one of the primary attractions of power is that it allows them to serve their *own* interests rather than those of others.

In contrast to the dependency view, the developmental approach is to see traditional forms of patron–client relations underpinning modern political mobilization thus focusing attention on traditional social and political institutions (Randall and Theobald 1985: 50). The problem with this view is that it assumes that there is a continuity between traditional political institutions and contemporary politics which is often more apparent than real. The growth of *modernization* in Third World societies – i.e. increased urbanization, industrialization and modern education – means that contemporary Third World societies are quite different in many respects from their pre-modern, overwhelmingly rural forerunners.

Whatever the precise role of clientelism in the contemporary Third World, it is beyond dispute that the widespread existence of patron–client relations means that there is no clear *social* boundary between state and society; each interacts, feeds off and helps sustain the other. State and society 'interpenetrate each other in more or less complex ways and at different levels (symbolic, normative, or structural), evolving over time into patterns' (Lemerchand 1992: 178). Political leaders are connected with allies throughout the state, sharing goals and orientations, although this should not imply an absence of conflict between different groups seeking state power. As economic crisis, triggered by the oil price rises of the 1970s, deepened throughout the 1980s in the Third World, so access to the state for resources became more and more difficult, even as it became increasingly desirable. As we shall see in chapter 4, often as a direct consequence of economic reform programmes imposed by the International Monetary Fund (IMF) in many Third World countries, state jobs become ever harder to come by; access to state resources via patronage mechanisms remains a better possibility for many individuals. One of the (unintended) effects of IMF programmes has been to produce extensive new opportunities for clientelistic interaction, giving increased opportunity for the disbursement of financial favours (Brittain 1994). In the context of increasing shortages of fungible resources, the state becomes ever more a patrimonial state, i.e. where authority is attributed to a person rather than the holder of an official position (Lewis 1992: 47).

At the same time, we need to be aware that groups in Third World states often organize themselves to challenge the state's monopoly of power. As we shall see in chapter 3, there has been a trend towards democratization in the Third World since the 1970s, led by elements of civil society in various countries. In the next section we examine the political importance of civil society in relation to the state in the Third World by examining their inter-actions in (a) Africa and the Middle East, (b) Asia, (c) Latin America and the Caribbean.

Civil Society and the State

One of the main functions of civil society – i.e. the group of non-state organizations, interest groups and associations, such as trade unions, professional associations, further and higher education student groups, churches and other religious bodies, and the media – is to maintain a check on the power of the state. If successful, civil society is able to balance the state's tendency to seek ever greater amounts of power. Civil society, in short, functions as the citizens' curb on the power of the state.

In the West, both France and Britain have powerful states *and* strong civil societies (Rudolph 1987: 734). Despite occasional tensions between state *and* society – for e.g. in France in 1968 and 1995, when higher education students and industrial workers united in a strong protest against state policy – there is a tenable presumption that Western nation-states embody a more or less binding congruence between the state-as-institution and the population-as-nation. In contrast to the situation in the West, civil society is weak and often fragmented in the states of Africa and the Middle East.

Africa and the Middle East

Civil society is often frail in Africa and the Middle East because of widespread ethnic and religious divisions, which serve to dissipate the ability to confront the power of the state (Haynes 1993a). The situation is exacerbated by low levels of economic development, especially in Africa, which limit the power of such groups as trade unions and professional associations. When civil society is weak, the state is often strong, although there is no clear-cut cause-and-effect process at work. For example, in countries recently wracked by civil strife, including Algeria, Mozambique, Burundi, Somalia, Angola, Liberia, Afghanistan and Zaire, the frailty of the state is matched by a corresponding weakness of civil society (Ayoob 1995: 69).[7]

While it is generally agreed that Africa has some of the weakest civil societies in the Third World, analyses of the relationship between states and civil societies in the Middle East tend to be dealt with in isolation from other Third World areas. The situation in the Middle East is said to be distinctive from other Third World areas because of three allegedly unique sets of circumstances: (a) the region is rich in oil reserves; (b) Islam is a ubiquitous – and powerful – cultural referent; (c) the Middle East was uniquely colonized by Muslims – Ottoman Turks – rather than by Europeans, although Iran and Saudi Arabia escaped foreign political control.[8] In short, there is said to be a number of singular political, cultural and economic characteristics of the states of the Middle East which set the region apart from other Third World areas (Owen 1992; Bill and Springborg 1994).

Despite claims for singularity, in fact both states and civil societies in the Middle East are much like those in Africa, for several reasons: (a) the state in the Middle East is rarely a coherent set of institutions with a shared sense of purpose; (b) civil society is often weak and fragmented; (c) the relationship of Middle Eastern states with the international economy, like those of Africa, is based on exchanges of raw materials for manufactured goods; and despite its alleged uniqueness, oil is actually a raw material much like coffee, cocoa or rubber, three of Africa's most important exports; (d) there is a general tendency for political elites to use their political positions for the amassing of personal power and wealth for themselves and their families.

Asia

As with Africa and the Middle East, the state in Asia is characterized by its pursuit of a central role *vis-à-vis* both domestic society and the international environment (Mitra 1990). Whereas in Western Europe, the state intervenes in societies whose basic structures were created at an earlier stage by civil society, a civil society whose strength had made the state act responsibly, in India, as well as most other Asian states, there was no prior civil society before colonial rule (Kaviraj 1991: 89). Mitra (1990: 3) claims that it is paradoxical that 'there was no common outcome' of colonialism in Asia; 'that comparable experiences produced a diversity of responses' in Asia in relation to the state and civil society. Common colonial control was certainly one important factor in the background to post-colonial state formation in Asia, but it was not the only one: there were also extensive, and sophisticated, pre-colonial political systems in a number of Asian countries, including China, India, Korea, Vietnam and Cambodia, which were not obliterated by the period of colonial control but lay dormant, resurfacing once foreign imperialists had retired (Bayart 1991: 52).

As a result, when post-colonial states in Asia emerged after World War II, there was not a complete 'discontinuity in the state tradition' as a result of the alleged wasting away of the pre-colonial political institutions as Mitra (1990: 3–4) argues, but rather 'colonial creations were . . . subject to multiple acts of reappropriation by indigenous social groups' (Bayart 1991: 52). In other words, many Asian states' political systems are characterized by their adaptation of pre-colonial political attributes in the post-colonial era. Distinctive social, cultural, ethnic, linguistic and religious mixes produced states whose politics reflect their historical past. There is, in addition, a variety of types of civil societies – from weak to strong – in Asian states, which reflect both the level of industrialization and economic development as well as the emergence of specialist interest groups as a result of modernization.

Latin America and the Caribbean

The state–civil society relationship had a much longer period in which to develop in Latin America than elsewhere in the Third World. Many Latin American states are more industrialized than most other Third World countries (World Bank 1995: 166–7, table 3). One result of economic growth and industrialization was the growth of politically active working classes and well-organized, powerful trade unions in many Latin American states.

There is a large proportion of democratic states in the Caribbean, although little industry compared to Latin America, with a few exceptions such as Trinidad and Tobago. Nevertheless, a consequence of long-standing democracies for the states of the Caribbean is the general development of strong civil societies (Rueschemeyer et al. 1992). As in the Caribbean, where pre-colonial political traditions were extinguished along with the political influence and in some cases the lives of indigenous peoples, the political history of independent Latin America has in some respects exhibited a strong element of continuity to the colonial past. In both areas post-colonial political and economic elites are often from the same racial stratum – light-skinned people of European origin – as dominated during the colonial era. After the liberation wars of the early nineteenth century in Latin America there was a general rise of *caudillismo* (Spanish for chieftain), a highly personalist form of government. Light-skinned *creoles* – i.e. people of European origin born locally – often managed to achieve power (Anderson 1991). Contemporary political and economic elites in Latin America are usually descendants of such people originally separated from others by skin colour, religious 'purity' and cultural affinities with Europeans. Below the lightest-skinned people in social status came the mixed-race *mesticos*, and at the bottom of the pile, the original indigenous inhabitants, the Indians. Accompanying the development of a distinctive political system in Latin America was an economic system which owed its origins to European influences in the second half of the nineteenth century.

Before the late 1920s, when economic depression caused a number of political and economic upheavals, the state in Latin America primarily represented the interests of raw materials exporters and large landowners. Following an economic crisis in the late 1920s, however, many states intervened to set up protective tariffs, and transferred funds from the export to the domestic sector. The aim was to create the necessary infrastructure for the development of import-substitution industry, i.e. manufactured goods produced locally rather than imported. During the 1930s state power was often jointly shared by large-scale capitalists who controlled the growing industrial sector and big landowners. There was very little say in the political process for ordinary people: civil society was underdeveloped.

In Latin America, the effects of the world wars and of global economic depression in the 1930s combined to produce significant political effects, especially after 1945. Whereas in Africa and Asia the result of the World War II was to galvanize nationalist challenges to imperial rule, in already independent[9] Latin America there were different results. Latin America's responses to war and economic dislocation involved a widespread, if tentative, democratization after 1945, followed by a period of 'new authoritarianism' (Rueschemeyer et al. 1992). From the 1950s, increasing industrialization and urbanization, coupled with strong population growth, combined to generate strong popular pressures for increased social spending and greater mass political participation. The result, however, was not more democracy, but the reverse: between 1964 and 1976 democratic regimes in a number of countries, including Brazil, Peru, Uruguay, Chile and Argentina, fell to military *coups*.

The resulting non-democratic governments were called 'bureaucratic authoritarian' (BA) regimes (O'Donnell 1973). BA regimes, O'Donnell argues, both guarantee and organize the political and economic domination of a small, exclusivist group whose chief loyalty is to itself rather than to the nation. This oligarchy sought to exclude the mass of people from political decision-making by banning elections and by directing state spending to areas to build up infrastructure attractive to foreign capital and to state bureaucracy, especially the military. There was a distinct separation between state and civil society during the BA era, which lasted until the late 1970s or later (Philip 1993).

During the 1960s and 1970s, developmental imperatives focused upon the utilization of capital to fuel industrialization. This ran contrary to the perceived interests of sectors of the highly politicized and vocal urban working and lower middle classes, who instead demanded that increased spending on welfare-oriented projects should take precedent. The military and their allies believed, however, that the way out of a growing economic crisis was for a small cohesive elite to retain power and to exclude the voices of the working and lower middle classes from pressurizing policy-makers. The governing coalition generally comprised big-scale landowners, capitalists and the military – i.e. the sectors of society who felt threatened by popular demands. In the late 1970s and early 1980s, however, as Latin America's economic fortunes declined in the wake of growing foreign indebtedness (as we shall see in chapter 4), a series of political and economic crises threatened the ruling elites' position and forced them to allow free elections. Moves towards democracy at this time were spearheaded by a bottom-up process rooted in civil society coupled with international pressure, principally from the United States.

In this chapter we have examined the decolonization process, with particular emphasis on the post-1945 period when most Third World states gained their independence. We saw that moves towards decolonization were a result of a dual process involving both international and domestic factors. After World War II the perception that colonization was acceptable changed to one where national self-determination was regarded as paramount. The weakness of war-weary colonial powers, coupled with the increasing confidence of nationalist politicians, was also instrumental in decolonization. Beginning with a trickle in the 1940s and 1950s, the pace of decolonization picked up in the 1960s. By the 1980s there were very few colonies left.

The states which emerged from the colonial period in the Third World were often qualitatively different from those created in an earlier epoch in Europe. Whereas in the latter the nation usually created the state, in the Third World it was the state's task to try to forge a nation. Because of social, political, economic and cultural divisions in many Third World societies, this was by no means an easy task. Many governments in the Third World became authoritarian, justifying this by the imperative of nation building.

Authoritarian attempts at nation building were by and large no more successful than earlier democratic efforts had been. In order for many Third World governments to achieve a measure of influence *vis-à-vis* their citizens, leading political figures frequently built up extensive patron–client relations to enhance their personal power. Over time, however, the undemocratic nature and poor economic position of many Third World states led to pressure from both civil society at home and international persuasion to democratize and reform economically. The processes involved in democratization are examined in chapter 3, those related to economic reform in chapter 4.

Notes

1 Initially, in 1947, Pakistan was in two parts: West and East Pakistan, the latter corresponding to present-day Bangladesh. The latter emerged as an independent state in 1971, following civil war with West Pakistan.
2 There is debate about the nature of political institutionalization in Communist countries: the swift, unexpected collapse of apparently comparable institutions in the late 1980s in Eastern Europe indicates that popular support for them was more apparent than real. On the other hand, the continued existence of Asian Communist systems with a combined population of more than 1.25 billion people is perhaps best explained by reference to the political cultures of those countries. They embody various religious and philosophical unifying elements – such as Confucianism and Buddhism – which were absent in Eastern

Europe; it is perhaps these cultural elements which help to explain the endurance of communism in Asia. It is unfortunately beyond the scope of this chapter, and this book, to seek answers to an important political question: why have some Communist systems collapsed, and not others?

3   Almost invariably, former colonial boundaries became those of new states.

4   When I refer to 'the West' in this book, I mean the group of highly industrialized, liberal democratic countries to be found in Western Europe, North America, the Antipodes and Asia (Japan).

5   In Mozambique and Angola, successful liberation wars in the 1970s were the *prelude* to 20-year civil wars.

6   'Neo-colonialism' refers to the belief that the political independence of Third World countries was not accompanied by economic independence from foreign control. It is said to be maintained by indirect means, such as multinational corporations and the fixing of commodity prices by the West. The late president of Ghana, Kwane Nkrumah, defined neo-colonialism thus: 'The essence of neo-colonialism is that the State which is subject to it is, in theory, independent and has all the outward trappings of international sovereignty. In reality its economic system and thus its political policy is directed from outside' (Nkrumah 1965: ix).

7   Zaire was a US client during the Cold War, useful as a conduit to supply arms to the rebel leader Jona Savimbi in Angola in his fight against the Soviet-backed government. Recently, however, Zaire was on the 'verge of becoming a massive case of state failure', as the American government no longer sees the need to support President Mobutu. The US State Department warned in early 1994 that Zaire could easily develop into 'Somalia and Liberia rolled into one' (Ayoob 1995: 69).

8   Some former Ottoman possessions, including Iraq, Palestine, Jordan, Kuwait, Lebanon and Syria, were taken over as League of Nations mandates by Britain and France. The fall of France in 1941 led to the independence of both Syria and Lebanon, while soon after the war Britain allowed independence to both Palestine (Israel) and Jordan.

9   Surinam (Dutch), Belize and Guyana (both British) were controlled by foreign powers until the 1970s or later. French Guiana is still a French possession.

3

Democracy

In the preceding chapter we were concerned with two issues: (a) the decolonization process after 1945 and (b) the relationship between state and society in the Third World. With regard to the former it was explained that it was a combination of international and domestic pressure which led to decolonization after World War II. Regarding the latter, we noted that many initially democratic post-colonial governments soon developed pronounced authoritarian tendencies as they struggled to build nation-states. The political terrain in the Third World became filled with heavily armed authoritarian states dominated by military governments, one-party regimes and personalist dictatorships. Recently, however, there has been a reversal of this authoritarian trend, with democratic governments taking over in many parts of the Third World.

In this chapter we are concerned with democracy. We begin with an explanation for the current wave of democracy in the Third World. Second, we describe several types of non-democratic regime, and explain why they endure at a time of democracy elsewhere. Third, we explore the views of dependency and developmental theories in relation to democracy. After that, we analyse the factors which are necessary for the current democratic transitions to be consolidated. We finish with an assessment of the democratic position of the states of each of the five Third World regions. Having appraised the democratic position, we will then be in a position to examine parallel moves towards economic reform in chapter 4.

Democracy and the Third World:
The Impact of the 'Third Wave'

The trend towards authoritarian government in the Third World began in the Middle East in the 1950s, when a series of military *coups* displaced a number of incumbent rulers. Following this, in the 1960s and 1970s, there were further military take-overs, especially in sub-Saharan Africa and Latin America. Elsewhere, however, the anti-democracy trend began to reverse itself in what Huntington (1991) calls the 'Third Wave'[1] of democracy.

The Third Wave began with democratic transitions in Greece, Spain, and Portugal in the mid-1970s after years of dictatorial rule. Buoyed by redemocratization in those countries, Third World democrats began to question the legitimacy of their often non-democratic governments. Redemocratization in southern Europe was followed by the end of dictatorial governments in Latin America a decade later. At the end of the 1980s democracy was given a further fillip by the demise of Communist governments in Eastern Europe.

The collapse of Communist governments in Europe removed not only the chief rationale for one-party rule, but also the main justifications for it: social and political stability and economic planning to smoothe out the cyclical hiccups of capitalism. As a result, in the Third World the legitimacy of single-party and other non-democratic governments was increasingly denied by important groups in civil society, such as trade unions and the Christian churches, and by international aid donors, especially the United States. The result of the combination of domestic and international pressure was that dozens of Third World states, often for the first time in decades, experienced national democratic elections in the early 1990s.

Before going any further, it is necessary to define what I mean by the term 'democracy'. I understand democracy to exist when three conditions are fulfilled: (a) regular, competitive elections take place; (b) there is free participation of individuals and groups in the electoral and political process; (c) democratic leaders and institutions are autonomous – i.e. they are able to govern without undue pressure from special interest groups in society like the military. Bearing this definition in mind, we can understand the significance of the current democratic wave when we note that the number of countries with democratic political systems increased from 44 in 1974 to 107 by 1994 (Shin 1994: 136). As there were then nearly 190 states overall, this means that about 56 per cent of them were democracies.

The main democratic 'growth area' is in the Third World. By 1995, all 23 Latin America countries were democratic; in Asia, seven formerly non-democratic regimes – Pakistan, Bangladesh, Nepal, the Philippines, Taiwan, South Korea and Mongolia – recently democratized; in Africa there were also clear signs of democratization, with more than half of the continent's nearly 50 countries holding democratic elections between the late 1980s and the mid-1990s. Only in the Middle East was there relatively little in the way of movement to democratic regimes, although there were some encouraging signs: the reintroduction of democracy in Lebanon after nearly 20 years of civil war and the deepening democratization of Jordan.

Having described the impact of the current, third wave of democracy on the Third World, and having learnt that increasing numbers of governments were democratic by 1994, we also need to be aware that while many Third World states are democratic, many others are not. It is necessary next to discuss the types of non-democracy in the Third World, in order to to draw contrasts between authoritarian and democratic rule.

Types of Non-Democratic Regimes

Fifty-six per cent of national governments were judged by Shin to be democratic in 1994; this implies that 44 per cent – about 84 regimes – were not. Four broad types of non-democratic regimes are common in the Third World: Communist governments, non-Communist one-party states, personalist regimes and military administrations.

Communist governments

After the demise of socialist regimes in Eastern Europe, five Communist governments remained; all were in the Third World:[2] China, Cuba, Laos, North Korea and Vietnam, collectively home to more than 1.25 billion people. The theoretical justification for Communist single-party rule is that only the party has the capacity to organize the defence of the revolution against counter-revolutionary forces, plan and oversee expansion of the forces of production, and supervise the reconstruction of society. In other words, the party, through the government, is the vehicle to build the framework for communism. In recent times, as a result of the changed international situation, Communist governments in the Third World have been obliged to change their tactics and, perhaps, their goals. Few would argue, for example, that the ruling Communist government in China, which has allowed the growth of capitalism to previously unexpected heights, still envisages a classless society. Similarly, Vietnam's and Cuba's governments also allow growing amounts of capitalism, while both Laos and North Korea desperately seek international aid to shore up their crumbling Communist systems. In short, while some one-party regimes in the Third World still label themselves 'Communist', it is by no means clear that the classic goals of communism are still of overwhelming importance.

Non-Communist one-party states

When Communist governments achieved power in the Third World, they did so as a result of revolutionary change. Non-Communist one-party regimes, on the other hand, gained power either through the ballot-box or by fiat. On the developmentalist view, as we shall see shortly, it was confidently expected after decolonization that Third World political parties would increasingly come to resemble those in the West. With the same forms and functions, they would be integral parts of multi-party systems offering an increasingly educated and discerning public an organized electoral choice and channels of accountability. What actually happened, however, was quite different: many post-colonial multi-party systems, particularly in sub-Saharan Africa and the Middle East, soon gave way to one-party systems. Some perceived this as a progressive development, regarding single-party governments as 'agents of national integration in states whose new and often arbitrarily imposed boundaries commanded less loyalty than "primordial" ties of language, religion or locality' (Randall 1988: 2). Huntington (1968: 91) saw the single party as the solution to the problem of how to construct political stability. The party, he believed, was the only modern organization which was likely to become the main source of authority.

Over time, however, it became apparent that single-party rule was by no means a panacea for the problem of how to build nation-states from a congeries of often diverse peoples. After a period in the 1960s and 1970s when one-party rule, like military government, became common, the numbers of one-party regimes later declined greatly. Nevertheless, one-party regimes still rule in a number of countries, including Syria, Iraq, Zaire and Indonesia. It is not necessarily the case that *constitutionally* only one party is allowed to function. Sometimes, more than the single party is allowed, but, by a variety of means, often involving fixing elections, it remains in power over long periods of time.[3]

Personalist regimes

One-party states, like other forms of non-democratic government in the Third World, are often linked closely to a powerful leader. 'Personalist' regimes are those which are headed by a dominant figure who wields a great deal of individual power, even though *formally* a party may well underpin the government's rule. Often the main justification for personalist rule is that it enhances economic development. The 'luxury' of multi-party democracy cannot be allowed because, it is argued, the resources and energy used to contest elections and fight political battles between parties detracts from the development effort. Paradoxically, however, the key to remaining in power for personalist rulers is not necessarily to deliver on promises of development – Zaire, led for 30 years by President Mobutu and his Mouvement Populaire de la Révolution (Popular Movement for the Revolution) has one of the world's lowest per capita gross national products (GNP)[4] (World Bank 1995: 228, table 1a) – but to retain the loyalty of the army.

There have been few concrete moves towards democracy in Indonesia, which is led by the personalist regime of President Suharto, for four reasons: (a) there is no powerful, mobilized working class or strong middle class pressing for democracy; (b) the power of the state is backed by a large, well-armed military; (c) the government has delivered good economic performance over time;[5] (d) there has been little international pressure for the government to allow democracy (Thompson 1993). In Zaire, on the other hand, a seemingly endless transition to democracy, which began in the early 1990s, involving *more than 200 political parties*, has not got very far. In both countries, the ability of governments to retain the loyalty of the military has been crucial to their longevity.

Military regimes

In the early 1990s 'about half' of all Third World countries were ruled by military regimes (Hadjor 1993: 196). Since then the number of overtly military regimes has declined, although the political power of the military in virtually all Third World countries remains great: the support of the military is often fundamental to a regime's survival, whether democratic or not (Frank 1994: 51–2). The political importance of the military in the Third World is due to (a) the poverty and lack of resources of other social strata; (b) the befriending of many Third World militaries by Western governments during the Cold War, if they purported to be 'anti-Communist'; (c) high levels of social conflict in many Third World countries controllable only by military forces kept powerful for this purpose.

The military not only deals with the suppression of dissent, but may also carve out new roles for itself: many Third World militaries have gone into business, trading in everything from missiles to real estate. For example, the Indonesian military runs an important economic sector with multiple interests, while the Chinese military runs 'more than 20,000 companies, including hotels, airlines, and shops' (Woollacott 1994).

When military personnel form a government, they usually claim to be only temporarily in power, asserting that they want to 'return to barracks' as quickly as possible, once the job in hand – dealing with civilian corruption and putting 'the ship of state back on an even keel' – is accomplished. Yet, despite such claims, and even though military governments usually have a narrow power base – they have of course come to power by force via the *coup d'état* rather than the ballot-box – and depend on authoritarianism and repressive tactics to rule, their period in power is often lengthy.

In conclusion, each of the four kinds of non-democratic regime has in common a desire to keep power in the hands of a small elite and to deny a voice in politics to ordinary people. The ultimate lack of success in this regard, however, is reflected by the increasing numbers of democratic regimes which have emerged in the Third World over the last decade.

Dependency and Developmental Perceptions of Democracy

Developmental theory

In the developmental view, Third World politics would come to look like politics in the West over time; i.e. they would become increasingly democratic. Three variables are believed to be the key factors leading to democracy: (a) good political leadership, (b) a political culture conducive to democracy, (c) long-term increases in economic well-being. Diamond (1993b: 4) asserts the importance of the first two factors: for him, democratization is the result of the 'gradual and incremental emergence of democratic culture, initially or predominantly at the elite level, [a] result of the instrumental, strategic choices of a relatively small number of political actors'. Higley and Burton (1989: 17) endorse his view, asserting that only a consensually unified national elite can produce a durable regime that will become democratic.

The third assumption of developmental theory is that increases in economic well-being over time will encourage democracy. Lipset (1963) argues that the wealthier a country's people, the greater chance there is that the country will be democratic. There is a strong correlation between wealth and democracy in Lipset's view because he believes that only a rich economy makes high levels of literacy, education, and exposure to mass media possible; all are conducive, he believes, to democracy. An affluent economy also mitigates political tensions through providing alternative opportunities for unsuccessful political leaders. For Lipset, a wealthy, complex economy cannot be governed efficiently by authoritarian means; rules and regulations must be based on the consent of those affected by them. Finally, Lipset argues, a state with a wealthy economy tends to have fewer poor people because income is distributed more equally than in unprosperous countries.

While not denying that a wealthy country is more likely to be a democracy, there is in fact no clear-cut process of cause and effect at work. Rich states like the United Arab Emirates, Singapore, or Kuwait, each with a GNP per capita in excess of $19,300 in 1993, are not democracies (World Bank 1995: 163, table 1); yet India, with a GNP per capita of $300 has been a democracy for 50 years. Using Lipset's single criterion for democracy – a certain level of national wealth – it is impossible to explain why low-income countries, like India, are democratic, and wealthy countries, like Kuwait, are not.

Huntington (1984) sought to provide a more sophisticated analysis of the pre-conditions for democracy than Lipset's one-variable analysis, highlighting four variables: (a) the choices that political elites make; (b) the pro-democracy pressures which a well-organized middle class can exert; (c) external pressure on non-democratic regimes; (d) cultural factors of a society conducive to democracy. In relation to the first factor, Huntington tries to reconcile the problems of equating the wealth of a country to its propensity to democratize by proposing the concept of a 'zone of transition'. What this amounts to is that, as countries develop economically they advance into a 'zone of transition', in which 'traditional' – i.e. non-democratic – political institutions are increasingly difficult to maintain. There is no certainty that increasingly wealthy countries will adopt Western-style democracy when in the transition zone. Huntington argues that there is a choice between democratic and non-democratic alternatives: the political direction is in the hands of political elites.

The second factor is the impact of social structure. If there is a well-developed civil society with widely differentiated, articulated autonomous groups, there will be a strong possibility that the power of the state will be checked by providing the necessary pre-conditions for democratic political institutions. For Huntington, the most important group is an autonomous, politically aware middle class. When economic development forges ahead of the development of a middle class, democracy tends not to develop.

Third, there is the impact of the external environment. Huntington claims that British and American influence is especially important in this regard, whether through settlement by nationals of those countries, the legacy of colonial rule, political arrangements imposed by defeat in war, or direct imposition for other reasons.

Finally, Huntington argues that the culture of the putative democracy is important. He claims that Christian countries tend to be democratic; that Hindu and Shinto-influenced cultures, such as India and Japan respectively, may be only lukewarm democratically but are not anti-democracy *per se*; and that Islamic, Confucian and Buddhist cultures are fairly unequivocally anti-democracy. Despite Huntington's assertions, the impact of cultural factors on democracy is not as straightforward as he thinks (Haynes 1993a, 1995c,

1996). Muslim Jordan, Malaysia, Egypt and Lebanon; Hindu/
Buddhist Nepal and Sri Lanka; Buddhist Thailand, Confucian
Taiwan and Confucian/Buddhist/Christian South Korea are all
functioning democracies.

In conclusion, a problem with Huntington's variables relating
to democracy is that his criteria resemble what Potter (1993: 355)
calls a 'shopping list which does not, as an ensemble, explain
democratization very well'. On the other hand, they do provide a
useful check-list of factors to be kept in mind when trying to
contend with detailed questions about democracy in individual
Third World states. Doubts coalesce around whether it is useful to
attempt to isolate distinctive and constant orderings of political
values, beliefs and understanding within societies in order to
explain democratization. There are aberrations – like India, a poor
country with a multiplicity of cultures, religions and castes – which
cannot be explained by reference to a simple 'democracy formula'.

Dependency theory

Dependency analysts argue that democracy is impossible under
the conditions of poverty and exploitation which characterize the
relationship of the Third World and the West; democracy can be
realized *only* by achieving economic and political autonomy (Frank
1984; Amin 1987). Yet, the democratic track record of those
countries which did come close to achieving such autonomy –
Albania, Myanmar (Burma), China, North Korea – leaves no
grounds for optimism that it is the best way to achieve democracy.
Economic autonomy may *theoretically* be desirable – it should,
after all, shelter an economy from the buffeting of international
economic forces – yet it is highly likely to require considerable
authoritarianism to cope with the resulting austerity. Democratization in the Third World did not come about as a result of increased
economic autonomy. In fact, the Third World countries which most
clearly democratized – those of Latin America and several in East
Asia: Taiwan and South Korea – were precisely those which greatly
expanded their exports and hence their involvement in the
international economic system.

The current trend towards democracy in the Third World forced
dependency analysts to revise their assessment that it could not
happen. They began to claim instead that apparent democratic
transformations were not leading to 'real' democracy. In the

dependency view, 'real' democracy involves substantial measures of power passing from the hands of a small political and/or military elite to the mass of ordinary people. Installation of formal democratic structures and procedures is thus only a first step in a more complex and interactive process. Democratic elections must be followed by a process of deepening democratization, which will occur only if the poor join with the middle classes to fight for it. In sum, 'real' democracy will emerge only as a consequence of three developments: (a) strong civilian control over the armed forces; (b) enhanced concern for human rights, economic equity, social justice and the rule of law; (c) greatly increased political participation by the poor, minority ethnic groups, women and young people (Garreton 1991: 106).

In conclusion, the dependency view that democracy would not be possible in the Third World under conditions of Western exploitation became increasingly untenable, as increasing numbers of Third World countries democratized. Attention was then focused upon the alleged superficiality of democratic transitions which did not, in fact, advance the material position of the poor and other excluded classes to an appreciable extent. What was required, in addition, was 'real' democratization which would serve to empower ordinary people.

What is Necessary for Democratic Consolidation?

The debate about what factors are necessary to consolidate democracy in the Third World — for developmentalism, the result of a pro-democracy culture and the efforts of a determined political elite; for dependency theory, the building of 'real' democracy — cannot be settled at the present time, because it is too soon to be sure whether the democratic trend in the Third World will endure or not. It is worth recalling that in the 1950s and 1960s many Third World countries were democratic; most, however, eventually succumbed to anti-democratic take-overs.

But not all. There were eight continuous democracies of more than 25 years' standing in Third World countries of more than one million people before the current wave of democracy — in Latin America and the Caribbean: Jamaica, Trinidad and Tobago, Colombia, Costa Rica and Venezuela; in sub-Saharan Africa: Botswana and Mauritius; and in South Asia: the world's second most populous state, India (Shin 1994: 160; Pinkney 1993: 83; Potter 1993: 370; Rueschemeyer et al. 1992: 189, 192–3).

The question is: how did long-running democratic governments preserve democratic structures, competitive elections and wide-spread civil liberties for long periods? As we have seen, it is not the case that the wealthiest Third World countries are inevitably democratic. The richest Third World country, the United Arab Emirates (UAE, GNP per capita in 1993 of $21,430) had a 'democracy rating' of 10 (out of 100) and a 'human development index'[6] (HDI) of 0.738 (out of 1) in 1993. One of the poorest, on the other hand, Benin ($430) had a 'democracy rating' of 74 and a HDI of 0.113 ('Bite the Ballot' 1994). In other words, economically poor Benin is a thriving democracy, while wealthy UAE has very few democratic credentials. As table 3.1 illustrates, continuous democracies are usually – but not always – good performers on the HDI.

The Third World countries featured in table 3.1 were able to consolidate democratic systems for decades as a result of three factors. First, the development of a democratic political culture is important. Second, a colonial legacy of representative institutions which carried over into the post-colonial period is advantageous. Third, a strong civil society, to provide a countervailing power to that of the state, and a high degree of consensus among political

Table 3.1 Democracy and the human development index (HDI) in continuous democracies of more than one million people, 1993–4

Country	GNP per capita (US dollars, 1993)	Population (millions, 1993)	HDI (0–1) (1993)	Democracy rating (1–100) (1994)
Trinidad and Tobago	3830	1.3	0.855	79
Costa Rica	2150	3.3	0.848	82
Venezuela	2840	20.9	0.820	58
Colombia	1400	35.7	0.813	54
Mauritius	3030	1.1	0.778	n/a
Jamaica	1440	2.4	0.749	64
Botswana	2790	1.4	0.670	74
India	300	898.0	0.382	63

Sources: World Bank 1995: 162, table 1; UNDP 1994: 129–31, table 1; 'Bite the Ballot' 1994

elites appear to be conducive to continuous democratization (Ayoade 1988: 113; Sisson 1993; Rueschemeyer et al. 1992; Sigmund 1993; Chazan 1993; Haynes 1995a). The level of economic prosperity in a consolidated democracy appears to be less important than other factors. To conclude this chapter, we examine the current democratic situation in each Third World region and assess the likelihood of new democracies becoming consolidated.

Democracy in the Third World: Regional Analysis

Latin America and the Caribbean

We shall be concerned primarily with Latin America in this section, because the islands of the Caribbean are noteworthy for a large proportion of continuous democracies, although populations for the most part are very small – well under one million people; as a result, there has been no recent democratic transition.

We noted earlier that in Latin America in the 1960s and 1970s a number of democratic governments, including those of Brazil, Peru, Uruguay, Chile and Argentina, fell to military *coups*. The result was a series of what O'Donnell (1973) called 'bureaucratic authoritarian' regimes, whose stated aim was modernization along Western lines. Such regimes 'attempted to "depoliticize" society in the name of economic efficiency, the nation and social order' (Carnoy 1984: 199). The mass of people were excluded from political decision-making, as there were no democratically elected political institutions; there was a distinct separation between state and civil society. In Chile between 1973 and 1989, Brazil between 1964 and 1984 and Argentina from 1976 to 1983, organized political opposition was not tolerated, human rights were widely abused, and civil society was denied a voice (Remmer 1993). A high proportion of state spending was directed to building up an infrastructure – roads, ports, railways, communications systems – to make Latin America attractive to foreign capital. Later, a series of interacting political and economic crises threatened the ruling elite's position; the result was the granting of elections and a new era of democracy for Latin America.

When the military's grip on power began to slacken, a combination of domestic and international pressures, the latter especially from the United States, resulted in redemocratization in the 1980s. It is sometimes suggested that there has already been a consolidation of democracy in Latin America, i.e. that the region is not experiencing just another event in the traditional rhythm of democratic and authoritarian alternations, but has entered a new historical stage in which democracy – regular elections, broad electoral participation and respect for oppositional rights – is now a widespread feature of regional politics (Diamond 1993a; Remmer 1993; Whitehead 1993).

Three factors suggest, however, that the democratic consolidation in Latin America may not be as widespread or as permanent as some think. First, there is the continuing political presence of the military. There were two serious military *coup* attempts in Venezuela in 1992, and sabre rattling from the armed forces in both Chile and Argentina in 1995 over the issue of the prosecution of military personnel for their human rights abuses during the 1970s. It cannot be ruled out that the military may decide that the time is ripe for their re-entry into politics, especially if economic indicators worsen and public outcry grows. Second, in many countries of the region democracy *has* failed to bring the promised economic rewards; many ordinary people may feel cheated by democracy and may lose faith in the democratic option. During the 1980s, Latin America 'experienced a negative per capita GNP growth rate of −8%', while an estimated three-quarters of the region's population – some 300 million people – suffer from some indication of malnutrition (J. K. Black 1993: 545). Third, there is a disturbing tendency for some democratically elected leaders to use authoritarian tactics to achieve political goals. For example, there was President Fujimori's *auto-golpe* (auto-coup) in Peru in 1994, which was, however, popularly legitimized by his retention of power in general elections in April 1995; the focusing of power in President Menem's hands in Argentina; and the slide into something approaching civil war in several regions of Mexico, including the deprived Chiapas region. Such developments serve collectively to show how democracy has limits in dealing with pressing economic and social issues in Latin America. On the other side of the 'balance sheet', the reinstallation of democracy in Haiti and Fernando Cardoso's convincing electoral victory on a platform of economic and social reform in Brazil, both in 1994, suggest that the redemocratization trend in the region has not yet run out of steam.

The answer to the question of whether democracy will endure in the region is unclear. Latin America's poor economic growth record in recent times is a cause for concern. Unemployment remains a problem in both rural and urban areas. It is by no means certain that ordinary people would choose democracy and poverty rather than authoritarianism and economic growth if offered the choice. It is a question of 'the wisdom of politicians, and the people who elect them, [in helping] to preserve democracy' (Pinkney 1993: 91).

Sub-Saharan Africa

If democracy's consolidation in Latin America is problematic, its chances of longevity in sub-Saharan Africa are even more so. Despite the almost miraculous creation of democracy in South Africa in 1994, in no small part due to the almost unparalleled statesmanship of Nelson Mandela, the states of the region are generally multi-ethnic and multi-religion countries with tiny middle classes, still embryonic civil societies, and without much encouragement from the West to democratize (Haynes 1993b, 1993c, 1995a, 1996). Add to this widespread economic underdevelopment[7] and poverty, and the situation is not auspicious for democracy to flourish.

Until recently, most of sub-Saharan Africa's governing regimes were either military, one-party or personalist in character. Nevertheless, from the mid-1980s popular demands began to be focused on democracy, economic reforms and human rights, reflecting an awakening of political voice on the part of a number of groups, including trade union and Christian church officials, higher education students, business people and some civil servants (Bratton and van der Walle 1991: 32). Such demands were later made integral parts of political programmes by professional politicians. The expectation was that popular efforts would force long-entrenched, usually venal, governments from office. Democratic regimes would take power. New leaders would tackle pressing economic problems with energy, resourcefulness and imagination; previously ignored political constituencies would be heard; human rights would be observed, including the precious freedom to criticize governments without fear of incarceration.

By 1995 agitation for change had resulted in the ousting of a number of rulers in about two-fifths of the region's more than 40 countries, whether by the ballot-box or by extra-constitutional means. Changes of regime occurred in Benin, Cape Verde, the Central African Republic, Ethiopia, the Gambia, Guinea-Bissau, Lesotho, Madagascar, Malawi, Mali, Namibia, Niger, Sao Tom, Sierra Leone, South Africa and Zambia. Elsewhere, regimes demonstrated an ability to stay put, either by winning often controversial elections – e.g. Ghana, Kenya, Burkina Faso, Gabon, Seychelles and Cameroon – or by simply refusing to budge – e.g. Togo, Zaire and Nigeria. A few dissolved into civil war: Somalia, Sudan, Liberia, Rwanda and Burundi.

Recent demands for political and economic changes in Africa parallel those of the 1950s in relation to colonial rule. In the era of anti-colonial agitation, coalitions of associational groups challenged imperial governments for power. Professional, student and labour groups led popular protest against rulers who were commonly perceived as unfit to govern: they were European, against African aspirations, and unrepresentative. In the 1950s the goal was overwhelmingly nationalist in focus; 'Self-Rule, Now!', often the rallying cry. Forty years later, European administrations had been replaced by African regimes, which proved disastrous failures at ruling, if we understand that term to include some responsibility to seek to increase citizens' well-being in a reasonably regularized, systematic way.

In conclusion, demands for democratization and economic change in Africa can best be explained by way of a rediscovery of political voice by long quiescent interest groups, encouraged by international developments, whose concerns were understandably exacerbated by years of popular frustration and disappointment that the promises of independence had turned out to be hollow. It is unlikely, however, that the chances for increasing the numbers of democratic states – or the consolidation of many of the existing democracies – is very high, because of the lack of strong working classes and middle classes, poor economic prospects, under-developed political cultures of tolerance, and a lack of consensus on the part of the political elites that democracy is the best way forward.

The Middle East and North Africa

Analysis of the political systems of the Arab countries of the Middle East and North Africa tend to be dealt with in scholarly analysis in isolation from other Third World regions. This is partly because of the political and cultural impact of Islam, partly because the region's countries were not widely colonized by Europeans, and partly because oil wealth is said to give the politics of the Middle East a unique flavour. Yet, while all countries in the region, with the exception of Israel, are predominantly Muslim, not all are oil-rich. Saudi Arabia, Algeria, UAE, Libya, Qatar, Oman, Kuwait, Iran, Iraq and a few others have significant oil reserves, while others, including Yemen, Syria and Jordan, have either very limited supplies or none. In fact, Middle Eastern countries are actually like many others in the Third World, in that their relationship with the international economy is linked to their export of primary products. Oil is a raw material much like any other; the region's countries do not always gain anything extra through having oil.

Adapting Huntington's (1991) terminology, we can discern two 'waves' of political liberalization in the region at earlier periods. The first occurred with the creation of national assemblies in Egypt, North Africa and the Arabian peninsular between the 1860s and the 1930s. This was followed by a second wave of political liberalization, manifested by the creation of parliamentary regimes in Egypt (1924–58), Iraq (1936–58) and Lebanon (1946–75). In the 1950s and 1960s, however, incumbent governments, often headed by unrepresentative monarchs, were overthrown in a number of countries, including Egypt, Iraq, Libya and Syria, by radical, often youthful army officers. They saw themselves as political modernizers, smashing the traditionalist political systems by overthrowing narrowly based governments regarded as unduly subservient to the West and opposed to social developments that threatened to undermine their dominance (Owen 1992). Yet, as far as the current period is concerned, there is no 'third wave' of democracy in the region. Apart from democratic Egypt, Lebanon, which democratized in the early 1990s after two decades of civil war, Jordan, tentatively democratizing under the tutelage of King Hussein, and Tunisia, currently allowing more political freedoms, the region's governments are authoritarian and unrepresentative.

We noted above three factors which appear to be of significance in democratic consolidation in the Third World: a suitable colonial legacy, a determination of political elites to democratize, and a relatively strong civil society. The explanation for the shortfall of democracy in the region is not to be found in levels of economic development – at $20,140, UAE's annual per capita GNP is greater than Britain's; at $7,820, Saudi Arabia's is four times that of democratic Poland; and at $6,120, Oman's is similar to that of Greece – but in the underdeveloped civil societies, small middle classes and low proportions of workers employed in industrial production – a traditional source of pressure for democracy. For example, Saudi Arabia and Oman had 14 and 22 per cent respectively of their work-forces employed in industry in 1991, while the figures for Poland and Greece were 41 and 28 per cent (Thomas et al 1994: 76–7, table 2).

There is also an important cultural factor in the failure of the region to democratize widely: it is sometimes argued that Islam is incompatible with Western conceptions of liberal democracy, and that Arab/Muslim society and political culture is predominantly 'patriarchal or patrimonial, [with] loyalties to religious sects, clans, or ethnic groups tend[ing] to vitiate any incentive toward the individual initiative and choice necessary to the democratic process' (Dorr 1993: 132). These factors are also thought to have a negative impact on the building of strong civil societies by restricting the growth of the particularistic and occupational interest groups which are usually regarded as essential building blocks of democracy (Esposito and Piscatori 1991).

Several countries in the region *do* have democratic systems, but these are exceptions to the norm. The chances for the widespread emergence – much less consolidation – of democratic regimes in North Africa and the Middle East seem slim, not only because the cultural conditions for them seem unpropitious, but also because incumbent state elites, often buoyed by oil revenues, retain a tight political grip. Significantly, democracy in Lebanon came after years of civil war, is underwritten by Syria, and may not endure, while Jordan's democracy centres on the whim of King Hussein. Not only do there not seem to be widely present sufficiently strong civil societies to force change, but most incumbent political elites seem unconvinced of the attractions of democracy.

South Asia

In contrast to the situation in the Middle East and North Africa, all of South Asia's main countries – India, Pakistan, Sri Lanka, Nepal and Bangladesh – are democracies. They have in common a British colonial legacy which may have been conducive to the establishment of post-colonial democracy. This factor should not, however, be overestimated. South Asian countries differ radically in terms of size, economic structure, geography, political traditions, religious affiliation, relations with external powers, diversity of peoples and forms of rule. In the post-colonial period these factors led rulers to seek a wide variety of solutions to the problem of building national unity, with democracy at times bypassed by military and other forms of non-democratic rule.

Rizvi (1995: 84) argues that the 'democratic transformation of South Asia in the aftermath of the Cold War has been breath-taking'. While both India and Sri Lanka have enjoyed long periods of democratic rule since independence, Bangladesh and Pakistan had years of military government, while, until recently, Nepal was a monarchical system with only a very limited degree of democracy. Yet, Bangladesh, Nepal and Pakistan now have democratic governments, while both India and Sri Lanka have shown that, despite political killings, upheavals and sectarian militancy, their democratic institutions are strong enough to endure.

As noted above in relation to sub-Saharan Africa, the election of a popular government is only the first step in democratic consolidation. The evidence from South Asia is that the democratic process in the new democracies – Nepal, Pakistan and Bangladesh – is not secure. Despite the impact of popular pressure which, as in sub-Saharan Africa and Latin America, helped to bring in democratic change, the masses of ordinary people still remain relatively marginal to the political process. The class composition of the leadership is still much as it was previously; in fact, many of the elites of the old order are still in or near power in the new arrangements. This is because the transfer of power was not a result of a comprehensive defeat of the old elites who stood behind the previous authoritarian rule. Rather, as in sub-Saharan Africa, the transfer of power was a result of negotiations between old and putative elites; in the end, the *status quo* prevailed. In other words, the new elites share many of the interests and concerns of their predecessors.

The result is that the newly democratic regimes in South Asia have actually not done much to give the mass of ordinary citizens a stake in the continuation of the new democratic order. Popular access to government is constrained by layers of bureaucracy. Bottom-up demands and fears do not usually filter through to a leadership which distances itself from the electorate. For democracy to survive and to thrive, as Rizvi (1995: 85) acknowledges, 'there has to be a continuing partnership between the elected leaders and the electorate'. This is necessary so that the latter can develop a real interest in the preservation of an elected government. At the moment this seems to be an objective not in easy reach in South Asia.

East and South-east Asia

As in the Middle East, there is no general trend towards democracy in the East and South-east Asia region. Many of the region's countries are either authoritarian or engaged in only the early stages of political liberalization. Nevertheless, two of the leading economic powers of the region, South Korea and Taiwan, are of particular interest in a discussion of recent democratization, since they manage to combine swift economic growth, as table 3.2 shows, with political liberalization and democratization. Because of their importance in terms of delivering simultaneous economic growth and democracy, we shall focus upon them below.

As we have already seen, dependency theory is concerned with the problematic of Third World economic growth in a capitalist international system. Contrary to the argument of dependency theory, however, both Taiwan and South Korea 'ha[ve] experienced one of the most profound records of development . . . in human history over recent decades' (King 1993: 141). Pye (1985: 3) is not wide of the mark when he notes that developmental 'theories had a close empirical fit with the experience of [some states in] Asia but not with those of either Africa or Latin America'. In South Korea and Taiwan, transition from authoritarian to

Table 3.2 South Korea and Taiwan: selected economic indicators, 1993

Country	GNP per capita ($, 1993)	Annual growth (%, 1980s)	Distribution of GNP, 1993 Industry	Agriculture
South Korea	7,660	8.7	45.0[a]	2.0
Taiwan	7,997	8.7[b]	42.3	8.0[a]

[a] 1991.
[b] 1980–2.

Sources: King 1993: 139; Thomas et al. 1994: 76–7, table 2; World Bank 1995: 164–5, table 2

democratic rule was a result of the development of elite consensus as to the virtues of democracy, political cultures tolerant to democracy, strong civil societies and expanding economic prosperity.

Taiwan

The most prominent characteristic of Taiwan's political system until 1988 was one-party rule. Until then, the Kuomintang (KMT), the only party allowed, had enjoyed supreme dominance since its leading cadres arrived in 1949 after suffering defeat at the hands of the Communists in mainland China. Initially, the KMT government was preoccupied with the issue of national security, since a military invasion by Communist China – to unify Taiwan with the mainland by force – seemed imminent in the 1950s, and still remains a possibility today. As a result of China's sabre rattling, Taiwan received copious economic and military aid from the United States (King 1993: 143–4). During the 1960s the KMT government transformed itself into a type of bureaucratic-authoritarian (BA) regime. As noted earlier in relation to Latin America, the chief characteristics of the BA state are that, first, it restricts political competition to a small elite, and general elections are not allowed, and second, when the limits of import-substitution industrialization are reached, the elite of military and civilian technocrats begins to work closely with foreign capital. A consequence is a demand for stringent sacrifices from the working class accompanied by political repression.

During the BA stage in Taiwan, the KMT government, unlike its counterparts in Latin America, made extensive land reforms, expropriating land from large-scale landowners and passing it to smallholders for cultivation. The result was a strong agricultural sector, which allowed growing profits to be invested in industrialization. Industrial growth was swift, with an average rate of more than 13 per cent a year between 1953 and 1982. As a result, huge balance of payments surpluses became common. By 1982, the GNP was twelve times greater than it had been 30 years earlier, while GNP growth rates averaged 8.7 per cent per annum. By 1995 Taiwan had the second largest foreign reserves in the world: an estimated $99 billion. Social indicators of living standards, including percentages of those in education at primary, secondary and tertiary levels, those with electricity, telephones, cars and television sets, showed huge increases.

The effects of swift industrialization, economic growth, increases in living standards, and the growth of strong middle and working classes led to demands for political liberalization. Following initial suspicion, the political elite gradually began to favour the idea of democracy. Egged on by the United States, Taiwan emerged as a democracy in the late 1980s.

South Korea

In 1950 Korea[8] had an annual GNP per capita of $146. Forty-five years later, South Korea was an impressive economic and industrial power, with GNP per capita of $7,660. As in Taiwan, strong economic growth was guided by the state, which was heavily authoritarian, but developmentally oriented. Between the 1960s and the late 1980s, a series of military governments centralized economic decision-making in the hands of technocrats who were delegated considerable economic powers, creating considerable state autonomy with respect to key social groups, especially labour. Government established a close alliance with the large business groups, the *chaebols*, while restructuring the bureaucracy and, as a result, bringing about considerable institutional transformation. The reformed development apparatus set about forcefully to encourage export-oriented industrialization.

Like Taiwan, South Korea was assisted by a Japanese colonial legacy of bureaucratization, centralization and the beginnings of an entrepreneurial class; by post-war land reform, in this case imposed by the United States; and by the presence of a major security threat and of a big power patron – America – that wanted an anti-Communist bastion. The United States provided considerable financial, economic and technical assistance. With good timing, South Korea also gained from the relatively open world markets and overall economic growth of the 1950s and 1960s. Compared to major Latin American countries, South Korea relied more on aid and borrowing from the international capital markets and less on direct foreign investment. Effected by substantial societal and cultural integration and by relatively high levels of educational attainment, South Korea managed to attain higher levels of both state competence and sophistication than did many Latin American states. These factors were central ingredients in the country's success. State leaders, as in Taiwan, successfully developed connections with the world economy. The country acquired and mastered new technologies, knowledge and institutions to build up local capacities. The result was that South Korea swiftly managed to transform its erstwhile position of dependence to become one of the world's leading industrial powers.

The Korean development model attracted a great deal of attention, due to its record of sustained economic growth, swift industrialization and, latterly, democratization. Wade and Kim (1978: 40) explain how economic growth in South Korea was facilitated by both a 'strong' – i.e. authoritative – state and by the development of an environment favourable to long-term decision-making: 'economic development [was] in large part due to the consolidation and stabilization of political power and the determination with which policy [was] implemented. . . . Constitutional reforms . . . tended to augment the authority of central and particularly executive institutions'.

To sum up developments in South Korea and Taiwan, one of the corollaries of swift economic growth in both countries was a strong authoritarian state. In both states growing per capita incomes, coupled with emerging working and middle classes, led to demands for democracy. In both countries, democratization proceeded through several stages (Robison 1988). First, military-dominated governments nurtured the development of industrial capitalism and initially fragile capital-owning classes. Second, non-democratic regimes were appropriate agents for undertaking a number of vital political and economic functions essential to the growth of capitalism in the late twentieth century, including the suppression of reformist and revolutionary groups, channeling state investment into heavy industry and infrastructure provision, offering cheap credit provision to nascent capitalists, building effective tariff protection and trade monopolies, and educating and skilling the work-force. Third, a 'pact of domination' developed between leading capitalists and the military bureaucratic leaders of the state apparatus. Fourth, capitalist industrialization led to a situation in which the governing regime came under growing pressure from capital-owning and middle classes who found state controls irksome. This led to a weakening of the 'pact of domination', a concomitant increase in intra-elite conflict, and, in time, the undermining of the social basis of authoritarian rule. Fifth, domestic structural transformations were reinforced by international leverage. Because of the growth of exports, both countries became strongly integrated into the international division of labour. Freer movement of goods, labour and capital were essential for continued capitalist expansion. Democratic, or at least liberalized, government was therefore necessary. Sixth, a contingent factor favouring democratization was that the 1980s was a period of general weakening of authoritarian governments in many parts of the world. Finally, in both Taiwan and South Korea prolonged economic success led to calls for political liberalization and democratization from the growing middle and working classes, who desired a say in governmental decisions. It is highly likely that democracy will be consolidated in both countries as international pressure, political elites and strong civil societies all favour it.[9]

Despite current democratic advances, it is not inconceivable that some Latin American countries will oscillate between unstable dictatorship and unstable democracy for the foreseeable future. Sustained, relatively equitably spread economic growth is important, although not necessarily sufficient on its own, to ensure the consolidation of democracy. Civil societies will need to keep a vigilant eye on government, while political elites need to remain convinced that their own interests are best served by democracy. The military's political influence remains strong throughout the region, while political parties are relatively unconsolidated. As we shall see in chapter 4, many Latin American state apparatuses were weakened by the adjustment policies imposed to deal with the burden of economic reform in the 1980s and 1990s. The result of a weakening of state capacity may be increasingly authoritarian government – as in Peru and Argentina – in the guise of democracy. Or the outcome may be serious political instability leading to the reintroduction of the military to government.

In sub-Saharan Africa, there is a reasonably strong democratic trend, which is, however, likely to be reversed due to continued economic crisis, weak civil societies and political elites not yet always convinced of the virtues of democracy. In the Middle East, on the other hand, there is no real sign of a decisive shift to democracy, so the issue of consolidation does not yet occur. Regarding South Asia, while currently democratic, it is by no means unlikely that some of the region's countries will revert to undemocratic forms of government; as in sub-Saharan Africa, not all the indicators for democracy's continuance are favourable. As far as the examples of Taiwan and South Korea are concerned, the development of a culture of tolerance and a desire for consensus on the part of political elites seems to be important in developing a climate conducive to democracy. In addition, both countries enjoyed sustained economic growth *relatively* equitably distributed, which led to pressure from growing middle and working classes for democracy. While Lipset was wrong to claim that prosperity is the *only* important variable which results in democracy, clearly it *is* significant.

Away from the newly industrializing countries of East Asia, many Third World countries experienced not only sometimes tentative democratization but also economic decline during the 1980s and early 1990s. Pressure for democracy was exacerbated in many states by a declining economic position. As a result, many embarked upon International Monetary Fund-sponsored economic structural adjustment programmes. The consequences nearly everywhere, however, were disappointing: declining living standards (especially for the poor), high inflation, growing unemployment and reductions in state welfare programmes where they existed. In the next chapter we examine the political and economic ramifications of attempts at economic reform.

Notes

1   The two earlier waves of democratization were in the late nineteenth century, with democratic government evolving throughout much of Western Europe, and after World War II, with the redemocratization of Germany, Italy and Japan.
2   India has had two communist state administrations – in Kerala and West Bengal – for years, while Nepal had a minority Communist government for a few months in 1995 before it collapsed.
3   Many believe, e.g., that national elections in Indonesia are routinely and extensively rigged. As Thompson (1993: 474) observes, the ruling Golkar party has won between 63 and 73 per cent of votes cast in five-yearly elections since 1971 against two 'opposition' parties tightly controlled by the state.
4   A country's gross *national* product (GNP) is closely related to its gross *domestic* product (GDP). The GDP is a territorial concept measuring value produced in a given country, while the GNP measures value produced by 'factors of production' – capital and labour – of a given country, wherever in the world they may operate.
5   Economic growth rates were an average 4.2 per cent a year during the 1980–93 period, delivering a gross national product (GNP) per capita of $740 (World Bank 1995: 162, table 1).
6   The concept of the human development index (HDI) will be discussed fully in chapter 4. The HDI is a cumulative index based on the following: life expectancy, infant mortality, mean years of schooling,

rate of illiteracy, 'real' GDP per capita. The HDI for each of the world's countries is reported annually in the *Human Development Report* published by the United Nations Development Programme.

7   Only five of sub-Saharan Africa's more than 40 states – Botswana, Gabon, Mauritius, Namibia and South Africa – had per capita GNPs greater than $1,000 in 1993, whereas of the 23 Latin American and Caribbean states with populations of over one million people in each, only six – Bolivia, Dominican Republic, Guatemala, Haiti, Honduras and Nicaragua – *did not* have per capita GNPs of more than $1,000 (World Bank 1995: 162–3, table 1).

8   Following an inconclusive civil war in 1950–3, Korea was divided into two halves, North and South Korea.

9   Opinions differ as to whether South Korea's and Taiwan's democratization is a cosmetic or a substantive process. I favour the latter. For the first view, see Gills et al. 1993: 226–57; for the second, see King 1993: 150–1.

4

Economic Growth
and Development

In this chapter we are concerned with measures necessary for managing the economy so as to increase economic growth and development. Like the problem of how to cultivate and consolidate democracy, the issues of economic growth and development are of central importance to analysis of Third World politics. This is not only because it is often empirically difficult to separate political and economic issues, but also the question of *how* the fruits of *economic* growth should be distributed is an intensely *political* controversy: the core of the 'development' issue.

Two things are necessary for sustained economic growth, whether in the Third World or elsewhere: economically competent governments and a favourable combination of international circumstances. Over the last 20 years, the former have seemed to be rather rare, while an often unfavourable international economic environment has been overcome by only a few. The result was that the 1980s were economically disastrous for most Latin American, African and Middle Eastern states, with only patchy improvements in the early 1990s, although better for many Asian states.

We begin with a brief historical account of the emergence of the Third World as a distinct economic entity. This will enable us to place the contemporary economic division *between* various Third World regions in perspective: the subject of the second section. Third, we examine the concept of *development*, arguing that the latter is not an inevitable consequence of economic growth, but that governments must not only direct sufficient resources to the attainment of development goals, but must also ensure that all sectors of society benefit from their policies. Finally, we assess the consequences of serious foreign indebtedness and the imposition of structural adjustment programmes on the people of Latin America and sub-Saharan Africa.

The Growth of an Economically Distinct Third World

What separates most Third World countries from their Western industrial counterparts is their *peripherality*. Peripherality refers to the division of the vast majority of Third World economies from, and their subordination to, the pivotal industrial economies of Western Europe, the United States and Japan. The Third World's peripherality is a consequence of a process which began in the late fifteenth century, when the previously scattered peoples of the world were gradually brought together into a global economic system dominated initially by a few European states seeking colonies to expand international influence (Dolan 1993: 259).

During the nineteenth and the first half of the twentieth century their colonial areas exported raw materials to the industrial economies, and manufactured goods were sent the other way. During the 1930s, however, a global economic recession developed, followed by World War II. Many governments felt that the slide into war had been facilitated by the effects of the Depression, which had encouraged states to act for their own short-term interests rather than helping to develop global solutions. After the war it was widely believed that rules to oversee international economic transactions were necessary to prevent a recurrence. As a result, economic rules were introduced under the aegis of the United States. They were regulated by the 'Bretton Woods'[1] organizations: the International Monetary Fund and the International Bank for Reconstruction and Development (popularly known as the World Bank), and, following a conference in Geneva in 1947, the General Agreement on Tariffs and Trade (replaced in January 1994 by the World Trade Organization).

As we have already seen, most Third World states gained their independence after World War II. As a result, they entered the global economic system when its structure was already determined. Compared with the period of Western industrialization in the nineteenth century, when most of the world was agrarian, the post-1945 situation was different. In the nineteenth century, newly industrializing countries did not have to compete with others: early industrializers, like Britain, were able to grow by monopolizing trade in manufactured goods, both at home and abroad.

By contrast, the states of the Third World did not start from a position where competition was minimal and no restraints existed on entering the world market. As Clapham (1985: 5) explains: 'The industrial economies . . . created the system, . . . developed the technology needed to work it, and . . . have the sophisticated productive capacity that holds it together.' I am not suggesting that this set of circumstances condemns *all* Third World countries to a subordinate economic position – there are several clear-cut economic success stories – but it *did* tie their economies to a global system of production and distribution controlled by the industrialized countries of the West.

During the 1950s and 1960s there was a generalized and sustained period of economic growth for virtually all countries, Third World states included. In the early 1970s, however, a further series of disruptions to the world economic system occurred. First, the American economy, the most powerful in the world, suffered strains following the country's reverses in Vietnam. Second, oil price rises in 1973 and 1979 led to the sudden prominence of Middle Eastern oil-producing countries.

The new influence of the latter was reflected in their backing for calls for a 'new international economic order' (NIEO). NIEO aspirations reflected demands for a comprehensive restructuring of the world economy in favour of the Third World, because it was felt that, despite strong global growth for more than two decades, the international economic system discriminated against Third World countries. The West, on the other hand, was united in the belief that the world economy did not need fundamental restructuring. Nevertheless, during the 1980s, the position of many Third World countries declined further, with growing foreign debt, falling aid, very little – if any – price support for primary products and a great deal of protectionism from Western countries.

Third World Economies in the 1980s and 1990s: Regional Analysis

The 1980s and early 1990s, as table 4.1 indicates, saw a sharp divergence in economic performance between Third World regions.

Table 4.1 GNP per capita average annual growth by region, 1980–93

Region	GNP per capita: average annual growth (%), 1980–93
East Asia and Pacific	6.4
South Asia	3.0
Latin America and Caribbean	−0.1
Sub-Saharan Africa	−0.8
Middle East and North Africa	−2.4

Source: World Bank 1995: 163, table 1

These years were especially disappointing both for the Middle East and North Africa, with GNP per capita declining by an average 2.4 per cent per annum, and for sub-Saharan Africa, with an average fall of 0.8 per cent a year. The 1980s and early 1990s were also disappointing for Latin America and the Caribbean – average GNP per capita dropped by 0.1 per cent per annum – although economic results elsewhere were better.

South Asia performed well, with 3.0 per cent growth during the same period, although mass poverty is present in Bangladesh, Bhutan and parts of India (Lane and Ersson 1994: 94). East Asia did best of all, recording a highly satisfactory average annual growth in GNP per capita of 6.4 per cent during 1980–93. These data indicate that East Asia is at one end of a performance continuum, and Africa and the Middle East at the other. It should be borne in mind, however, that these are *average* figures: some countries in each region outperformed others in the same area. Nevertheless, the regional economic performance indicators show that the idea of a Third World united by its collective economic peripherality and weakness is outdated.

Middle East and North Africa

There were various reasons for poor performances. The oil-producing countries of this region experienced economic downturn as the world price of oil fell, halving in price from $26 to $13 per barrel between 1985 and 1986, before settling down to around $17 a barrel in the early 1990s (Bill and Springborg 1994: 423). As a result, many of the region's states sought to reform their economies, although some had begun a reform process earlier (Owen 1992: 138). The results, however, were generally disappointing.

The reformist trend began with the Tunisian government's attempt to reverse the process of state-led development in the late 1960s. This was followed by Egypt's *intifah* ('liberalization' or 'opening up') policy, introduced by President Sadat in 1974, the challenge to 'socialist' planning which resulted from Chadli Benjedid's accession to power in Algeria in 1978, and by the structural adjustments begun in Turkey just before the military *coup* of 1980. Later, during the 1980s, 'many more regimes, including oil producers, began a process of attempting to reduce the state's share of national resources consumption' (Owen 1992: 138).

Attempts to alter statist systems of economic management in the Middle East and North Africa ran into problems. Both 'demand side' – involving changes in the exchange rate or reduction of budget deficits – and 'supply side' – concerning attempts to increase exports – ran up against a web of vested interests which made fundamental change impossible (Owen 1992: 141).

Sub-Saharan Africa

The 'quality of life' indicators for this region are far below those of the West or even of more affluent Third World areas such as East Asia. Angola, Benin, Ethiopia, Guinea, Liberia, Mozambique, Niger, Sierra Leone, Somalia and Zaire are some of the poorest states in sub-Saharan Africa.[2] Despite widespread poverty, many of the region's governments were slow to embark on systematic economic reforms; once again, the power of vested interests helped to prevent change. Yet, the need for socio-economic change in sub-Saharan Africa is obvious: each year in the region more than 4 million children die before they reach the age of 5, a third of all African children are malnourished, one in eight is disabled, and one in three has no primary education.

To help combat such conditions, the region's share of global aid more than doubled from the early 1970s. Despite this, the vast majority of the region's economies performed poorly. The problem is that increased aid flows on their own are not enough: as we shall see later, without debt relief to put the region's economies on a sound footing, there is little hope of an economic turn around. With gross debts now more than 100 per cent of annual export output, and with service payments over three times annual export earnings, the continent is stuck in a vice from which it cannot easily escape. Sub-Saharan Africa, increasingly peripheral to the world economy, is suffering most in the harsh international climate of the 1990s, because it is by far the weakest region economically (Callaghy 1993: 180).

Latin America and the Caribbean

This region falls in the middle range of Third World regional economic performance during the 1980s and early 1990s. Those years were relatively poor for the region, largely because of a foreign debt crisis which reversed the previously positive trend in per capita income and brought about a general and severe setback. The debt crisis, as we shall see below, was partially brought under control by the early 1990s via a reduction in the foreign debt of most Latin American countries in return for adoption of market-oriented reforms. One result was to save governments money; another was to bolster both national and international confidence. By the early 1990s, the general trend was for the majority of the region's economies to show some signs of economic recovery (Philip 1993: 555). Yet, as we shall see by focusing on Mexico, economic recovery was sometimes short-lived.

South Asia

Like Latin America, most of the countries of South Asia, embarked on extensive economic reforms in the 1980s or 1990s, with reform focused on rethinking the role of the state. Such a turn of events was especially surprising in India, where state control was for many years the core of economic policy.

After many years of prevarication, India finally engaged in serious economic reform from the second half of the 1980s. Until then, India had a very inward-looking, heavily statist economy, whose direction, according to Callaghy (1993: 194), was justified and defended by a commanding ideological mix of 'socialism, self-reliance, nationalism and Third World pride'. The immediate cause of the reforms was a debt crisis, although larger economic pressures had been building.

Even though economic growth in the 1980s was respectable, it was little more than a third that recorded by South Korea. In the mid-1950s, however, India and South Korea had both had the *same* per capita income; three decades later South Korea had surged ahead with a figure *ten times that of India*. With exports accounting for less than 5 per cent of GDP, the Indian government began to realize that – like South Korea – the way forward was to focus on export-led growth. A succession of weak governments in the 1980s, however, lacked the ability and political will to reorientate the economy. Balance of payments imbalances and inflation grew, while foreign exchange reserves dropped; as a result, a debt crisis loomed. By the early 1990s, India's foreign debt – $83 billion – was the third highest in the world; only those of Brazil and Mexico were greater. The country's debt service ratio – i.e. the proportion of export earnings devoted to paying the interest on foreign debt – was 30.1 per cent, four times South Korea's manageable 7.1 per cent on a debt of $35 billion (World Bank 1995: 200–1, table 20). On top of this came the Gulf Crisis of 1990–1 which (temporarily) led to higher oil prices and hence increased price inflation. India's reluctance to restructure economically was finally dispelled in mid-1991, when $600 million was due to be repaid in debt servicing which the government did not have. The result was serious economic restructuring which, while leading to rapid growth, nevertheless exacerbated the already serious socio-economic divisions between rich and poor.

East and South-east Asia

The best economic performance of any Third World region in the 1980s and early 1990s was that of East and South-east Asia. In particular, South Korea, Taiwan, Hong Kong and Singapore performed well, managing to offset shortfalls in raw materials' earnings by substantial increases of exports of manufactured goods. In order to appreciate South Korea's success as the region's leading economy (in terms of overall output), it will be useful to compare its economic performance with those of countries which, a few decades ago, were at the same developmental stage.

As noted above, Korea's economic situation was similar to India's in the 1950s; it was also akin to those of two sub-Saharan African countries, Kenya and Nigeria. In 1950, Korea had a GNP per capita of $146, while Kenya and Nigeria managed $129 and $150 respectively. By 1993, South Korea's per capita GNP had grown to $7,660, while Nigeria's and Kenya's were a mere $340 each (Callaghy 1993: 185). In other words, in little more than

40 years South Korea's per capita GNP had grown from parity to a figure *more than eighteen times* greater than those of Kenya and Nigeria. It is evident that South Korea enjoyed impressive economic success, while Nigeria and Kenya fell far behind. What explains the difference in economic outcomes between South Korea and Kenya and Nigeria?

One factor in the success of South Korea was that, because of its status as chief bastion against communism in the region, the country received 6 per cent of the global aid allocated in 1960, even though its population was less than 1 per cent of that of the Third World as a whole. Aid was used to build up local industry, while the approval signified by relatively large resource transfers from Western donors encouraged foreign investors to risk long-term commitments. On the other hand, Nigeria had extensive oil deposits, yielding over $150 billion, which South Korea lacked (Naanen 1995). The disparity in performance between Nigeria and South Korea or between the latter and India cannot be explained by natural resource endowment or levels of foreign aid alone. Rather, the crucial issue is: how *effective* is government in pushing through its policies? While reserving a discussion of such issues until chapter 5, it is worth noting that a lack of religious and/or ethnic divisions in a country may well be conducive to economic growth. For example, the homogeneity of South Korean society contrasts sharply with the cultural, ethnic and religious fragmentation of India, Kenya and Nigeria. As a result, given that each state had to work within the same international economic system, it is plausible to suggest that (a) the higher the level of societal homogeneity and (b) the more expert government is in directing the national economy towards universal goals, the more likely there is to be (1) not only sustained economic growth but also (2) relative equity in distribution of resources. In sum, the example of South Korea suggests that it is crucial for sustained economic growth and development that governments deal expertly with actors both inside and outside their country's borders.

In conclusion, Third World regional economic outcomes in the 1980s and early 1990s differed widely, ranging from 'highly disappointing' in the Middle East and Africa, to 'poor' in Latin America and the Caribbean, 'satisfactory' in South Asia, and 'highly satisfactory' in East and South-east Asia. The newly industrializing countries of the latter region are especially noteworthy, because they are the paradigmatic cases of both rapid local industrialization and effective adjustment to a changing international economic situation. Apart from the ability to deal with international actors – i.e. the external dimension – their success shows that it is crucial for Third World governments to exhibit clear signs of purpose and capability in relation to internal factors.

Problems of Development

Explanations of Third World economic outcomes focus on domestic factors in developmental analysis, with the external dimension in dependency analysis. Having discussed the economic views of the traditional analytic paradigms in chapter 1, we need only briefly restate their views now. We will then be in a position to turn to an exploration of the problems of 'development'.

The main presumption of the developmental perspective is that economic growth will take place in Third World countries whose governments manage to adopt and operate *appropriate*, i.e. *capitalist, economic mechanisms*. Such an expectation appears to be borne out by the experience of both South Korea and Taiwan. A further assumption of developmental theory is that societies go through the same *stages* of development: the contemporary Third World represents a stage through which the West passed several centuries ago. But this ignores not only cultural and economic diversity *within* the Third World, but also the fact of a volatile international economic system which some governments deal with competently and others do not. The dependency view, by contrast, argues that the very *structure* of the capitalist world economy effectively prohibits general Third World economic growth. The successes of East Asia's newly industrializing countries refute this argument. Neither view is overly concerned with development issues. Nevertheless, we need to explore the concept of development before we can properly place differing economic outcomes for Third World regions in social context.

Development and the Third World

When many Third World states were emerging from colonial servitude in the 1950s and 1960s, 'development' was equated with Western industrial capitalism, except in the socialist world. In the West, development was seen as a process of change making

'traditional' Third World societies more 'modernized', i.e. industrialized, urbanized, and educated (Randall and Theobald 1985; So
1990; Cammack et al. 1993; Marchand and Parpart 1995).

More recently, what 'development' *actually* connotes has become
both a complex and a contentious issue. It is complex, because it is
no longer clear what 'development' involves. Is it a question of
economic growth alone? Or does it relate to *redistribution* of the
fruits of growth as well? In what ways is development beneficial,
and to whom? The issue has become contentious, because there
are differing opinions about how to designate development. Is it
simply a *quantitative* process, measured, e.g., by the number of
cars and television sets in a country? Or is it more of a qualitative
process, e.g., what is the rate of literacy in a society? How many
children are in the educational system? While there is no objective
answer to this conundrum, it is perhaps best to think of development as a twofold process involving *both* economic growth *and*
significant changes in various aspects of social life.

Development conveys not only the idea of technological change,
but also increases in people's material resources and their 'quality
of life'. Lack of development, on the other hand, means that most
people in a society have insufficient material resources and are
'obliged to struggle even to survive' (Hadjor 1993: 100). There is a
strong argument that development is really only a meaningful
concept if it measures improvements in humanity's well-being.
Quantitative economic growth on its own does not necessarily
produce *generalized* development. Some Third World countries –
such as oil-rich United Arab Emirates (UAE) and Kuwait and the
East Asian industrialized island states of Singapore and Hong Kong
– had per capita GNPs of at least $18,000 in 1993, i.e. the same or
better than Britain's (World Bank 1995: 162–3, table 1). The
governments and citizens of UAE, Hong Kong and the others do
not, however, necessarily share the idea that a *welfare* state is
necessary to redistribute wealth: in Kuwait, UAE and Hong Kong
especially, much national wealth remains largely in the hands of a
small elite (Hadjor 1993: 100).

The quandary of how to perceive and measure development led
the United Nations Development Programme (UNDP) to devise the
human development index (HDI) in 1990. The HDI is an attempt to
arrive at an *objective* conception of development, by combin-
ing indicators of economic and social welfare. The HDI, now published annually, seeks to apportion equal weight to a number of

development attributes, including life expectancy at birth, educational attainment and the 'utility derived from income' – i.e. citizens' purchasing power.

In terms of *life expectancy* at birth, in 1992 Sierra Leone scored the lowest of any country, with a figure of 42.4 years; in Japan, the highest, it was 78.6. For *educational attainment*, two variables are combined: adult literacy (two-thirds weight) and average years of schooling (one-third weight). The *'utility derived from income'* score is measured by a composite formula. It assesses a country's *real (GDP) per capita*, i.e. people's 'purchasing power' (PPP), rather than GNP per capita, to indicate average income. Then it assumes that as income increases, there are diminishing returns for human development. What this means is that once a certain point is reached, double the purchasing power means much less than twice the well-being. By averaging the three indicators, a country's HDI value, from 0, the lowest, to 1, the highest, is calculated. The UNDP's *Human Development Report* for 1994 gave Canada the highest HDI: 0.983, while the West African state of Guinea had the lowest: 0.191 (UNDP 1994: 129–31, table 1). Table 4.2 presents, for comparative purposes, the HDIs for a group of Western and Third World countries in 1992–3.

Table 4.2 indicates, unsurprisingly, that a high GNP per capita often accompanies a good score on the HDI, although this is not axiomatic. For example, Brazil's HDI is almost the same as UAE's, but its per capita income is only one-seventh. Cuba's GNP per capita is almost certainly at the bottom of the 'lower-middle income' category, say $650 per annum, yet the country's HDI of 0.711 is only marginally less than UAE's and quite close to South Korea's 0.872. This indicates that it is what governments *do* with the national income at their disposal in terms of economic and social welfare, rather than the absolute figures, which are of most importance in development terms. In relation to 'real GDP', most Third World countries represented in table 4.2, as well as others, have considerably higher real GDPs than GNP per capita figures would indicate. This is partly because the value of goods produced and consumed which do not have a monetary value – i.e. they are not sold – are not counted in conventional GNP per capita indices.

In sum, the idea of development is more complex than a comparison of countries' GNP per capita shows. The HDI offers the best indicator yet devised of how to 'score' a country's level of development. While the overall wealth of a society is important,

Table 4.2 HDI and GNP per capita for selected countries, 1992–3

Region	Country	HDI (1992)	GNP per capita ($, 1993)	'Real' GDP per capita (1992) (PPP$)[a]
Industrially	Canada	0.932	19,970	19,320
developed	Japan	0.929	31,490	19,390
countries	United States	0.925	24,740	22,130
	Britain	0.919	18,060	16,340
Third World				
Middle East and	UAE	0.771	21,430	17,000
North Africa	Kuwait	0.809	19,360	13,126
South Asia	India	0.382	300	1,150
	Nepal	0.289	190	1,130
East and South-	South Korea	0.872[b]	7,660	n/a
east Asia	China	0.644	490	2,946
Latin America and	Brazil	0.756	2,930	5,240
Caribbean	Cuba	0.711	LM[c]	2,000
Sub-Saharan	Mauritius	0.778	3,030	7,178
Africa	Guinea	0.191	460[b]	500

[a] Purchasing power parity (PPP) or real GDP per capita: 'The method of using official exchange rates to convert the national currency figures to US dollars does not attempt to measure the relative domestic purchasing powers of currencies. The United Nations International Comparison Project (ICP) has developed measures of real GDP on an internationally comparable scale using PPP rather than exchange rates as conversion factors, which is expressed in PPP dollars' (UNDP 1994: 221).
[b] 1990.
[c] Lower-middle income: $696–$2,785.
Sources: UNDP 1994: 129–31, table 1; World Bank 1995: 162–3, table 1

there are also other indicators, such as literacy levels and individuals' purchasing power, which help us to perceive a country's level of development.

In addition to the issue of development indicators, there is a further – social and political – dimension to the development question: which groups are to benefit? As we have already discussed, the demand for democracy is central to political debates in the Third World; as we shall see in the forthcoming chapters, other social and political concerns, including women's and human rights, religious and ethnic identity, and the issue of environmental sustainability, are also intimately connected with the question of development: *Who* is to benefit? and *Who* loses out? In the next two sections we look at what happens when there is a serious lack of economic growth and development. We examine, first, the impact of international indebtedness and, second, the social costs of economic reform in the Third World, with particular emphasis on Latin America and sub-Saharan Africa.

The Third World Debt Crisis of the 1980s and 1990s

The Third World collectively is burdened by a huge amount of international debt, which rose nearly *fifteen* times from about $100 billion to an estimated $1,450 billion between 1970 and the early 1990s (George 1993: 59). A number of scholars, including Sweezy and Magdoff (1984), Pool and Stamos (1985), and Magdoff (1986) have presented a dependency perspective on the debt trap ensnaring many Latin American and African states. To Magdoff and others, the foreign debt problem represents an intensification of *financial* dependency, 'a process that has played a crucial role in the shaping of the development of [many Third World] countries' (So 1990: 116). The circumstances surrounding Third World countries' foreign indebtedness appear to Magdoff and the others to be a clear-cut case of peripheral countries' economic policy being dictated by the West, in two ways. First, there is the failure to come up with a comprehensive policy on debt, which means that many countries send huge proportions of their export proceeds – more than 50 per cent is not unknown – to Western creditors to service debts. Second, there is the imposition of economic policy by the IMF in indebted Third World countries who apply to it for financial assistance.

In order to assess where the 'blame' for Third World indebtedness lies, we next identify the origins of the Third World's debt crisis and the impact of the debt problem, focusing on one of the biggest debtors, Mexico. We then survey some of the proposed solutions to the debt problems. After that, we examine the social consequences of attempts to solve the Third World debt crisis by the application of structural adjustment programmes.

Causes of the debt crisis

Latin America's external debt grew from $354 billion to $470 billion between 1982 and 1993, while sub-Saharan Africa's increased from $15 billion in 1974 to $57 billion in 1982, before rising to $144 billion in 1993, about 11 per cent of the global total (George 1993: 60). While Latin American debt rose to be the largest in terms of volume – both Mexico and Brazil currently owe more than $85 billion each – many sub-Saharan African countries have been greatly affected by debt burdens even though, in relative terms, individual countries' debts are small, as table 4.3 indicates.

While for both Latin America and sub-Saharan Africa most of the external debt was accrued largely because of rocketing world oil prices between 1973 and 1982, the total continues to rise for four reasons. First, international banks, as a consequence of oil price rises in the 1970s, found themselves with huge amounts of 'petrodollars', i.e. profits from oil sales. They were obliged to lend their petrodollars quickly or risk losing profitability. They had such a plethora of funds because the banks' traditional customers, Western businesses, were forced to modify their spending plans

Table 4.3 The Third World debt burden, 1993

Region	Country	Total external debt ($ millions)	Debt per capita ($)	Debt service ratio[a] (%) 1985	1993
Sub-Saharan Africa	Côte d'Ivoire	13,167	1,031	17.4	31.9
	Ghana	3,378	270	12.2	26.7
	Nigeria	28,558	304	30.8	28.9
	Tanzania	6,746	259	16.7	31.5
Latin America	Argentina	61,534	2,041	41.8	34.4
	Chile	16,031	1,423	26.2	20.9
	Brazil	105,283	787	26.5	23.1
	Mexico	85,960	1,334	44.4	30.9

[a] A country's debt service ratio is the proportion of export proceeds it must pay annually to service its external debt.

Source: World Bank 1995: 200–1, table 20

due to economic recession caused, in part, by the oil price rises. Second, the United States government encouraged the banks to lend to Third World countries as a way of keeping up demand for US exports at a time of reduced demand elsewhere. Third, the debt crisis took deep hold because ruling Third World elites 'saw a way of using debt to convert their wealth into liquid form and to ship it out of the country' (Hadjor 1993: 91). Finally, many states were content to accrue large external debts because, initially, the conditions of indebtedness did not look too onerous. Nominal interest rates were low, because the banks had a lot of cash to lend; and real interest rates were lower, because international inflation was high in the mid-1970s.

In the early 1980s, after a large volume of debt had been accumulated, the conditions of indebtedness suddenly changed for the worse. Real interest rose sharply, largely as a result of the burgeoning American deficit caused by increases in military spending and cuts in taxes, while the price of exported raw materials from the Third World dropped rapidly as a result of economic recession in the West. Suddenly, the debt burden became unsupportable: in August 1982 Mexico and then Brazil indicated that they could no longer pay the interest on their external debt. The announcements forced Western governments, banks and the international financial institutions to make some attempt to deal with the problem, as the default involved over $200 billion. The debt crisis had arrived.

Debt crisis: the West's response

The West's primary fear was that the debt crisis would undermine the leading banks so much that there would be a global monetary collapse. This did not happen, however, and the banks gradually adjusted their balance sheets so as to be less vulnerable if Third World states were unable to service their debts. A number of essentially stopgap solutions were introduced, including debt renegotiations and rescheduling of debts for nearly all Third World debtors, unilateral moratoriums on repayments, fixed proportions of export earnings to service debt, and structural adjustment programmes (SAPs). But none was sufficient to end the crisis. Debt continues to be an enormous economic burden with serious social consequences, especially in Latin America and sub-Saharan Africa.

The response of the West to the debt crisis was very disappointing. Countries grouped in the Organization of Economic Co-operation and Development converted about $5 billion from debts to grants, while SAPs injected roughly $5 billion. In addition, following a Toronto summit meeting in 1988, concessions amounting to a further $5 billion were made to 'low-income' Third World countries – i.e. those with GNP per capita of less than $635 in 1991 (Dolan 1993: 266). For a few 'middle-income' countries – i.e. with per capita GNP between $636 and $2,555 in 1991 – some commercial debt was restructured. Yet, relative to the scale of the debt – nearly $1,500 billion – total assistance of little more than $15 billion – i.e. little more than *1 per cent* of the total debt – was quite insufficient.

Mexico: the travails of a seriously indebted country

Mexico was one of the few countries which the West was keen to help out of its debt crisis. This was not only because of the size of its debt, but also because the US government was keen to develop a regional economic grouping, the North American Free Trade Area (NAFTA), with Mexico as a partner in the venture. The results, however, were mixed: short-term economic recovery followed by a crash in early 1995. In order to examine the socio-economic and political ramifications of serious external indebtedness in the Third World, we focus on Mexico.

With hindsight it is clear that Mexico's economic problems began in the 1970s. At that time, the government commenced a series of extensive social spending programmes, including improvements in health care, education and welfare services, to be paid for by the country's oil wealth. It also began to promote the development of heavy industry and the building of infrastructural improvements, including roads, ports and airports. It believed that it was only possible to develop Mexico's economy swiftly by importing many of the raw materials and manufactured goods that it needed. As a result, products were imported from abroad, including machinery, vehicles, computers and steel. Because this resulted in a trade imbalance, the government needed to find sources of foreign exchange to pay for the imports (Callaghy 1993: 195).

The government thought that it had a solution to its problem: it would use its oil, located in one of the world's richest fields, to amass the foreign currency necessary to pay for imports. Suddenly, with oil prices rising more than fivefold during the 1970s, the government had more money at its disposal. On the strength of its actual and anticipated oil earnings, the government borrowed money from the IMF, the World Bank and American commercial banks, in order to finance its oil exploration programme. Once oil output and domestic product for export grew, the government reckoned that the country's exports should enable Mexico to earn sufficient foreign currency not only to solve its balance of payments problem but also to reduce the government's deficit. By the mid-1970s Mexico was borrowing between $4 and $6 billion *a year*, buoyed by optimism that expanding exports would allow it to service the external debt easily. In the early 1980s, however, the world price of oil halved, from over $30 to $15 a barrel. As a result, Mexico earned much less for its oil exports than the government had anticipated.

The result was that Mexico fell into a debt trap. Borrowing around $5 billion dollars a year would obviously be no problem as long as exports were expanding at a sufficient pace. When the oil price declined rapidly and new export earnings failed to materialize, the country's debt burden quickly became intolerable. Due to compound interest, once the debt reached a certain size, it would automatically continue to increase even if no new debts were accrued.[3] By 1982, after borrowing for a few years, the country had a foreign debt of $55 billion, which required paying $9 billion each year in interest and other servicing payments (UNRISD 1995: 41). Before long, the debt burden was unsupportable: in August 1982 the Mexican government announced that it could no longer pay the interest on its external debt.

A rescue team from the IMF, World Bank and several American banks came up with the following: Mexico was allowed to reschedule loan repayments, and the banks lent the government more money. This time, however, the loans were short-term, at higher interest rates than the prevailing market rate. What this amounted to was that (a) the US banks were bailed out, not Mexico; (b) rescue policies provided increased profit for the banks; (c) the supervision of the Mexican economy by the IMF was a negation of its sovereignty as it could – and did – inspect the national accounts and demand austerity policies and the right to approve budgets.

Austerity policies, as we shall see below, led to massive reductions in government spending, increased governments' tax take, reduced foreign imports to diminish the balance of payments problem, and increased exports to acquire more foreign currency. Due to reductions in state investment in the industrial sector and in imports like machinery, crucial to economic growth, the optimistic projections in the 1970s of economic growth were not realized. Mexican GNP growth rates went from 8 per cent per year in 1978 to −5 per cent in 1983. The national currency, the peso, was devalued. Its value fell eightfold between 1982 and 1984, from 25 to 200 pesos to \$1. Many Mexicans responded by converting their pesos into dollars, thus exacerbating the currency's weakness and adding to inflationary pressures. Annual price inflation in Mexico reached 80 per cent in the early 1980s, doubling to 160 per cent in 1987.

Despite these problems, by the early 1990s the Mexican government appeared to have turned the economic situation around. Growth of 3.9 per cent was recorded in both 1990 and 1991. Inflation fell to under 20 per cent in 1992. Exports were growing swiftly; wage levels were stabilizing; privatization of state-owned businesses was proceeding smoothly. Perhaps most encouraging, the debt crisis seemed to have been brought under control, largely by an agreement – the Brady Plan (named after Nicholas Brady, then US Secretary of the Treasury) – 'with the international banks in 1990 that cut the overall size of existing debt and extended new credits, and rescheduling' (Callaghy 1993: 198). A current account deficit remained, which was partially financed by a variety of means. These included capital formerly invested out of the country gradually returning, enhanced foreign investment, the proceeds of privatization, improved tax collection and, significantly as it turned out, large flows of short-term foreign capital. Much of the latter comprised dollars from Wall Street searching for high returns in Latin America stock markets or buying dollar-denominated Latin American debt issued by banks and governments. Mexico's central bank exchanged large quantities of pesos for dollars, building up substantial reserves which would be used to support high exchange rates. As Scott (1995b) notes, however, these reserves were, in effect, a continuation of the 1980s debt crisis by other means: 'Mexico may not be in hock to the banks like it was in 1982, but its banks and government have issued \$67 billion of paper – mainly the so-called Tesobonos – on which interest had to be paid to [American] insurance companies and unit trusts.' In December 1994 President Clinton hailed Mexico's role as the vanguard of economic reform in Latin America. He pledged that if the region followed Mexico's example it would be integrated into a giant free trade zone – NAFTA – along the lines of the European Union, by the year 2005.

The danger for the Mexican government was that if the US insurance companies and mutual funds asked to be repaid – $26 billion of debts on short-term loans fell due in 1995 – and then did not buy fresh bonds, Mexico would be left defenceless. This is what happened: the current account deficit of $27 billion a year was no longer tenable; investors rushed to protect themselves; and the Mexican economy wobbled and then crashed. By January 1995, foreign reserves of $25 billion had shrunk by three-quarters to just $6 billion: the much-vaunted Mexican economic miracle had fallen apart, necessitating a $40 billion rescue programme arranged by the US government (Scott 1995b; Balls 1995). Mexico's external debts were still well over $80 billion in 1995, with a debt service ratio in excess of 40 per cent.

Two conclusions emerge from Mexico's economic débâcle. First, it is almost impossible for national governments to run unsustainable domestic policies as Mexico did in 1994. Second, the fickleness of international investors can quickly turn the perception of unsustainability into a self-fulfilling prophecy if remedial action is not taken promptly enough. Both problems emerged precisely because the Mexican government was trying to make the best of an 'unfair' world by seeking to appeal as much as possible to international capital (Balls 1995). Results were disappointing; by no stretch of the imagination had Mexico's debt crisis been solved.

Prospects for Solving the Third World Debt Crisis

Nearly 15 years since its inception, the Third World debt crisis remains unresolved. A general pardoning of the debt (an act of the creditors) or general default (an act of the debtors) has been suggested, but so far they have not been accepted by either side. In relation to Mexico and other Latin American countries, the 1989 Brady Plan, which involved requesting the debtor banks to forgive portions of the loans and to swap other parts of the debt for new securities – an exchange to be backed up by World Bank and IMF guarantees – was less successful than it appeared at the time. This was because the banks' response was lukewarm. They wished to continue to receive their profits from Third World debts; the best way to do this was not to reduce the debts appreciably.

Because Latin America owes most of its debt to the banks, whereas sub-Saharan Africa owes most of its debt to governments and international organizations, it means in effect that the former's debt dependence is more financial, and the latter's more political. Because sub-Saharan Africa's debt is small in absolute terms, there is a lack of interest in the West in dealing with its economic repercussions. In global terms, Africa's debt, George (1993: 61) explains, 'is so modest as to be a threat to [no] one except Africans themselves'.

Africa's debt crisis continues, first, because of a mixture of creditor and debtor mistakes. The main creditor mistake is not to forgive the countries of the region their debts. The debtors' chief error is not to come together to press the creditors to pardon their loans. Not that this is too surprising: African governments have not been notable for their ability to resolve differences for long enough to act in unison over issues of mutual concern. The 'inability to arrive at a common stance makes it easy for creditors to isolate and browbeat individual debtors' (George 1993: 64). The debtors' inability to unite to challenge their creditors gave the latter a major opportunity to apply orthodox neo-classical economic policies, an economic experiment which had a number of unfortunate economic, political and social consequences.

Second, Africa's debt crisis continues because the main prescription offered by the West to deal with it – viz. increasing exports to accumulate the foreign exchange in order to service debts and, in the longer term, to pay off the debt principal – has not been successful. Africa cannot hope to emerge from debt crisis by continuing to rely on exports of traditional products like cocoa, coffee, tea, sugar, rubber and minerals (Brown and Tiffen 1992).

Third, the non-resolution of Africa's debt crisis is good for the industrialized economies. Raw materials can be bought very cheaply. This is so because very many African countries are competing among themselves to sell similar raw materials in pursuance of SAPs. The result of glut and low prices for raw materials is that debtors attempt to export even more, in the vain hope of keeping revenue levels constant.

In sum, the non-resolution of Latin America's and Africa's debt crisis is due to a mixture of a lack of debtors' ability to organize to force the issue to a conclusion and a relative lack of urgency on the part of the West and the commercial banks to find a way out of the crisis. The main mechanism to deal with the conditions which helped to create the debt crisis – poor economic policy and over-spending by affected Third World governments – was the SAP. As we shall see in the final section of the chapter, the social, political and economic consequences of SAPs in Latin America and Africa have been profound.

Structural Adjustment: Social Costs of Economic Reform

The 1980s were a period not only of growing international Third World indebtedness, but also of 'economic liberalization'. Strong pressure was exerted by Western aid donors on Third World governments with balance of payments difficulties to reform their economies. Economic liberalization primarily involved a reduction in the role of the state in the economy. The purpose of con-centrated economic liberalization – structural adjustment – was 'to generate "surplus" cash so that debt can be serviced'. In effect, the IMF and the World Bank served as 'collection agencies for the creditor countries' (George 1993: 63).

International indebtedness was the lever used by the IMF to force the indebted countries of the Third World to change economic direction. IMF financial assistance to governments of ailing economies comes with a panoply of conditions; it is in no way a gift. Governments which draw upon its resources are required to submit their economic plans for approval, and if they do not conform to the institutions' established norms, modifications are usually required. Because of the nature of IMF financing, such modifications tend to take the form of reductions in consumption, rather than increases in investment. The IMF's austerity measures – SAPs – are in broad outline the same for all countries to which they are applied, although there are some local differences.

The IMF makes the adoption of debt rescheduling programmes conditional on the introduction of various measures, a position known as *conditionality*. The Fund urges debtor governments to take action in five broad areas. *Trade barriers* are to be drastically lowered, exposing local producers to foreign competition. *Subsidies and price controls* are to be reduced or withdrawn completely, to remove 'distortions' in local prices for goods and services. By withdrawing controls on capital movements, *financial systems* are to be restructured. *State-owned enterprises* should be privatized, and private foreign investment encouraged, by removing controls. Finally, *state intervention* in both the management of the economy generally as well as in the provision of social services is to be minimized (UNRISD 1995: 38).

The World Bank works closely with the IMF, but is also a powerful economic actor in its own right. In 1990 the Bank had total outstanding loans of $89 billion, 6 per cent of total Third World debt, giving it considerable clout with debtor governments. In that year the net flow of funds from the Bank to the Third World was nearly $6 billion in ordinary loans and more than $3.5 billion in 'soft' – i.e. low interest – loans.

The dependence on the IMF, the World Bank and major Western countries for the design of economic reform packages and the resources needed to implement them is seen by some as a new form of neo-colonialism. Western leverage converts into intensive economic policy conditionality and specific economic policy changes in return for borrowed resources. The problem is that the authority of Third World governments is linked to the way that they react to the adverse social effects of attempts at economic adjustment. The social effects of externally imposed economic adjustment programmes were among the most important stimuli for political challenges to Third World governments in the 1980s and early 1990s. The IMF claimed that economic stabilization would lead to a situation in which a recipient country's economy would become largely self-regulating via more open competition between private businesses. The public sector would retract and be relatively passive; it would aim to provide the minimum necessary services to enable private business to conduct its affairs efficiently and to protect society's weakest members. In general, however, the programmes caused severe recessions in the short term and, as a result, much suffering among the poor in the Third World.

In conclusion, the IMF's prescription for economic reform involved a combination of reducing the economic role of the state and reforming the structure of the economy, with a stress on liberalizing markets, increasing competition, and building strong linkages to the world economy via increases in exports. The result, it was hoped, would be increased development and prosperity in countries which had pursued misguided strategies of economic growth for too long. Economic reform would be underpinned, it was hoped, by 'new globalized capital markets and a reborn world trading order, so that the gap between the world's rich and poor [would] not continue to widen' (Callaghy 1993: 161).

The IMF demand was that indebted Third World economies open themselves to investment from outside before loans could be granted. States were to retain control over their currencies and their non-economic policies only in so far as both were compatible with the free flow of money and goods. It was, in effect, the demand that governments surrender their economic sovereignty in order to be 'guided' by the IMF and the World Bank. Such attempts to compel Third World countries to adjust to economic liberalism were made, however, without embedding the policies in the realities of domestic state–society relations. In their efforts to cope with the Third World debt crisis, Western states and actors attempted to apply the 'mono-economics' of the dominant neoclassical orthodoxy about development to countries dependent on the IMF and the World Bank. Despite the doubtless good intentions of the Bank and the Fund, the result of sometimes insensitively applied conditionality was to force many Third World countries to adjust to full orthodox liberalism without allowing the pace or thrust of liberalization to be tempered by the peculiarities of local state–society relations. Results were often disappointing, with serious social and political repercussions. Global economic conditions were such that governments that tried to use deflationary policies to deal with economic crises were not able to rise out of recession, while at the same time their populations endured economic and social upheaval. We examine the outcome of SAPs in four countries: Mexico, Argentina, Zambia and Ghana.

Latin America: Mexico and Argentina

The characteristics of Mexico's economic crisis in the 1990s were a huge trade deficit, an over-valued peso followed by devaluation, extensive foreign currency borrowing, a drop in financial market confidence, sudden hikes in interest rates, a deepening recession, a sharp rise in unemployment, an austerity budget and a sharp rise in VAT and fuel prices. The result was that more than 800,000 people lost their jobs between December 1994 and July 1995, while for those still fortunate enough to have work, living standards plunged. Mexico's experiences were replicated elsewhere in Latin America. Sometimes, in addition, social costs of the effects of indebtedness and SAPs also included strikes, hunger riots and demonstrations (So 1990: 120). Even in the relatively prosperous country of Argentina the effects of structural adjustment included strikes and demonstrations against rising unemployment. The country's unemployment rate rose from 12 to 18 per cent in the three months from May 1995. In order to keep in the IMF's good books, Argentina had to achieve a $2 billion surplus in its current account balance following the flight of $8 billion in 'hot money' from Argentina after the collapse of the Mexican economy. Economic cuts were achieved by cutting jobs (Scott 1995a).

Sub-Saharan Africa: Zambia and Ghana

Attempts at economic adjustment produced widespread hardship in Africa. An example of a government which embarked zealously upon economic reform via SAPs was that of Zambia. The rise to power of President Chiluba's Movement for Multiparty Democracy (MMD) in October 1991 was a result of widespread political and economic disillusionment with the United National Independence Party (UNIP) government of Kenneth Kaunda, who had taken the country to independence in 1964.

On attaining power, Chiluba's government speedily implemented structural adjustment. As is usual with IMF packages in the Third World, resources were disproportionately extracted from the poor and near-poor. The economic reform programme of the MMD government was so stringent that the local World Bank representative counselled caution and a greater concern with the issue of social instability which he judged was being caused by an overly fervent application of adjustment policies (M. Hall 1993: 15). These included: the abrupt elimination of state subsidies on the staple food, maize flour, which led to a tenfold price increase; major reductions in governmental expenditure, especially the sacking of state employees; the merging of the official and free market rates of the local currency, the *kwacha*, involving a 29 per cent devaluation. The government's reward was $1.1 billion in foreign aid. Domestically, its policies were less well received: less than 10 per cent of the electorate bothered to vote in the local elections of December 1992.

By mid-1995 disillusionment with the Chiluba regime had spread. Agriculture 'had collapsed'; 220,000 of 360,000 'jobs in the manufacturing industry and parastatals had been lost' due to the effects of foreign competition; the 'crucial mining sector was in an alarming state of decline'; while serious corruption allegations were made against Chiluba and members of his government (Beresford 1995).

The only attempt at structural adjustment in sub-Saharan Africa which has been defended by the IMF and the World Bank as a success story – Ghana's – has been effective as a growth strategy but not as a development blueprint; it has been a *social* failure (Haynes 1993c). Ghana received more than $9 billion in foreign loans, principally from the IMF and the World Bank, between 1984 and 1993. During much of that period, Ghana's economy grew by an average of 5 per cent annually, while population increased by about 2.6 per cent a year. Resulting real growth of nearly 2.5 per cent a year was one of the best achievements in sub-Saharan Africa. Yet, most ordinary Ghanaians found that macro-economic success was not reflected in increases in their purchasing power. By 1993 the minimum day's wage was 460 *cedis* ($0.33) – the cost of a bottle of beer. Petrol was 1,600 cedis per gallon; hence a minimum-waged worker earning 12,420 *cedis* a month could buy 7.76 gallons of petrol with his or her monthly salary and could afford *nothing* else.

The fact that this macro-economic success was not translated into a clear increase in well-being for ordinary Ghanaians was a source of worry both for the government and for the international financial agencies (Haynes 1993c: 465). Given that Ghana needs economic growth rates of around 10 per cent per year *for a generation* to drag its fast-growing population of about 17 million people from poverty, a comparatively good performance of 2.5 per cent a year – which in any case slowed in the 1990s – is nowhere near good enough (Haynes 1995b).

The fact is that it is the impact of foreign loans which gave Ghana the *illusion* of economic recovery. Diversification of exports was at best a highly qualified success, while foreign investment was very slow to arrive. Ghana's problem in the latter respect was common in Africa: endemic political instability (five successful *coup d'états* between 1966 and 1981 and innumerable unsuccessful ones from 1982) is not conducive to building the confidence of foreign investors, who prefer a country like China, politically stable, with a weak labour movement and assured repatriation of profits (Hutton 1995).

In sum, the targeting of recipient states like Mexico, Argentina,

Zambia and Ghana as the main cause of the success or failure of SAPs fails to take into account the importance of global factors. Had the international financial institutions carried through on the original intention that adjustments be system-wide – implying adjustments by both deficit and surplus countries, including debt relief, more open trade and a greater focus in the SAPs on human resources, especially women – and that the developed countries deliver the other components needed to make adjustment relief work, SAPs would have been much less painful. But since adjustment has addressed only the deficit countries, its impact has necessarily been recessionary, requiring governments to curb demand, cutting or restraining wages and/or limiting government expenditure. By encouraging higher interest rates, it has also curbed investment, and restricted new employment opportunities.

East Asia's newly industrializing countries, including South Korea and Taiwan, are unusual in that they managed to offset shortfalls in raw materials earnings by substantial increases of exports of manufactured goods. The reliance on raw materials exports alone was highlighted in the case of oil-producing countries like Mexico and several Middle Eastern states. While their incomes from exporting oil were buoyant in the 1970s and early 1980s, they later declined. By 1994 the price of a barrel of oil in real terms was as low as it had been 15 years earlier. In order to get over the problem of putting all the export eggs in one basket, IMF advice to *all* Third World countries who asked it was the same: diversify raw materials exports to maximize foreign exchange earnings. But there were serious problems with such advice. In 1980, for example, three-quarters of Malaysia's export proceeds came from just five commodities: crude oil, palm oil, tin, rubber and timber. Five years later those commodities' share of total exports fell to little more than half of the total. What this amounted to was that Malaysia had successfully begun to diversify its exports in line with IMF advice; yet, by 1985 it had to export *19 per cent more* than it did in 1980 in order to buy the same amount of manufactured goods: running hard in order to stand still, Malaysia's terms of trade had dropped by a fifth in relation to the West's manufactured goods.

Malaysia's experience is not unique: most raw materials-exporting Third World states saw their terms of trade fall throughout the second half of the 1980s and the first half of the 1990s; a result was increased poverty, especially among the poor and middle-income earners, the vast majority in every Third World country. In developmental terms, the impact was to reduce the well-being of millions of people. The political impact of the widespread impoverishment of many Third World peoples was variable, but a common result was the growth of opposition groups claiming that economic mismanagement was the root cause of citizens' poverty. In the next chapter we focus upon the causes and consequences of ethnic and religious conflict in the Third World, phenomena which increased in the 1980s as a result of growing political and economic tensions.

Notes

1   Bretton Woods, New Hampshire, was the venue of the United Nations Monetary and Financial Conference attended by representatives of 45 states between 1 and 22 July 1944. The declared purpose of the conference was to forge a co-operative approach to international monetary issues, to be instituted after the war.
2   With the exception of Benin, Guinea, Niger and Zaire, these states have endured periods of civil war since the 1970s.
3   The principal of compound interest is as follows. If a country borrows $1,000 a year for 7 years at an interest rate of 10 per cent and the loan is to be repaid after 20 years, when the state borrows again – in the eighth year, the $1,000 it receives would be just enough to cover the interest and 'principal amortization' payments on the loans it took out during the previous 7 years. In other words, after the eighth year, the country which had borrowed the initial $1,000 would have to continue to borrow in order to meet the deadline for interest and amortization payments (So 1990: 117–18). This example is relevant to Mexico's position.

5

Religion, Ethnicity and Identity

In chapters 3 and 4 we focused upon the democratic challenges and economic problems affecting most Third World countries in the 1980s and early 1990s. The growing distance between rulers and ruled led to democratic challenges. Third World democrats were encouraged by the demise of communism in Eastern Europe. International support for democratic challenges helped to lead to the gradual – and partial – democratization of many formerly non-democratic Third World countries.

Economic problems were the result of a combination of domestic and global factors. The difficulties which many Third World countries have of finding a niche in the international economic system in the post-war period were added to by the effects of growing external indebtedness in the 1980s and 1990s. Attempts to solve economic problems usually necessitated calling in the IMF, but were almost invariably domestic social and political failures, even if in some cases, e.g. Ghana, they led to macro-economic stability.

While economic and political instability characterized many Third World countries in the 1980s and 1990s, their emergence also both reflected and sustained a growing societal desire to change things more generally. Apart from pressures to democratize and reform economically, a third indication of both upheaval and instability were widespread ethnic and religious conflicts.

Ethnic conflicts are very frequent in sub-Saharan Africa and widespread in South Asia. Religion is also an important factor in

Third World politics (Haynes 1993a). Recent examples of political conflict with a religious dimension are to be found in many areas, including the Middle East, South Asia and Africa. In the Middle East militant Islamic groups – often drawing inspiration from Iran's Islamic revolution of 1978–80 – fight the state in a number of countries, including Israel (Palestine), Algeria and Egypt. In South Asia, internecine conflict erupted between Buddhists and Hindus in Sri Lanka in the 1980s; while in India, Hindus and Muslims confront each other; in addition, Sikh separatists in Punjab and Muslim militants in Jammu-Kashmir challenge the state's authority. In sub-Saharan Africa, civil war in Sudan is expressed in religious terms, while in Nigeria political divisions are increasingly polarized by a Muslim–Christian divide.

In this chapter we examine the causes and consequences of ethnic and religious conflicts in the Third World. The term, 'ethnicity', relates broadly to the perceived shared characteristics of a racial or cultural group, while the idea of religious particularity is that a group regards itself as distinctive because of its religious identity. Very often, however, groups have *both* ethnic and religious characteristics in their world-views. As a result, we refer to some groups' 'religio-ethnic' characteristics, which involve a mix of religious and ethnic individuality.

We begin by examining how the developmental and dependency paradigms perceive the issues of ethnicity and religion in Third World politics. After describing the effects of 'incomplete' modernization on politics in the Third World, we proceed to explore the frequency and ubiquity of ethnic and religious conflicts in relation to two factors: first, as a result of only incomplete national identities forged in many Third World countries, and second, as a consequence of the degree of religious or ethnic fragmentation in a country. Third, we discuss four broad types of religious and ethnic groups: culturalist, fundamentalist, community-orientated and syncretistic. In the final section we look at religious and ethnic challenges to the *status quo* in the Third World regions.

Religion and Ethnicity: Developmental and Dependency Views

Many political scientists were taken by surprise by the sudden resurgence of ethnic and religious issues in the Third World in the

1980s, for two reasons: (a) the traditional paradigms stress the importance of either the individual, the state or the international economic system as the relevant context and subject for analysis, rather than cultural factors; (b) both contemplate a linear tradition–modernity transition, seeing ethnicity and religion as belonging to an earlier, pre-modern stage of tradition and as bound to disappear as society modernizes.

The developmental perspective

The sudden salience of religion and ethnicity in Third World politics was unexpected for developmentalist analysts, because it was thought that a group's ethnic or religious identity was a traditionalist obstacle to development which would disappear as a country modernizes (Haynes 1993a: 18–43). It was a great surprise to see an *Islamic* revolution in modernized Iran. Evidence of burgeoning religious and ethnic issues in Third World politics is often interpreted as symptomatic of a fundamentalist, anti-modernist backlash against science, industrialization and liberal Western values. It is seldom recognized as part of a larger global phenomenon (Haynes 1995c; Sahliyeh 1990).

The state's project in relation to modernization is understood to be primarily concerned with the evolution from 'traditional' to 'modern' society, during which there would be fundamental change in the nature of people's occupational roles and associated values (Mamdani et al. 1993: 102). As Stiefel and Wolfe (1994: 25) explain: 'If capital formation and transfer of technology were to generate self-sustaining "development", they would have to go hand in hand with cultural, political and social "modernization", such as the conveying of democratic political institutions from the West and the transfer of values emphasizing "efficiency" and consumerism.' To build a nation-state from a congeries of often culturally diverse peoples, modernizing elites – whether a civil bureaucracy, armed forces or political party – had to develop the capacity to achieve order and to develop society towards modernization. Social movements coalescing around ethnic, religious or class concerns are identified as a 'problem' of 'incomplete' state building while traditional community and extended family ties are distrusted as forms of participation (Stiefel and Wolfe 1994: 26).

The dependency view

Because dependency analysis traditionally emphasizes external factors, it has little to say about ethnic and religious conflicts. It does, however, stress that such conflicts may be activated in situations of 'internal colonialism' – e.g. where an ethnic community is subjugated by a dominant group. When there is no internal colonialism apparent, such conflict is regarded as a facet of the manipulation of ordinary people by cynical politicians who whip up 'atavistic' ethnic sentiments for their own political purposes (Hettne 1995: 7).

A good example of this way of thinking is to be found in some of the contributions to a recent book entitled *New Social Movements in the South*, written with a broadly dependency orientation. The book's editor, Ponna Wignaraja, argues that people 'withdraw' into religion as 'the anarchy in their lives develops'. The withdrawal is then 'used by vested interests and immature political leaders to manipulate the people' (Wignaraja 1993: 33). In another contribution to the same volume, Kothari (1993: 68) claims that those who look for religious solutions to their material and social problems are duped by the 'ruling class (which) has set in motion a completely new canard . . . to distract attention from the socio-economic sphere . . . releasing strong regional, linguistic and cultural sentiments'. The writer of a further chapter in the book, Samir Amin (1993: 77), explains the *raison d'être* of people turning to religion in the following way: they are movements of 'religious revival' which appeal to the 'heritage of the past' overlain by the 'modern world'; they are symptomatic of 'crisis . . . products of disillusionment. They will eventually lose steam as they reveal their powerlessness in the face of the real challenge' – i.e. how to build socialism. Thus, those who belong to political groups informed by religious or ethnic concerns, with the exception of those motivated by liberation theology,[1] are duped either by opposition politicians (Wignaraja), by the ruling class (Kothari) or by appeals to a (probably mythical) 'golden age' (Amin).

Neither Amin, Kothari, nor Wignaraja give credit where it is due. Class organizations often seem to appeal rather minimally to many people in the Third World; religion or ethnic solidarity, on the other hand, offers ideological belief systems with spiritual, material or community benefits which may appeal across otherwise prominent social or class divisions.

In sum, neither of the traditional paradigms is able satisfactorily to explain the salience of religion and ethnicity in contemporary Third World politics. Developmental analysis, believing that development and modernization are linear processes involving a transition from tradition to modernity, was unable to explain the Iranian revolution and other manifestations of ethnicity or religion in Third World politics. Dependency analysis, for its part, concerned with the effects of the international economic system, is content to regard religion and ethnicity in politics as a sign either of 'internal colonialism' or the duping of unsophisticated people by manipulative politicians. Neither of the paradigms is willing to see religion and ethnicity as symptoms of incomplete or partial modernization in the Third World.

Modernization and Political Change

The idea of modernization is usually linked to a number of developments, including the spread of modern – i.e. Western-style – education, a money economy, urbanization and industrialization, and to a rationalization of previously 'irrational' views, such as religious beliefs and ethnic separatism.

Amin is correct to stress how attempts to modernize often cause crisis for many people in the Third World; he is wrong, however, to claim that such people are passive in the face of it. In the West, social changes accompanying modernization led to significant shifts in the behaviour and prevailing choices of social actors, with such particularistic traits as ethnicity or caste losing importance in relation to more generalistic attributes such as nationalism. The emergence and growth of formal political organizations (e.g. parties) and procedures (e.g. the rule of law) bolstered national identity. In short, the advent of social change corresponding to a process of modernization led to a general jettisoning of older, traditional values and the adoption of other modern political practices and institutions.

In the Third World, on the other hand, the adoption of Western traits in many Third World countries is only skin-deep: Western suits for men rather than traditional dress, the trappings of state-hood (flag, constitution, legislature, etc.), a Western lingua franca and so on. The important point is that social change has not been even throughout most Third World societies during modernization;

rather, social and political conflicts are highly likely, owing to the patchy adoption of modern practices. This is because such change destabilizes, creating a division between those who benefit from it and those who do not. In addition, new social strata arise whose position in the new order is decidedly ambiguous. Examples include recent migrants from rural to urban areas in many Third World societies who find themselves between two worlds, often without an effective set of anchoring values. Such people may be particularly open to political appeals based on religious or ethnic precepts.

Over the last 15 years or so, three broad developments have exacerbated the stresses and strains of modernization in the Third World: the collapse of communism, widespread economic crisis connected with population movements, and the diffusion of democracy linked to a questioning of the idea of nation building. Together these developments served to encourage large numbers of people to question their political, social and economic identities.

The collapse of communism

Until recently, most Third World civil wars were routinely interpreted as *de facto* clashes between socialist and anti-socialist forces, a symptom of the way that global political developments were interpreted in terms of the East–West conflict. The demise of communism in Eastern Europe in the 1980s removed the supposedly dominant issue of class ideology which had formerly overlain ethnic differences in several Third World Marxist states, including, in sub-Saharan Africa, Angola, Mozambique and Ethiopia, and in the Middle East, South Yemen. With the collapse of communism and the end of the Cold War, ethnic and religious dimensions of conflicts often reasserted themselves.

Economic crisis and the movement of peoples

Global migration flows have been a common feature of the post-World War II period. Often the direction of the process is from the Third World to the rich economies of North America and Western Europe, encouraged by the poor economic conditions in many Third World countries. As we saw in chapter 4, painful social effects were the ubiquitous results of attempts at structural adjustment. As economic chances diminished in the Third World in the 1980s, millions of people tried to remove themselves to more economically congenial surroundings. Migrants, whether internal or cross-border, often became a political issue, because they brought with them their different looks, cultures, languages and religions. In other words, 'they are easily visible – and their ethnic identity sets them apart as easy scapegoats whenever there are social or economic problems' (UNRISD 1995: 99).

The diffusion of democracy and the question of 'nation building'

The impact of structural adjustment not only affected many people's ability to afford the necessities of life, it also often delivered a significant blow to the idea of 'nation building', the aim of all post-colonial states. Many governments, under economic pressure to pursue structural adjustment, could no longer deliver the resources or the jobs to ensure social stability. In addition, there was change in the structure of the state in many Third World countries. The spread of democratic ideas, which accompanied the diffusion of economic reform, served to undermine the authority of previously autocratic governments, weakening civic-based forms of identity and encouraging many previously suppressed divisions to emerge.

In sum, these developments – the collapse of communism, economic crisis and the accompanying movement of peoples, and the diffusion of democracy and the demise of the idea of 'nation-building' – served to encourage many people in the Third World to question their identity in a number of ways. Because the concept of 'identity' is a fluid and multi-faceted one, we need to discuss its relevance to ethnic and religious conflict. Identity crisis became a facet of politics in many countries, representing a serious threat to national integration and development. A result was the exacerbation of religious and ethnic cleavages, with often serious impacts upon a country's political stability (Habermas 1976).

Identity, Religion and Ethnicity

The orientations and sentiments people have towards politics in general, and toward existing political arrangements in particular, are formulated within the context of the views they have of themselves and of their concept of their identity. As Kamrava (1993: 164) notes, 'it is their sense of identity which largely determines how people behave politically and in turn view their own political environment.' The absence of widely accepted, enduring arrays of norms and social values makes it difficult for many people in the Third World to form solid opinions about what exactly their identity is, both at a personal level and in a national context.

Rather than leading to the development of a *national* identity, the social and political characteristics of many Third World countries – political repression, economic crisis, rapid social change, uneven industrialization, swift urbanization – often instead foster feelings of disappointment and an identity crisis, prompting people to question their social and political values.

Religious and ethnic sentiments may well accentuate negative aspects of politics, but this is not always the case. Sometimes the mobilization of both religion and ethnicity are towards progressive goals of societal enhancement. We discuss the meanings of the terms 'religion' and 'ethnicity' before presenting a typology of religious and ethnic groups which will show the various and varied goals they pursue in the contemporary Third World.

The term 'religion' has two distinct, yet related, meanings. First, in a spiritual sense, religion pertains to models of social and individual behaviour that help believers to organize their everyday lives. In this sense, religion has to do with the idea of transcendence – i.e. it relates to supernatural realities; with sacredness – i.e. as a system of language and practice that organizes the world in terms of what is deemed holy; and with ultimacy – i.e. it relates people to the ultimate conditions of existence. Second, in a material sense it refers to religious establishments (i.e. institutions and officials) as well as to social groups and movements whose *raisons d'être* are to be found within religious concerns. Examples include the conservative Roman Catholic organization Opus Dei, the radical Front Islamique de Salut (FIS) of Algeria, and India's Hindu chauvinist Bharatiya Jana Party (Haynes 1995c).

By contrast, ethnicity concerns the perceived shared characteristics of a *racial or cultural group*.[2] A group's religion *may* be one of its particularistic characteristics; others include language, race, territory and/or culture. Ethnic problems often stem from a basic contradiction involving the idea that each sovereign country should be filled with a *nation* of people sharing a common language or culture. The problem is that in reality *all* countries are to a lesser or greater extent multi-ethnic; it is impossible for every self-proclaimed ethnic group or 'nation' – i.e. *large* ethnic group – to have its own state.

The concept of a tight 'fit' between country and nation emerged during the process of industrialization in Europe in the eighteenth and nineteenth centuries; since then the 'nation-state' has been regarded as the superior form of political entity. In the Caribbean, Asia and Africa, imperial powers bequeathed post-colonial states to societies often with large numbers of ethnic groups. Not every ethnic group was big enough or powerful enough to grab its own state. As a result, the concept of the 'nation-state' in virtually all countries of the Third World was – and is – problematic. This is because many ethnic groups did not perceive themselves in relation to other ethnic groups as belonging to the same *nation*. This helps to explain why people in the contemporary Third World still put so much emphasis on their own ethnic identity.

It is sometimes argued that contemporary ethnic consciousness expresses basic, primeval human sentiments along the lines that communities have *always* been divided by either language, custom, religion, race or territory or by a combination of these factors. This idea is interesting but fails to answer four important questions: (a) Why does such consciousness form in the first place? (b) Why does ethnic consciousness vary in strength from one group to another? (c) Why do individuals of the *same* group vary in fervour? (d) Why does it rise and fall over time? The answer to these questions is that ethnic identities are not predetermined or inevitable. Rather, they can be constructed by skilful, if unscrupulous, politicians who perceive that their goal of power is best facilitated by the creation of a receptive political constituency. It is no coincidence that the recent ethnicization of politics has come at a time of great social and economic upheaval in many parts of the world.

Not everyone believes that they have a strong ethnic identity which bonds them inextricably with others of 'their' group. It is only when an identity meets an explicit demand or situation that such ties become important. Unsurprisingly, some of the most powerful ethnic-orientated identities emerge out of a subordinate or super-ordinate position in a social hierarchy. In sum, the relation of ethnicity to politics changes; its appeal does not remain constant but is determined to a great extent by the level of material well-being and security – i.e. the 'feel good factor' – which members of a community collectively enjoy.

Important as ethnic or religious identity is to many people, it is, in

Table 5.1 Types of religio-ethnic groups and their political interaction with the state in the Third World

	Culturalist	Fundamentalist	Community-orientated	Syncretist
Objective	To use cultural separateness to seek to achieve autonomy in relation to centralized state (e.g. Sikhs, Tibetans).	To protect self-proclaimed groups of the 'religiously pure' against governmental attempts to belittle religion (e.g. HAMAS, Islamic Salvation Front).	To direct community activities for enhancement of local groups' self interest (e.g. Basic Christian Communities, Latin American Indians).	To achieve higher political standing within national culture of diverse groups (e.g. Napramas, Holy Spirit Movement).
Perceptions of state and society	Aggregation of diverse groups with state structure dominated by one particular group.	Society is dichotomized between 'believers' and 'non-believers'. State aims to extend its power at the cost of believers.	Society comprises diverse interests. Local groups need to be aided so that self-interest can be protected and furthered.	Society comprises diverse groups with one or a few often dominating at state level.
Perceptions of role of government	To prevent the full flowering of diversity.	Regarded as seeking to undermine religion's role in society.	Seen as hostile or indifferent to plight of local communities.	Seen as hostile or indifferent.
Role in political process	May use vehicle of political party if government permits; non-constitutional means may also be employed.	May fight elections if permitted. In addition, a wide range of means of gaining political ends may be employed.	Formally uninvolved, although activists may ally themselves with most progressive political parties.	Will often remain outside any formal political process, pursuing goals through direct action, negotiation and lobbying.
Citizen participation	Active participation of group members will be encouraged by group leaders in seeking political goals.	Individual interests seen as subordinate to the interests of the religious entity.	Popular participation essential to offset elite dominance of politics and society.	Individual interests seen as synonymous with community goals.
Tactics to achieve objectives	Any means necessary considered, constitutional or non-constitutional, including terrorism.	Depending on the ideology of the fundamentalist group, most tactics would be regarded as legitimate.	Lobbying of political elites, and as widespread as possible popular mobilization.	Defensive mobilization of community interests, which may become more aggressive.

fact, only *one* form of identity. People have simultaneous member-ship in some or all of the following: families, clans, communities, nations, classes, occupational, gender and age-groups. None of these defines itself by ethnicity or religion. The distinctive capacity of ethnicity and religion is to be found in the way they can sometimes 'totalize', i.e. they have the potential to transcend other loyalties and obligations so as to become the sole basis of identity, which may lead to conflict. This is because when people's multiple identities become focused in this way, social divisions appear deeper and rigid. Because ethnicity and religion are deeply emotional bases of identity, distinguishing one's group from 'outsiders', they have the capacity to demonize and dehumanize 'enemy' groups, encouraging atrocities against them. Alternatively, as we shall see shortly, groups with a central religious or ethnic concern *may* be useful to help individuals cope with the stresses and strains of modernization.

Types of Religio-ethnic Groups in the Third World

Religio-ethnic groups can take a large variety of forms. Below we examine four broad types: 'culturalist', 'fundamentalist', 'community-orientated' and 'syncretist'[3] groups. The political differences between them and their relationship to government are shown in table 5.1. Each type of group has two elements in common. First, leaders of each type utilize religious and/or ethnic concerns to offer a message of hope and a programme of action to their followers. Second, each type of group tends to be oppositional in character. Leaders try to capitalize upon dissatisfaction with the *status quo* – whether with government or with rival groups – to galvanize the support of actual and putative group members. Two types of groups – fundamentalist and culturalist – tend to be particularly antipathetic to government for reasons we shall discuss shortly; community-orientated groups are concerned primarily with self-help efforts rather than political issues *per se*, while syncretistic groups tend to be involved in defending their way of life and religious beliefs from outside interference or attack.

Culturalist groups

A culturalist group emerges when a community, believing that it has particular ethnic, religious and other cultural characteristics, identifies itself as a powerless and repressed minority within a state dominated by others. Domination is reflected by one group's control of political and economic power, land, employment and public resources to the detriment of others; in other words, the dominant group benefits from development, while others do not to the same degree.

The mobilization of a minority group's culture may be directed towards more than achieving development goals. Such groups may also seek political autonomy or self-government. Examples include numerous groups in South-east Asia, as we shall see below: Sikhs in India, southern Sudanese Christian peoples fighting both Islamization and Arabization, Tibetan Buddhists in China, and the mostly Muslim Palestinians[4] of Israel's occupied territories. In each case, the religion followed by the ethnic minority provides part of the ideological basis for action against representatives of the dominant group.

Whether separatist groups seek autonomy within, or withdrawal from, a country depends largely on what appears to be possible as much as on what is desirable. The achievement of autonomy within a state may be a good platform for eventual secession. The possibility of separatism obviously depends upon the existence of a specific territory that a secessionist group can call its own. Particular problems exist when, as with the Kurds, their land lies across several countries: Iran, Iraq, Syria and Turkey. Not all separatist struggles are pursued through unconstitutional means, but because a government will be most unlikely to grant such groups' goals because that would diminish the 'nation-state', very often what begins as a goal to be achieved through persuasion ends up as an objective to be gained by any means necessary.

Separatist culturalist groups are common in Asia and Africa, but until recently were rare in Latin America. Many Indians in Latin America, who now constitute only about 10 per cent of the population, exist on the margins of society; many are poor and uneducated and, as a result, politically powerless. Lately, however, groups have emerged pressing for the rights of the indigenous peoples; one of their goals may well be autonomy. Defence of land, cultures and languages are also focal points of conflict. As populations grow and the amount of vacant land fit for agriculture diminishes, pressure on the land occupied by indigenous peoples increases. Indigenous peoples may control land which the state, farmers or national or transnational corporations want for their own purposes.

In short, Latin American Indians are fighting back, working with others to press for land redistribution, economic opportunities and civic rights. Rubber-tappers and Indians join forces in Brazil to defend forests against logging companies, while in Chiapas, Mexico, and on Nicaragua's eastern Pacific coast Indian peasants take part in armed uprisings against the state to press for social and land reforms.

Syncretist groups

Syncretistic groups are commonly found among rural dwellers in many parts of the Third World, especially sub-Saharan Africa and Latin America. Their systems of religious belief typically feature a number of elements found in pre-modern forms of religious association, such as ancestor worship, healing and shamanistic practices. Sometimes ethnic differentiation forms an aspect of syncretism. A syncretist community group will use both their religious beliefs to help defend their individuality and their way of life in the face of a threat from outside forces − often, but not invariably, the state. Examples include the cult of Olivorismo in the Dominican Republic; Sendero Luminoso in Peru, whose ideology, a variant of Maoism, also utilizes aspects of indigenous (i.e. pre-Christian) cultural religious belief to attract peasants in Ayacucho; the *napramas* of north-eastern Mozambique, who combine traditional and Roman Catholic beliefs, and were temporarily successful in defeating the South African-supported guerrilla movement, the Mozambique National Resistance (RENAMO) in the early 1990s; and a number of groups in Uganda and Zambia, led by charismatic, often female, figures, who led struggles against government in pursuit of regional autonomy (Haynes 1995c).

Religious fundamentalists

Religious fundamentalism is by no means an exclusively Third World phenomenon: millions of religious fundamentalists live in North America and Western Europe. Fundamentalist groups in the Third World are to be found among followers of Buddhism, Christianity, Hinduism and Islam (Haynes 1993a, 1996). Fundamentalists tend to live in population centres − or are at least closely linked with each other by electronic media. What they all have in common, irrespective of religious belief, is that they perceive their way of life to be under serious threat. A common aim, as a result, is to *reform* society in accordance with their religious tenets: to change the laws, morality, social norms and political configurations of the country where they reside. The aim is to create a tradition-orientated, less modern(ized) society.

Fundamentalists often struggle against governments, because the latter's jurisdiction encompasses areas which the former hold as integral to the building of an appropriate society, including education, employment policy and the nature of the extant moral climate. They also attack both 'nominal' co-religionists, whom they perceive as lax in their religious duties, and members of opposing religions, whom they often perceive as ungodly.

Community-orientated groups

Whereas each of the groups we have discussed so far target governments and other power-holders, community-orientated groups, by contrast, work principally towards material improvements for their members. Usually, this does not involve conflict with government, because often the groups undertake to provide themselves with services which are officially the responsibility of government to provide. The most prominent example of Third World community-orientated groups are the tens of thousands of Basic Christian Communities (BCCs) which mushroomed over the last 25 years in many Roman Catholic areas of the Third World, especially Latin America and the Caribbean, parts of East Asia and sub-Saharan Africa. Many BCCs undertake a range of self-help projects, including literacy campaigns, environmental improvement efforts and basic health endeavours, which help to transform their lives for the better. Although for the most part apolitical, the basic idea behind the BCCs comes from the tenets of 'liberation theology'.

First articulated in Brazil in the early 1960s, liberation theology is an ideology which grew as a response to poor social and economic conditions. It is a radical form of Christianity exhorting the dispossessed to take their futures into their own hands rather than relying on governments to change things for them (Haynes 1993a: 95–121).

In conclusion, each of the four broad types of religio-ethnic groups is primarily concerned with the well-being and solidarity of communities feeling themselves under threat, whether from the state or from a lack of development. It is necessary to bear in mind, however, that the characteristics of the groups described are not necessarily exclusive to each. For example, fundamentalist groups may also be community-orientated, while culturalist groups may also be syncretistic (Haynes 1995d).

What emerges from the analysis is that group perceptions of ethnic and/or religious separateness may lead to conflict with the state. We might expect it to follow from this that the political stability of a country with *extensive* religious and/or ethnic schisms will normally be low. Many countries in Latin America and the Caribbean, South and South-east Asia, sub-Saharan Africa and the Middle East have serious religious fragmentation and multiple ethnic cleavages, while in many East Asian states, on the other hand, there is a relatively high degree of ethnic and religious homogeneity (Lane and Ersson 1994: 133). Table 5.2 indicates which Third World countries have high levels of ethnic and religious fragmentation.

Table 5.2 shows that a dozen countries, including Angola, Cameroon, Chad, Côte d'Ivoire, India, Kenya, Liberia, Malawi, Nigeria, Tanzania, Uganda and Zaire, score very high, i.e. 0.8 or more, on the ethnic fragmentation index. Religious divisions, on the other hand, are pronounced in Cameroon, Central African Republic, Chad, Côte d'Ivoire, Kenya, Liberia, Malawi, Mozambique, Rwanda, Tanzania, Togo, Trinidad and Tobago, and Uganda. It will be noted that 18 African countries, plus Indonesia and Malaysia, have to accommodate serious ethnic *and* religious cleavages. The data in table 5.2 do not, however, make it easy for us to give a clear-cut response to the question: does ethnic and/or religious fragmentation in a country lead to violent conflict between groups? The answer is: sometimes. Of the 20 countries in table 5.2 which score high on both ethnic and religious fragmentation indices, relatively few – only six, all in Africa – Angola, Chad, Ethiopia, Liberia, Mozambique and Uganda – have experienced civil war over the last 20 years. Recently there was also serious civil conflict in Burundi, Rwanda and Somalia: in the first two countries the cause was ethnic rivalry – Hutu versus Tutsi – while in Somalia it was a result of inter-clan[5] discord, rather than ethnic or religious contest. None of these three countries appears in table 5.2 in relation to the ethnicity criterion, while only Rwanda is noted for its 'religious fragmentation'.

Table 5.2 Ethnic and religious fragmentation in the Third World

Region	Country	Ethnic fragmentation[a]	Religious fragmentation[b]
Sub-Saharan Africa	Angola	0.80	0.49
	Benin	0.75	0.53
	Botswana	0.51	0.54
	Burkina Faso	0.72	0.59
	Cameroon	0.86	0.73
	Central African Republic	0.74	0.63
	Chad	0.80	0.70
	Côte d'Ivoire	0.87	0.67
	Ethiopia	0.70	0.61
	Kenya	0.86	0.69
	Liberia	0.86	0.64
	Malawi	0.65	0.73
	Mozambique	0.75	0.62
	Nigeria	0.88	low
	Rwanda	low	0.64
	Sierra Leone	0.78	0.57
	South Africa	0.68	0.48
	Tanzania	0.95	0.73
	Togo	0.72	0.64
	Uganda	0.92	0.66
	Zaire	0.80	low
East and South-east Asia	Indonesia	0.77	0.59
	Laos	0.61	low
	Malaysia	0.71	0.55
	Philippines	0.79	low
South Asia	India	0.90	low
	Nepal	0.69	low
	Pakistan	0.63	low
Latin America and the Caribbean	Bolivia	0.70	low
	Ecuador	0.60	low
	Guatemala	0.58	low
	Peru	0.63	low
	Trinidad and Tobago	0.61	0.70
	Uruguay	low	0.49
	Venezuela	0.54	low
Middle East and North Africa	Afghanistan	0.63	low
	Iran	0.76	low
	Jordan	0.52	low
	Lebanon	low	0.51
	Morocco	0.53	low

[a] Ethnic fragmentation index: over 0.55 signifies a high level of ethnic fragmentation.
[b] Religious fragmentation index: over 0.45 signifies a high level of religious fragmentation.

Source: adapted from data in Lane and Ersson 1994: 134–5

We cannot claim with confidence, according to the data in table 5.2, that countries with apparently the most serious ethnic and religious divisions are those which will most likely erupt into civil conflict. Rather, the propensity of Third World countries to religio-ethnic clashes seems to depend on the extent to which their governments are able to deal with the effects of widespread, rapid, social and economic changes on both local power structures and societal forces.

For example, the post-colonial Indian republic not only inherited a Western-style system of democracy and rapidly industrialized, but it also had in place a number of factors apparently conducive to societal conflict: ethnic, caste and religious diversity: Islam, Hinduism, Sikhism, Christianity, Jainism and Buddhism. Despite occasionally serious outbreaks of ethnic and religious conflict, however, the Indian state has, for 50 years, managed to keep the country both intact and democratic. What seems to be significant is the degree of governmental skill in dealing with factors conducive to social conflict.

In religiously and ethnically diverse East Africa, on the other hand, there was a different outcome. There, late nineteenth-century European colonialism interacted with Arab and Islamic influences which pre-dated it by some 800 years. The states which the colonialists left were, like India, based on Western models, but the level of governmental skill in dealing with societal schism was much less. Very few states in East Africa were, until recently, democratic, while ethnic conflicts are at a high level: in Somalia civil war broke out in the early 1990s, while in October 1995 ethnic riots left five Kenyans dead (Barrow 1995).

Regarding South-east Asia, another region of religious and ethnic fragmentation, ancient religious and cultural determinants – especially Buddhism and Confucianism – were juxtaposed with the Western idea of statehood and its accompanying institutions: centralized government, monopoly of the means of force, and a comprehensive administrative structure. These factors tending towards social homogeneity were not sufficient, however, to eliminate ethnic and religious challenges to governments in many countries in the region, as we shall see below. Finally, as already noted, in relatively religiously and ethnically homogeneous Latin America, several countries, including Nicaragua, Peru, Bolivia and Mexico, have important ethnic minorities whose influence on national-level politics is significant.

In conclusion, modernization has contributed to a resurgence of religious and ethnic identity in many parts of the Third World. It did not impinge upon an otherwise blank or uniform cultural and political situation; rather, the struggle to establish modern political institutions and a developed economy often conflicted with pre-modern social norms and traditions. Sometimes, but by no means invariably, ethnic or religious schism led to serious conflict. It is not possible, however, accurately to predict where ethnic or religious conflict will break out by the use of a simple fragmentation model. Sometimes civil war erupts in a religiously and ethnically *homogeneous* country – e.g. Somalia – but not in a country – e.g. Tanzania – with high levels of religious and ethnic fragmentation. The level of governmental skill in achieving sufficient social solidarity to transcend potential cultural schisms seems to be an important factor in whether or not serious conflict develops.

Having examined some of the reasons why religious and ethnic factors may or may not lead to societal conflict, in the final section we examine the regional political impacts of ethnic and religious tensions.

Religious and Ethnic Challenges: Regional Analysis

Latin America and the Caribbean

As we saw above, Basic Christian Communities (BCCs) represent attempts by predominantly poor communities to improve their material situation. Yet, whereas thousands of BCCs emerged in Latin America, they were much less common in the islands of the Caribbean. Part of the reason for this is that many Caribbean governments have been democratically elected for decades, unlike Latin American regimes until recently. The result was that the former had to be concerned with winning – and maintaining – the support of a large proportion of the poor if they wanted to ensure re-election; one way of achieving this was to make certain that living standards were as high as possible, with reasonable community amenities provided by government. Recently, however, due to downturns in the global economy, many Caribbean countries experienced economic problems, which sometimes led to religio-ethnic tensions surfacing in political conflict. In Trinidad, such tensions were reflected in a *coup* attempt by a splinter Muslim group, the Jamaat al Muslimeen, in the early 1990s. In Jamaica, on the other hand, economic downturn and political polarization are less recent phenomena; a syncretistic religious cult, Rastafarianism, epitomized for decades the desire of many Jamaicans for redemption from, first, colonial rule and second, a poor post-colonial socio-economic situation.

Jamaica's 2.5 million people, mostly descendants of West African slaves, are predominantly Christian, although about 100,000 describe themselves as Rastafarians (Wiebe 1989). The emergence of Rastafarianism in the 1930s was fuelled by the unacceptability for many Jamaicans of the image of a white-skinned God promulgated by the British Christian colonists. Rastafarians regard the last Ethiopian emperor, Haile Selassie ('Ras Tafari'), who ruled from 1932 until his overthrow and death in 1974, as God; and the black American, Marcus Garvey, is recognized as his greatest prophet (S. Hall 1985; Haynes 1993a: 58–9). The militant message of liberation preached by Garvey until his death in the early 1940s was highly influential in helping to spread Rastafarianism as the route to emancipation from British rule for Jamaicans.

Following independence in 1962, serious riots occurred in 1965 and again in 1968, touched off by the polarization of society between a small rich elite and the mass of poor people in the country. At this time the Rastafarians' idea of a new type of society based on equality and communitarian ideals offered a radical alternative. As a result, Rastafarianism enjoyed a period of growing popularity, aided by the popularity of the great reggae artist, Bob Marley, a member of the Rastafarian faith. Following the death of Marley in 1980, however, the influence of the Rastafarian movement declined precipitously. It lost much of its direct political influence and is currently of only marginal political significance in Jamaica.

Just as Rastafarianism was initially no more than a marginal creed, which later achieved short-lived political influence, so Islam in Trinidad has gone through a series of developments. A line of the national anthem of Trinidad and Tobago, 'Here every creed and race finds an equal place', illustrates the country's desire for religious and ethnic tolerance. The two islands of 1.3 million people have a racially and religiously diverse culture: about 40 per cent of the people trace their ancestry to Africa, while the same proportion have their cultural roots in the Indian subcontinent.

There are smaller communities of Lebanese, Syrians, Chinese, Portuguese and Jews. Racial complexity is paralleled by religious diversity, with Christianity, Hinduism, Islam and a variety of Afro-Caribbean religions present. About 60 per cent of the population is Christian, one-quarter Hindu and around 5 per cent Muslim.

The country prospered in the oil boom of the 1970s, but during the 1980s real GNP per capita (i.e. purchasing power) fell by more than a third to $3,830 (World Bank 1995: 163, table 1), with GNP per capita declining by an annual rate of 2.8 per cent, one of the worst performances in the Caribbean. Unemployment rose to 22 per cent, while crime and violence increased as living standards and job availability dropped (Rueschemeyer et al. 1992: 250–2).

The deteriorating socio-economic position was the background for an armed Muslim insurrection. On 27 July 1990 a group of about 100 members of a radical Muslim group, Jamaat al Muslimeen, burned down the police headquarters, occupied the television station, took over parliament and held the Prime Minister, A. N. R. Robinson, and most of his cabinet hostage. The Muslimeen were black converts to Islam who acted, according to their leader, 'for the sake of our community and the good of Trinidad' (Mullin 1994). The Muslims' leader, Yasin Abu Bakr, demanded an amnesty from arrest for his followers, the formation of an interim government which would include Abu Bakr, and elections within 90 days. Five days later they gave themselves up, convinced that they would go free and that Abu Bakr's demands would be met. Instead they were arrested. The government claimed that an amnesty promised during the siege was invalid because granted under duress.

Abu Bakr, ex-policeman and former goalkeeper for the national football team, believed that his group's action would precipitate a popular uprising. Instead, widespread looting ensued, with 20 people killed and 500 injured in the violence, most of them wounded by gunshots allegedly fired by police. For their pains the members of the Jamaat al Muslimeen involved in the *coup* attempt spent two years in prison (Mullin 1994). The attempted governmental take-over did, however, have some popular support. The unpopular coalition government, the National Alliance for Reconstruction (NAR), had swept to power in 1986, but had been unable to tackle the country's pressing socio-economic problems. In elections in early 1992 the NAR lost all of its 31 seats. Abu Bakr formed a political party, the New National Vision (NNV) party, whose chief aim was to build an Islamic state in Trinidad. His electoral appeal was very limited, however; the NNV came third in a by-election in early 1994 in Laventille, a poor area of the capital, Port of Spain, which might have been expected to be natural territory for his anti-establishment message. While the Islamic message of deliverance preached by the NNV failed, at least in the short term to gain popular acceptance, the *coup* attempt exemplified how serious were the social divisions in the country, and illustrated the failure of the party system to integrate and articulate effectively the interests of all sections of society. Like the Rastafarians in Jamaica, the NNV in Trinidad showed an alternative to the poor, based on a message of religious deliverance and redemption.

The Middle East and North Africa

Whereas the radical message of Trinidad's Jamaat al Muslimeen was directed to a relatively small Muslim minority, the political importance of Islam in the Middle East and North Africa reflects the faith's predominant cultural significance. The widespread emergence of Islamic fundamentalist groups is symptomatic of the failure of many regimes to institute mechanisms of accountability, to spread the fruits of economic growth, or, in some cases, to stimulate development, reflected in extensive internal migration from the country to the town, growing unemployment and declining living standards for many people.

Although little research has been completed in relation to the growth of fundamentalist Islam in Algeria, where a civil war erupted in 1992 following the disallowing of an Islamic party's election victory, much more is known about the situation in Egypt, another country troubled by conflict between the state and Islamic fundamentalists. In Egypt, five alleged members of the al Jihad ('Holy War') group responsible for the assassination of President Sadat in 1981 were sentenced to death, in March 1982. In 1984, over 300 al Jihad members were arrested, and some were executed for their alleged involvement in the murder of state security forces in the town of Asyût. From 1986, the group has been engaged in guerrilla war against the authorities, most recently turning its attention to Egypt's foreign tourists and the Christian minority, some of whom were murdered.

Dessouki (1982: 10–13) notes that Islamic political activism in Egypt has the aim of the reinstitution of Islamic law. What this amounts to is that the Islamists, irrespective of the extent to which they differ in terms of tactics, leaders and, to an extent, the precise vision of an Islamic society, have as their main aim the desecularization of societies which they perceive have departed from the religiously correct path. They also seek the removal of modernizing elites from state power and their replacement by Islamists. What is involved, then, is not only grabbing power in order to introduce Muslim law for *moral* and *religious* reasons, but also the achievement of *political* goals through the creation of a fully *Islamic* society.

Ayubi (1991: 118) explains that Islamic fundamentalist movements 'appear to be more vigorous in countries that have openly discarded some of the symbols of "traditionalism" and have clearly declared a schema for Western-style modernization'. Overtly modernizing governments have been in power for years in many countries of the region, including Algeria, Tunisia, Syria and Libya, although the strength of the fundamentalists in the first is not replicated in the latter three countries. What this suggests is that the relative weakness of Islamic movements in some modernizing countries has more to do with the ability of the state to create a political system which has the support – or at minimum, the quiescence – of most people. Libya achieved this by the shrewd use of massive oil revenues, Syria by the control of a single-party state, and Tunisia by gradual, yet discernible, increases in living standards for most citizens. Neither Algeria nor Egypt, on the other hand, had governments which were able to maintain societal support, whether through authoritarian tactics or through the sensible use of oil revenues.

In sum, the Islamist movements in the Middle East and North Africa have as their goal the creation of an Islamic society to replace the current, modernizing one. The division between secular and Islamist forces is a comprehensive conflict between two different conceptions of society and social change. The division is manifested in the fields of politics, economy, religion and social affairs. The success of the fundamentalists in achieving their goals is to a large extent a function of the ability of incumbent governments to deflect them by either societal control or palpable amounts of development or a mixture of the two.

Sub-Saharan Africa

Unlike the Middle East and North Africa, largely populated by Muslim Arabs, sub-Saharan Africa is filled with an array of religious and ethnic groups. While ethnic and religious conflicts are common in the region, it would not be correct to assume that they are primordial, ages-old phenomena, firmly entrenched at the time of European colonization in the nineteenth century. In fact, as Bayart (1993: 46) explains, 'most situations where the structuring of the contemporary political arena seems to be enunciated in terms of ethnicity relate to identities which did not exist a century ago, or, at least, were then not as clearly defined.' What this suggests is that the emergence of religio-ethnic rivalry is a manufactured phenomenon, which is linked to post-colonial modernization.

While it would be going too far to argue that every manifestation of contemporary ethnicity is a product of the colonial period, the speed of the formation of ethnic identity in sub-Saharan Africa becomes incomprehensible if it is divorced from the circumstances of colonial rule. The colonizers regarded their often arbitrarily carved out colonies, peopled with myriad groups, as embryonic nation-states. At the same time, colonial authorities *invariably* created and maintained their dominance by coercion. They controlled migratory movements, and more or less artificially fixed ethnic details through birth certificates and identity cards. Yet, ethnic identity was not only imposed by colonial administrations for their own convenience. Of just as much importance was the way in which Africans themselves sought to adjust to prevailing circumstances by using the Europeans' rules to their own advantage. Although many communities did not traditionally have a 'chief' to rule them, because Europeans believed that *all* societies have at their head a leader, many chief-less communities produced a *de facto* leader when required. In the Belgian Congo (now Zaire), for example, the function of chief was quickly taken up by a community elder, who then drew an administrative salary from the Belgian authorities as well as a 'customary' tribute from his people. These payments, proportional to the numbers of people and sub-chiefs which a chiefdom could boast, in time led chiefs to seek increasing numbers of people to rule over. Over time, such communities became 'ethnic groups' as they grew in size. Indications of political power, manifested in the figure of the chief, became tied to important structures of power, as well as allocation of resources, the size of which was tied to the size of communities under individual chiefs' control. Kasfir (1976) has shown how in both Uganda and northern Nigeria originally mutually hostile communities were organized as 'ethnic groups' by their traditional (or neo-traditional) leaders for the latter's pecuniary benefit.

Bayart (1993: 52–3) notes the case of the Aïzi, a small group of about 9,000 people living in 13 villages by the lagoons of the Côte d'Ivoire. Each of the groups of Aïzi was different: different language, different traditions of origin, and so on; and each of the villages had an original configuration; yet, during the colonial era, there grew what became known as 'Aïzitude', a sense of Aïzi ethnicity based on both cultural similarity and fear of outsiders. Since the notion of ethnic group was one of the ideological premises of the colonial administration, it became the chief means of affirming one's own existence in relation to other (rival) groups and hence the language of relationships between the subject peoples themselves.

Such examples could be extended, but hopefully the point is clear: Africans worked out their own ways of community life, of living together and governing themselves, over the course of many centuries. They created a very large number of different communities and, in some cases, states. Each of the communities had its own territory, language, beliefs and loyalties. European colonizers understood little or nothing about the long and complex development of African socio-political units. To them, Africans lived in 'tribes' or larger, self-contained ethnic groups. How could Africans be controlled as cheaply as possible? The answer was that each tribe must have its own chief; if there were none, one must be created. The cultivation or invention of chiefs had two results: one was that several communities would unite under a single chief; the other was treating these combined communities as though they formed a single people. Inventing chiefs led to 'inventing' ethnicity. A good deal of modern ethnic conflict in Africa began in this way.

East and South-east Asia

Several East and South-east countries have minority religio-ethnic groups seeking to achieve autonomy or independence (Encarnacion and Tadem 1993). In these countries, as elsewhere in the Third World, governments aim to build nation-states in which all ethnic and religious minority groups feel a sense of national identity. As we shall see, however, many governments have failed in their goal. To illustrate this and to explain the reasons why, we focus upon culturalist groups in Myanmar,[6] Thailand and the Philippines.

Until recently, rebel groups were active in 12 areas of Myanmar. Most dynamic were the Karens and Shans, who were nevertheless defeated by the state's forces in 1994. The Christian Karens had fought for independence since 1947, when the Karen National Union was formed, following the granting of independence to Burma – Myanmar from the late 1980s – by the British. A common characteristic of the groups fighting the central government is that they consider themselves excluded from power in a state dominated by the Buddhist Burmese. In other words, their marginality is exacerbated by their religious distinctiveness from the dominant group in the country (Encarnacion and Tadem 1993: 150).

Like Myanmar, the Philippines is home to many ethnic groups – in fact, more than 100. Muslims, concentrated in the southern islands, number about 4 million of the southern population of 14 million, and about 7 per cent overall. Thirteen ethno-linguistic groups make up the Muslim population, with the Tausugs, Maranaos and Maguindanaos the three largest; all are active in a Muslim secessionist movement. Muslim separatists contend that their people have been forcibly included in a state which is dominated by foreign capitalists and their Filipino counterparts (Encarnacion and Tadem 1993: 152). The Muslims are divided among themselves, however, in relation to both tactics and organization, with the largest separatist group, the Moro National Liberation Front, 'having to contend with other groups with differing agendas' (von der Mehden 1989a: 217). Over time, the conflict has become internationalized, with Muslim states such as Libya allegedly supplying military equipment to the Muslim rebels.

Muslim agitation occasionally resorts to terrorist tactics. The separatist Abu Sayyaf ('the sword-bearer') group was formed in 1990 in the southern Philippines, and has between 250 and 600 members. The Philippines authorities suspected that Abu Sayyaf was receiving funds from Islamic groups in the Middle East. From April 1992 the group unleashed a number of terrorist assaults, beginning with a hand grenade attack on the Roman Catholic cathedral in Iligan City, killing five and wounding 80 people. In 1995, 200 alleged Abu Sayyaf activists attacked the southern town of Ipil, killing 53 people (Shenon 1995).

As in the Philippines, religion combined with ethnicity plays a political role in southern Thailand among a Malay Muslim minority that comprises about 4 per cent of the overall population of the country of about 60 million. According to Encarnacion and Tadem (1993: 153), the Malay Muslim minority's 'strict aderence to Islam has alienated them from the mainstream' of predominantly Buddhist Thai society, and has made them resentful of the chauvinism of the government in Bangkok. Estrangement is exacerbated by the fact that many among the Malay Muslim minority engage in non-lucrative small-scale farming, which serves to marginalize and impoverish them in a national economic situation dominated by Thai Buddhists and ethnic Chinese.

One result of Muslim alienation has been armed conflict with the state. Muslim rebels have fought Thai authorities for more than 40 years, in a conflict which has nevertheless failed to deliver the results the Muslims desired. Two groups, the Pattani National Liberation Movement and the Path of God, were at the forefront of demands for separatism (Encarnacion and Tadem 1993: 154; von der Mehden 1989b). By the late 1980s about 200 cadres of the two main Muslim separatist groups, were serving long prison sentences. Thai authorities claimed that by the mid-1990s there were fewer than 200 Muslim fighters in the field compared to around 2,000 at the end of the 1970s. The government claimed that it had tried to meet Muslim demands by increasing government services and local participation in political activities, but that its attempts were thwarted by aid from Iran and Libya to the Muslim separatists which helped to keep the flame of revolt alive.

In conclusion, minority groups in Myanmar, the Philippines and Thailand believe that they are increasingly coerced into conforming with the requirements of the dominant national group. Such groups do not perceive themselves as fully part of the nation, believing that their ethnic, religious, political and economic rights are violated.

South Asia

Religio-ethnic conflicts are also common in South Asia. In Pakistan, the capital, Karachi, is frequently rent by ethnic conflict between Pathans and Mohajirs, recent migrants from India. Nationally, traditional Punjabi dominance is challenged by the regions of Sind and Baluchistan. In Sri Lanka a long-term civil war is being fought between Buddhist Sinhalese and Tamil Hindus. Bangladesh endures ethnic conflict involving Buddhist Chakmas from the hill tracts and Muslim Bengalis from the crowded plains. In India, clashes take place between 'tribals' and Hindus in Bihar, while in Assam indigenes defend their land and jobs against what they see as an 'invasion' of outsiders from Bangladesh, Bihar and West Bengal (Hettne 1995: 7).

One of the most serious, and long-running, challenges to the state in India has come from the Sikh minority. The assassination of Prime Minister Indira Gandhi in October 1984 followed 'Operation Bluestar', an assault by security agents and soldiers to end the occupation of the Golden Temple, Amritsar, by the Sikh extremist Jernail Singh Bhindranwale and a large number of his followers. In the process more than 2,000 people were killed. This catastrophic event focused attention on Sikh designs for an independent state, Khalistan. Over time, however, Sikh unity fractured in the struggle for dominance among a number of competing groups, whose ideologies ranged from 'extremist', using terrorism in pursuit of political aims, to 'moderates', whose chief tactic was negotiation. Although the Sikhs failed in the short term to gain their state, their exemplary opposition to what they perceived as the 'Hinduization' of India helped to stimulate other religio-ethnic separatist movements in the country. Some of these, like Muslim radicals in the state of Jammu-Kashmir, used appeals to religious solidarity to focus opposition to the central government.

Religious and ethnic issues have considerable impact upon politics in many parts of the Third World. Confidence that the spread of urbanization, education, economic development, scientific rationality and social mobility would combine to diminish significantly the socio-political position of religion and ethnicity was not well founded. Instead, religio-ethnic concerns, reflected in culturalist, fundamentalist and syncretistic entities, serve as vehicles of opposition bolstering ideologies of group self-interest. Threats from powerful outsider groups or from unwelcome symptoms of modernization (e.g. breakdown of moral behaviour, over-liberalization in education and social habits) also encourage such responses. In addition, the failure of governments to push through programmes of social improvement leads to the emergence of community-orientated groups which develop their religion-based ideology of solidarity towards the goal of community development.

The overall thrust of this chapter has been that one of the most resilient ideas about societal development after World War II – that nations would inevitably secularize as they modernized – was misplaced. It was believed that modernization would lead to the development of a new kind of national society. Instead, increasingly common religio-ethnic conflicts reflected the widespread loss of faith in central government extant throughout the Third World. In the next chapter, we examine a further important manifestation of society's demands on the state: calls for enhanced human rights.

Notes

1   As we shall see below in the regional analysis of Latin America in this chapter, liberation theology became a widespread feature of socio-political division and struggle within the Catholic Third World. Liberation theology is an intensely political phenomenon, a response to the appalling social and political conditions widely found throughout Latin America and in other Third World Roman Catholic areas. Central to the concept are the notion of dependence and underdevelopment, the use of a class struggle perspective to explain social conflict and justify political action, and the exercise of a political role to achieve both religious and political goals.

2   There is a vast literature concerned with ethnicity and its impact upon politics. There is little agreement, however, about the basic concerns of ethnicity; this is because most of the words used to describe types of ethnic groups are open to multiple interpretations, including 'tribe', 'ethnic group' and 'minority group'.

3   'Syncretism' is a term used to describe a fusion or blending of religions to produce a new hybrid. Syncretistic religions are particularly common in the Third World, where the impact and forms of the so-called world religions – Islam and Christianity – are very often moulded by pre-existing religious forms. For further discussion of the concept of syncretism, see Haynes 1995c.

4   In September 1995, in response to the Palestinian campaign for increased autonomy, it was announced that Palestinian Arabs would henceforward enjoy increased autonomy in a number of towns in the Israeli-administered West Bank of the River Jordan area.

5   A clan is smaller than an ethnic group. It is generally thought of as a collection of families under the control of a single chieftain, often bearing the same family name.

6   The Myanmar government claimed in 1995 to have crushed all ethnic challenges to its rule, including that of the Karens, who fought for 20 years for independence from Rangoon's control.

6

Human Rights

So far, we have been concerned with states and societies in relation to democracy, economic development and religio-ethnic tensions and conflict. In this chapter we move on to a further area of state–society friction: the pursuit of human rights. Earlier, we noted that post-colonial states in the Third World are often qualitatively different from those created in an earlier epoch in Europe. In the latter, the nation usually created the state, whereas in the former the state, often unsuccessfully, tried to create a nation. One aspect of the failure to construct nation-states was that a large number of Third World governments became progressively more authoritarian. One of the manifestations of this was that many routinely incarcerated and/or tortured those perceived as political 'trouble-makers'.

Twenty years ago, Emerson (1975: 207) noted that most Third World governments abuse many of their citizens' human rights. He noted then that the

intricate set of provisions outlawing arbitrary arrest or detention, asserting the right of anyone arrested or detained to take proceedings before a court, and seeking to guarantee humane treatment, presumption of innocence till proved guilty, and fair and speedy trial are remote from a world in which . . . preventive detention without right of access to any court is a standard part of the procedure. In much of the Third World . . . recourse to torture is so common as to attract little attention.

A decade later, Jackson (1990: 139) portrayed a similarly bleak picture of human rights abuses in the Third World, arguing that many governments are a threat to their citizens' well-being. Over the years, humanitarian organizations, like Amnesty International in their annual Report, have catalogued the arbitrary detentions, beatings, political killings, torture, terror, political prisoners, disappearances, refugees, death squads, destruction of livelihood and various other human rights violations around the world.[1] The Third World regularly features in the Amnesty Reports with political killings, massacres, abductions and disappearances being common in every region (Jackson 1990: 140).

In the first four sections of this chapter we examine: (a) the state of human rights in the Third World in the 1990s; (b) differing – i.e. individual and collective – interpretations of human rights; (c) the ways that human rights are perceived in the traditional development paradigms; (d) how we can *measure* states' human rights records by assessing the veracity of Mitchell and McCormick's (1988: 477) statement that 'countries that enjoy higher levels of economic well-being ha[ve] . . . better human rights records than those that d[o] not'. The final section is a regional survey of human rights; we explore Islamic, Hindu and African conceptions. We do not discuss the plight of women in the Third World in the current chapter, preferring to devote chapter 7 to that purpose.

Human Rights in the 1990s: The Third World Situation

As we noted in chapters 3 and 4, two of the most pressing issues for many people in the Third World are democracy and economic growth. Each is associated with a basic human right: the first involves the right to choose one's government, while the second is connected to the right to have a sufficiency to live on. During the 1980s and 1990s, as we have seen, these human rights concerns emerged as central to political debates and economic struggles in many Third World countries. As a result, it is no longer as easy as it once was for Third World governments to deprive their citizens of basic human rights. For one thing, increased numbers of governments are democratic; in addition, a range of international and domestic factors helps to set human rights standards.

Regarding international factors, events of recent years have combined to produce international diffusion effects encouraging demands for rights. Six are of particular importance: (a) in the post-

Cold War era, Western governments no longer routinely try *to justify Third World allies' human rights excesses as they once did in the name of fighting communism;* (b) *the collapse of many authoritarian governments,* exemplified and symbolized by the failure of the Soviet bloc, has encouraged people everywhere to express their opinions openly and to participate in decision-making; (c) *the dominance of market forces,* illustrated by the widespread adoption of structural adjustment in the Third World, while sometimes producing greater economic efficiency, has reduced the already weak economic position of the poor; (d) *the integration of the global economy* has allowed capital, labour and goods to cross national boundaries while increasing international competition; (e) *the transformation of production systems and labour markets* has the potential to weaken greatly the power of organized labour to ensure that governments enforce labour standards, such as minimum wage legislation and to fund welfare programmes; (f) *the media revolution and consumerism* have not only helped to erode particularistic cultures and values, replacing them with a 'global culture' of Coca-Cola, Hollywood and Michael Jackson, but have also served to stimulate demands for a wide array of rights in the Third World, a result of the spread of Western individualistic values. In sum, these six international diffusion effects were important in encouraging people in the Third World to demand their rights.

International agents and forces have interacted with domestic factors. Of particular importance in relation to the latter is the spread of modernization and Western-style education, resulting in an increasing proportion of educated people and of those with access to television and radio. Democratic and economic struggles also help to strengthen civil societies, providing a focal point to demands for widespread change. Finally, the experience of many people in the Third World of living for years under vicious military dictatorships, characterized by brutal, wholesale violations of human rights 'justified' in the name of national security, has also encouraged many to call for enhanced rights.

Increasing human rights awareness in the 1990s was reflected in the holding of a global human rights conference under the auspices of the United Nations (UN) in Vienna in 1992. As a result of the higher international profile for human rights, the human rights industry became both fashionable and astute about publicity. Organizations like Amnesty International put the relationship between individual citizens and the state on to international conference agendas. As we shall see in chapter 7, the fourth UN conference on women held in Beijing in September 1995 was concerned with Third World females' rights (Brittain 1995b).

In conclusion, the effect of both international and domestic developments was to put human rights issues firmly on political and developmental agendas in the Third World. Governments which failed to address such human rights concerns were likely not only to be ousted at the ballot-box, but also to attract the opprobrium of international aid donors. The latter increasingly tied aid pro-grammes to governments' human rights credentials, especially those relating to democracy and the treatment of minority groups.

Collectivist and Individualist Conceptions of Human Rights

So far we have discussed the extension of human rights conscious-ness in the Third World. While human rights as a *concept* has become internationalized, there are problems with the assumption that there is *one* objective set of human rights standards applicable to all cultures which is simple to detail. There are, in fact, wide-ranging, definitional disagreements over the content of human rights, especially the comparative status of *individual* and *collective* rights. Sometimes, for example, Third World governments will seek to defend harsh treatment of individuals in the name of the *collective* or national good. The question we need to ask is: *which* human rights are appropriate to the Third World?

Individualistic conceptions of human rights have historically been dominant in the West. Collective concerns, on the other hand, are of most importance to socialist and many Third World govern-ments. Because of differing interpretations of what human rights entail, beyond a commonly agreed minimum it is very difficult to come up with a list of human rights which would attract universal support. Fukuyama (1992: 42–3) offers a list of what he terms 'fundamental' rights, which fall into three categories: *civil rights* – i.e. 'the exemption from control of the citizen in respect of his person and property'; *religious rights* – i.e. 'exemption from control in the expression of religious opinions and the practice of worship'; *political rights* – i.e. 'exemption from control in matters which do not so plainly affect the welfare of the whole community as to render control necessary', including the right of press freedom.

Fukuyama has nothing to say about economic and social rights such as the 'right' to food or to a job.

Ajami (1978: 28–9) identifies three different, more basic rights, which, while allowing for cultural diversity, amount to what he calls the 'maximum feasible consensus': (a) the right to survive, (b) the right not to be subjected to torture, (c) the right to food. The first two are civil and political rights, the third an economic and social right. Ferguson (1986: 211) also seeks to identify 'universally accepted . . . basic or primary rights, which apply regardless of cultural differences or social order'. His list includes the right to life and the right to freedom from torture, slavery or summary execution, and, if a state has the resources, freedom from hunger, a minimum standard of living, basic education and health care.

Both Ajami and Ferguson agree that the right to food and the right to life are interdependent, necessary for 'something resembling a minimally satisfactory human life to be lived' (Vincent 1986: 26–7). Fukuyama, on the other hand, denies the veracity of this inter-dependence. Despite these differing views, many people would probably agree that a range of human rights is both inherent in the individual and socially derived by development; i.e. political freedoms are not possible without some reasonable degree of economic and social development.

A concern with individual rights is the core of liberal democracy; a concern with collective rights is the heart of socialism. A central issue of the Cold War era was which system, liberal democracy or socialism, was best poised to deliver human rights. In other words, was socialism, a system built on the premiss of providing collective benefits to all citizens who accept the legitimacy of the socio-political system, 'better' at delivering human rights than liberal democracy? Whereas Western individualistic conceptions of human rights, exemplified by Fukuyama's list, focus on the freedom of the individual *not* to be controlled by the state, socialist formulations are more concerned with various economic rights, such as the right to employment, housing and health care.

In relation to the Third World, where there were until recently many self-described 'socialist' regimes and where a handful survive, it was quite uncontroversial for Shepherd to write in the 1980s that 'socialism and the control of individual rights in the interests of the whole has become generally accepted' (Shepherd 1981: 214). Falk (1979: 5) argued at this time that socialism was the most appropriate ideology for development in the Third World, and that human rights would be better fulfilled within a socialist system than in any feasible alternative.[2] White et al. (1983) pointed out, however, that there was a problem with accepting the claims of self-proclaimed socialist regimes at face value. It was unacceptable, they explained, that 'socialist' regimes routinely denied individual rights, because such 'human rights cannot be dismissed as "bourgeois", but must be incorporated into a truly humane socialism'. They noted, in addition, that 'democratic rights of individuals or groups as *citizens*, able to influence the direction of society as a whole through electoral processes, representative institutions and sectional associations' must become considerably stronger in such states (White et al. 1983: 29, emphasis original).

White et al.'s prescient concerns found an echo in the demise of socialist regimes throughout the world in the late 1980s. The downfall of socialism in the Soviet bloc was, at least in part, due to the unacceptable restrictions placed on individuals by Communist regimes. Communist regimes in Eastern Europe were, it is necessary to remember, imposed by force at the hands of the Red Army; they did not spring from local cultural traditions. As a result, it is not that surprising that over time they were rejected by large numbers of people. In effect, Eastern Europeans were denying the centrality of collective rights and asserting their commitment to individualistic human rights. As far as the Third World is concerned, many 'socialist' regimes wanted to enjoy the authoritarian control which 'socialism' offered; they were much less willing – or able – in many cases to deliver promised collective rights.

Human Rights and the Development Paradigms

Liberal democracy's concern with the individual and socialism's focus on the collective also animate the conceptions of rights in the two traditional development paradigms. Dependency writers tend to be impressed by the achievements of socialist regimes, while those of the developmental school look favourably at those of the West.

Developmental theory

As noted earlier, developmental theorists argue that once societies throw off the 'dead hand' of tradition, they will be able to progress to a modern stage. Many hope that the modern stage will be characterized by the full panoply of individual rights, although some argue that the modern stage is just as likely to be authoritarian as democratic (Almond 1970: ch. 5). Developmental theorists like Lipset, while not arguing the causal directionality of liberal democratic development, assert a strong empirical connection between economic development and democracy: 'It seems clear', he wrote in 1959, 'that the factors of industrialization, urbanization, wealth and education are so closely interrelated as to form one common factor. And the factors subsumed under economic development carry with it the political correlate of democracy' (quoted in King 1993: 142). The problem, however, is that an apparent empirical connection between socio-economic factors and democracy do not imply a causal relationship. Industrialization and economic development in Brazil between 1964 and 1984, in Chile between 1973 and 1989, in South Korea and Taiwan from the early 1950s to the late 1980s, and in Indonesia at the present time were pursued under the aegis of military regimes with little apparent concern for human rights. In short, the appeal of democracy and human rights for developmentalist theory is a normative one; there is no 'iron law' that links the two.

Dependency theory

Dependency theory is inherently economistic. As a result, neither social classes, the state, politics, ideology nor human rights receive concentrated attention. At the same time, given human rights abuses in many Third World socialist countries, dependency analysts have been obliged to pay some attention to human rights issues. On the dependency approach, democracy is a sham unless it is 'true' or 'real' democracy – i.e. unless it leads to a substantial degree of power passing to ordinary people and their mass organization in decision-making bodies and assemblies. Socialist democracy was regarded as the ideal, while the Western conception of democracy involving meaningful and extensive competition, a high level of participation, and extensive individualistic civil rights was regarded as an inferior form of democracy. In short, the best form of democracy in the view of many dependency writers was socialist democracy; individual liberties were less important than collective rights to a job, housing and food.

As already noted, the dependency view is that the West's

development was possible only as a result of the exploitation and accompanying 'underdevelopment' of the Third World. The idea that 'real' democracy, grounded in economic autonomy and socialism, is better than liberal democracy is, however, difficult to accept. Those socialist countries which came closest to achieving economic autonomy – North Korea, Albania and Burma – showed few democratic tendencies and did not appear especially concerned with human rights. Economic autonomy *may* be a desirable end, as it shelters the economy from international economic forces, *but* it is highly likely to require considerable authoritarianism to cope with the austerity which results.

In sum, developmental theory believes that liberal democracy is best equipped to deliver individualistic rights, while dependency analysis argues that economic autarchy and a humane socialism are the best way forward. Both understand that economic growth is the first essential pre-condition for modernization, to be followed by increasing human rights, whether based on individualistic or on collective concerns.

Cultural Relativity and Human Rights

Just as dependency and developmental theories differ in their conceptions of which rights should be predominant, so there are claims that human rights are culturally grounded. In other words, in culture-based arguments few rights have *universal* application beyond the following: nobody of whichever culture would believe that it is right to kill people without justification, to let people starve wilfully or to imprison people for no reason. On the other hand, not all would agree that everyone has the right to a house guaranteed by government, to paid holidays or even to clean water. These are obviously desirable, but they are not necessarily *rights*.

As we noted earlier, Third World governments, often accused of extensive human rights violations, must increasingly take account of both domestic and international opinion in relation to their human rights records. The most common means of defence is either (a) to deny that they are infringing human rights at all, or (b) to seek to justify human rights violations by arguing that they should not be judged by 'inappropriate' – i.e. individualistic, Western – conceptions but by the standards and concerns of their own culture's societies.

The first defence – that they are not infringing basic human rights: locking up people for no good reason and torturing them to confess to a 'political crime' – does not hold water simply because of the extent of documented proof to the contrary. The second is more problematic. Discussions about human rights in the Third World sooner or later come up against the issue of *cultural relativity*. The notion of cultural relativity is that because each individual culture has its own norms and rules of social and individual behaviour, *which* human rights are observed in society is a function of its unique cultural characteristics. In other words, cultural relativity is the idea that because different cultures have differing cultural reference points, it is not appropriate to judge all societies according to one, universal standard. It is not for those from other cultural milieus to pronounce judgement, so the argument runs, because their different world-views preclude them from objective assessment. If we deny the logic of the applicability of universal rights, then governments rooted in specific cultural contexts have strong grounds to rule as they see fit – as long as they do not violate their society's cultural norms. This raises an important question which we turn to next: to what extent are supposedly *universal* human rights norms any more than Western ethnocentric interpretations of essentially individualistic rights?

Are there universal human rights?

The centrality of the notion of universal human rights was placed definitively on the international agenda in 1948, when the United Nations General Assembly adopted the Universal Declaration of Human Rights (UDHR) (Sikkink 1993: 414). Many decolonizing Third World countries, including India and more than 20 sub-Saharan African states, later adopted constitutions which expressly referred to the 1948 Declaration.

The UDHR itself is an intricate document expressed at three separate levels. The first sets out the basic principles which every government should satisfy. The second reduces those principles to the language of rights, and lists different kinds of rights. The third lays out which institutions and practices, in its view, can guarantee and safeguard these rights. Parts 2 and 3 have a liberal democratic bias. In the second part this is reflected in its use of the language of rights and the kinds of rights it stresses, while in the third it is reflected in the suggested kinds of institutions and procedures, which 'presuppose and are specific to liberal democracy' (Parekh 1993: 173–4).

The general philosophy of the Declaration falls into two categories. The first groups a number of principles which are both liberal and culturally specific. These include, e.g., the declaration that marriages must be rooted in the 'free and full consent' of the proposed partners, the right to freedom of expression and the strong concern expressed in relation to the importance of private property. The second group relates to vital human interests which are objectively valued in all societies. These include 'the respect for human life and dignity, equality before the law, equal protection of the law, fair trial' and, less certainly, the 'protection of minorities' (Parekh 1993: 174). These concerns are emphasized as core themes of the world's great religions and are commonly practised in most non-Western societies.

The claim that there *are* universal human rights, worth championing in *all* cultures, can be illustrated in three ways. First, as already noted, the 1948 Declaration was signed by a large number of non-Western governments. Second, when decolonized Asian and African countries joined the United Nations in the 1950s and 1960s, they demanded changes to the UDHR, which were finally accepted in 1966. Three were important: the rejection of the right to property and to full compensation in the event of nationalization, the toning down of the individualistic basis of the 1948 Declaration, and the acceptance of the principle that it might on occasion be necessary to set aside individual rights in the national interest. In other words, negotiations about the content of the UDHR led to a final version with universal applicability. Third, people have constantly appealed to the principles of the UDHR in their struggles against authoritarian governments. The latter have usually sought to *deny* 'the existence of unacceptable practices rather than shelter behind relativism and cultural autonomy. In their own different ways both parties are thus beginning to accept the principles of the UDHR as the basis of good government, conferring on them the moral authority they otherwise cannot have' (Parekh 1993: 174–5). Parekh (1993: 175) explains how these 'principles are increasingly becoming "a common standard of achievement for all peoples and nations" as the UN Declaration itself had hoped'. As a result, they provide a valuable basis for a freely negotiated and constantly evolving consensus on *universally valid* principles of what is sometimes called *good government*.

In sum, several factors – the general acceptance and partial renegotiation of the UDHR by Third World states and attempts by some to deny that they are infringing rights rather than sheltering behind cultural relativity – suggest that it is widely recognized that there *are* universal human rights. This obviously logically denies governments the 'right' to ignore those they do not like.

Good Government and Human Rights: Regional Analysis

The idea of good government does *not* necessarily imply that all countries have to have liberal democratic regimes in order to be just or representative, or that only Western-style rulers respect human rights; in other words, different countries should remain free to determine their own appropriate forms of government *if* they are acceptable to their citizens; the latter *may* choose liberal democracy, or not. The point is that for a regime to exhibit the fundamentals of good government, it should have concern for the public good uppermost in its mind. The notion of good government refers to effective, 'user-friendly' rule, respectful of human rights and beneficial to those living under a its jurisdiction.

Good government has four qualities. It is (a) at the core of the exercise of power, (b) central to political accountability, (c) purposive and development-oriented, and (d) seeking with vigour to improve the mass of people's quality of life. Good government, in short, describes a situation where state–society relations are bounded by political relationships of reciprocity and authority, trust and accountability (Haynes 1993b). The 'amount' of good government in a country can be gauged, at least roughly, in terms of the extent of *liberty* and *socio-economic fairness* present.

The degree of 'liberty' in a country is the relative occurrence of civil and political rights. A 'political freedom index' (PFI) has recently been compiled to measure the variation by country in the institutionalization of the rights and freedoms that seek to confirm the abstract concept of liberty. The question of the extent of liberty in a country begins with the question: how much democracy is there? Democracy has two fundamental components: (a) the implementation of human rights of various kinds and (b) a legitimate probability that the power position of the ruling elite may be regularly contested (Lane and Ersson 1994: 84).

A second measurable element of good government is: to what extent does a regime seek to instill a reasonable degree of socio-economic fairness? Many states attempt to increase the general level of affluence in their country, perhaps by supporting a welfare state or by seeking to introduce a progressive taxation regime. While a standard indicator like gross domestic product measures the *overall* economic output in a country, it says nothing about the 'quality of life', i.e. the level of human development and the distribution of welfare, which would allow us to assess the level of socio-economic fairness in a country. A widely accepted indicator of 'quality of life' is the United Nations Development Programme's human development index (HDI) already referred to in chapter 4. The HDI measures life expectancy, level of literacy and people's purchasing power: when these indicators are combined, we can gauge the 'quality of life' within a country.

Next we present data on the Third World's 'freedom' and 'liberty' position, measured by the 'political freedom index', and on the 'quality of life' situation, measured by the HDI. For reasons of space, we focus upon the most populous Third World states: those with over 10 million inhabitants, except for Caribbean countries, where the criterion is a population of 1 million.[3]

The aim is twofold: first, it is to examine Mitchell and McCormick's (1988) contention that countries enjoying higher levels of economic well-being have better human rights records than those that do not. Another way of putting this is the World Bank's claim that 'for a given level of income, improvements in social indicators are associated with freedom and liberty' (World Bank 1991: 134). In other words, if these hypotheses are correct, we should note a strong correlation between a country's PFI and its HDI. Table 6.1 shows the average scores for the PFI and HDI for each of the five Third World regions. As we shall discuss, there are a number of correlations between the HDI and PFI which we can note from table 6.1: e.g. Latin America and the Caribbean does best on both indicators, while the Middle East and North Africa does reasonably well in terms of the HDI but worst in terms of the PFI; South Asia, on the other hand, performs well on the PFI but poorly in relation to the HDI.

We shall not attempt to offer a definitive answer to the old question: what is necessary for sustained economic development: democracy or authoritarian rule? Some argue that the first is necessary – examples include the United States and Britain – while others maintain that the latter is best – examples embrace Chile and

Table 6.1 Average regional scores for the HDI and PFI in the Third World, 1994

Region (no. of states in brackets) (n = 53)	Average HDI (0–1)	Average PFI (1–100)
Latin America and Caribbean (14)	0.74	54.5
East and South-east Asia (10)	0.65	40.8
Middle East and North Africa (9)	0.61	24.0
South Asia (5)	0.41	58.2
Sub-Saharan Africa (15)	0.36	35.6

Sources: data derived from UNDP 1994: 129–31, table 1; 'Bite the Ballot' 1994

South Korea during the 1970s and 1980s. It is difficult to establish a durable connection between authoritarian rule and protracted economic growth; there are too many examples of authoritarian governments with appalling records in this respect. On the other hand, while the link between freedom and development is not really in dispute, it is problematic to decide whether freedom leads to development, or whether development begets freedom. What is clear, however, is that *sometimes* sustained economic development leads to increasing demands for democracy and human rights, as we have already noted is the case for both Taiwan and South Korea. On the other hand, a sustained economic downturn in the 1980s led to redemocratization in Latin America! Regarding Middle Eastern oil-producing states, there were high levels of economic growth until recently, but little democracy and a poor human rights record (Bill and Springborg 1994: 295–6). This leads us to the second focus: to what extent do cultural factors impinge upon both the 'quality of life' and the extent of freedom in a society?

Latin America and the Caribbean

In general, Latin American and Caribbean countries perform better in relation to both the PFI and the HDI than any other Third World region, as table 6.1 indicates. Table 6.2 shows a breakdown of PFI and HDI indicators in selected states in the region. Apart from Haiti, the poorest country in the Western hemisphere, none of the countries scores less than a 'medium human development' rating on the HDI.[4] In terms of the PFI, only Cuba and Haiti achieve very poor ratings, 3 and 5 respectively.[5]

Table 6.2 Latin America and the Caribbean: human rights indicators, 1992–4

Region	Country	Population (millions, 1993)	Life expectancy (1992)	Adult literacy rate (%, 1992)	'Real' GDP per capita ($, 1993)	HDI[a] (1993)	Global HDI ranking out of 173 states	PFI (1994)
Latin America[b]	Argentina	33.5	71.1	95.5	5120	0.853	37	74
	Chile	13.8	71.9	93.8	5208	0.848	39	73
	Venezuela	20.7	70.1	89.0	8120	0.820	46	58
	Colombia	34.9	69.0	87.4	5460	0.813	50	54
	Mexico	91.6	69.9	88.6	7170	0.804	52	57
	Brazil	159.1	65.8	82.1	5240	0.756	63	68
	Ecuador	11.0	66.2	87.4	4140	0.718	74	63
	Peru	22.9	63.6	86.2	3110	0.642	95	48
Caribbean[c]	Trinidad and Tobago	1.3	70.9	96.0	8380	0.855	35	79
	Costa Rica	3.3	76.0	93.2	5100	0.848	39	82
	Jamaica	2.5	73.3	98.5	3670	0.749	65	64
	Cuba	11.0	75.6	94.5	2000	0.666	89	3
	Dominican Republic	7.6	67.0	84.3	3080	0.638	96	45
	Haiti	6.6	56.0	55.0	925	0.354	137	5

[a] The constituents of the HDI are life expectancy, adult literacy rate and 'real' GDP per capita.
[b] Countries with over 10 million inhabitants.
[c] Countries with over 1 million inhabitants.

Source: UNDP 1994: 129–31, table 1; 'Bite the Ballot' 1994

Trinidad and Tobago, Costa Rica, Argentina and Chile do very well in terms of both the HDI and PFI, with more than 0.8 in the former and more than 67 in the latter.[6] Venezuela and Jamaica do well with respect to both indices. The rest, with the exception of Cuba and Haiti, perform reasonably well in relation to both the HDI and the PFI. The average PFI for the countries in table 6.2 is 54.5, for the HDI, 0.74. Haiti, one of the worst performers in both respects, recently redemocratized following a two-year period of military rule. This development would no doubt now allow the country to achieve a higher rating on the PFI. Cuba, with a PFI rating of 3, is estimated to be a 'medium development country' in terms of the HDI. It is, of course, the Western hemisphere's only Communist country, but performs badly according to the PFI not only because of the absence of genuinely competitive elections but also because of the propensity of the regime to deny people their rights by, e.g., locking them up without adequate cause (Pinkney 1993: 149).

In relation to the correlation between freedom and economic well-being, the data in table 6.2 are not conclusive. The problem is that Latin America's currently satisfactory democracy rating may not last. The term 'Latin-Americanization'[7] was coined to refer to an oscillation between democracy and authoritarian rule which was characteristic of Latin America in the 1970s and 1980s (O'Donnell et al. 1986). There is no guarantee of course that the same process will not occur again. What this suggests is that it is too early to tell whether the region's relatively good freedom position will endure, or whether democracy is more conducive to economic develop-ment than authoritarian rule. Both Chile and Argentina, e.g., made good economic progress during periods of military dictatorship in the 1970s and 1980s.

In relation to our second issue – i.e. the link between culture and human rights – it is claimed by Huntington (1991) that the predominance of Christianity is an important factor in the region's recent redemocratization. For him, 'it seems plausible to hypothesize that the expansion of Christianity encourages democratic develop-ment' (Huntington 1991: 73). Witte (1993: 11) notes that 24 of 32 new democracies which emerged between 1973 and 1993, many of which were in Latin America, were Christian. The great majority, including Argentina, Brazil, Chile and others in the region, were, like the Philippines, South Korea, Poland, Hungary and Lithuania, countries which received a great deal of diplomatic and sometimes

Table 6.3 East and South-east Asia: human rights indicators, 1992–4

Country[b]	Population (millions, 1993)	Life expectancy (1992)	Adult literacy rate (%, 1992)	'Real' GDP per capita ($, 1993)	HDI[a] (1993)	Global HDI ranking out of 173 states	PFI (1994)
South Korea	44.2	70.4	96.8	8320	0.859	32	55
Taiwan	21.0	74.0	91.0	8000	0.800+[c]	–	56
Thailand	58.3	68.7	93.8	5270	0.798	54	61
Malaysia	19.1	70.4	80.0	7400	0.794	57	61
China	1185.0	70.5	80.0	2946	0.644	94	8
Philippines	63.8	64.6	90.4	2440	0.621	99	50
North Korea	22.6	70.7	95.0	1750	0.609	101	4
Indonesia	187.7	62.0	84.4	2730	0.586	105	44
Vietnam	70.4	63.4	88.6	1250	0.514	116	23
Myanmar	43.5	56.9	81.5	650	0.406	130	46

[a] The constituents of the HDI are life expectancy, adult literacy rate and 'real' GDP per capita.
[b] Countries with over 10 million inhabitants only.
[c] Estimated by the author because Taiwan is not widely recognized as a country, but is perceived by many governments as part of China. As a result, its HDI is not calculated by the UNDP.

Sources: UNDP 1994: 129–31, table 1; 'Bite the Ballot' 1994

material support from the United States for their redemocratization processes. Several African Christian countries, on the other hand, such as Zaire, Togo and Rwanda, which are not democracies, were not objects of United States' strategic interest in the same way and did not experience prolonged American pressure for democratization. In sum, Christianity may well be a feature in democratization and human rights observance in Latin America, but equally so is strong US encouragement.

East and South-east Asia

As table 6.3 shows, of states in the East and South-east Asia region with populations greater than 10 million, only South Korea (and probably Taiwan) are 'high human development' countries, while Thailand and Malaysia just fail to enter that category. All other countries in table 6.3, with the exception of Myanmar, are 'medium human development' countries.

None of the countries scores a sufficiently high rating on the PFI to categorize it as having a 'high' level of political freedoms, although Thailand and Malaysia both score 61, which puts them in the 'moderate' category. The worst performers are China, Vietnam and North Korea, the Communist triumvirate, with 8, 23 and 4 respectively. In relation to the HDI, however, each does better than military-run Myanmar. In relation to the hypothesis about the correlation between freedom and economic development, the data are once again inconclusive. Most of the region's states were authoritarian until recently; several still are, although most with a few exceptions have reasonable ratings on the HDI.

Whereas the average PFI for Latin America and the Caribbean was 54.5, that for the East and South-east Asia region is only 40.8. As far as the HDI is concerned, the East and South-east Asia region achieves an average of 0.65, compared to Latin America and the Caribbean's average of 0.74. Thus, in both rankings Latin America and the Caribbean outdo East and South-east Asia.

The relatively poor PFI rating for many of the region's states led to recent American attacks on its human rights record. Inoguchi (1995: 131) claims that many people in the region regard American attacks on human rights as politically or racially motivated, aiming to undermine political and social stability, an essential element in economic success. A 'senior diplomat', speaking anonymously in early 1995, claimed that there was growing concern about

Table 6.4 The Middle East and North Africa: human rights indicators, 1992–4

Country[b]	Population (millions, 1993)	Life expectancy (1992)	Adult literacy rate (%, 1992)	'Real' GDP per capita ($, 1993)	HDI[a] (1993)	Global HDI ranking out of 173 states	PFI (1994)
Saudi Arabia	17.5	68.7	64.1	10850	0.742	67	8
Turkey	60.1	66.7	81.9	4840	0.739	68	54
Syria	13.5	66.4	66.6	5220	0.727	73	5
Iran	61.7	66.6	56.0	4670	0.672	86	16
Iraq	20.7[c]	65.7	62.5	3500	0.614	100	3
Algeria	27.2	65.6	60.6	2870	0.553	109	15
Egypt	56.4	60.9	50.0	3600	0.551	110	45
Morocco	27.0	62.5	52.5	3340	0.549	111	25
Yemen	12.1	51.9	60.0	1374	0.323	142	45

[a] The constituents of the HDI are life expectancy, adult literacy rate and 'real' GDP per capita.
[b] Countries with over 10 million inhabitants only.
[c] Includes Iraqi Kurdistan.

Sources: UNDP, 1994: 129–31, table 1; 'Bite the Ballot' 1994

American intrusiveness in the region: 'They want us to swallow an American culture of CNN and Hollywood, insist we welcome their rude and intrusive media, while they lecture us on human rights. The cultural arrogance of a country with such problems of race and crime is breathtaking to people on our side of the Pacific' (quoted in Walker 1995).

As Thompson (1993: 481) notes, leaders of economically success- ful countries in the region win support at home by attacking 'foreign interventionists' and delivering economic growth that is fairly equitably spread. In other words, Asian authoritarians often argue from a position of economic success. On the other hand, the region's countries *are* vulnerable to violations of human rights charges when viewed from a Western perspective, because many Asian states put the collective interest foremost, while individual interests are subordinate. Economic development is the priority, and social redistribution is downgraded in many of the region's countries (Inoguchi 1995: 131).

The Middle East and North Africa

None of the countries in table 6.4 manages to gain a 'high human development' rating or a 'high' PFI score. The average HDI for the region is 0.61, that for PFI, 24. In terms of the PFI, only Turkey, Egypt and Yemen, with respectively 54, 45 and 45 do better than poorly; in terms of the HDI, all, with the exception of Yemen (with a 'low' HDI) achieve a 'medium' ranking. On both measures, the region's states on average do worse than both Latin America and the Caribbean and East and South-east Asia. Thus, despite the asset of considerable oil wealth, the governments of the region's most populous countries have managed to deliver their citizens only a medium level of human development, while only a few have managed to develop even moderate political freedoms.

The region offers little support for the notion that freedom and economic development go together. Two of the three best performers in terms of the HDI – Saudi Arabia and Syria – are in the bottom three where freedom is concerned, while three of the four countries which score best in relation to freedom – Yemen, Egypt and Moroco – are at the bottom of the HDI range.

It is sometimes argued that the low level of democracy in the region is due to the influence of Islam (Huntington 1991; Fukuyama 1992). The social importance of Islam cannot be denied: every country in the region, with the exception of Israel, has a population at least 89 per cent Muslim (Beeley 1992: 296–7). What impact does Islam have on human rights in the region? The first point is that Islam is both premissed and rooted in the importance of *collective* over *individual* rights; in other words, there is a high regard for social solidarity. The Muslim community – the *umma* – is said to be a 'compact wall whose bricks support each other'. The role of the individual 'is not merely to act so as to ensure [the community's] preservation, but also to recognize that it is the community that provides for the integration of human personality realized through self-abnegation and action for the good of the collectivity' (Vincent 1986: 42). As far as girls and women are concerned, as we shall see in chapter 7, this means that they must not act in ways which are outside the norms of recognized Muslim conventions.

Second, in relation to Islam, Vincent (1986: 42) argues that the 'language of duty seems more natural than that of [individual] rights'. Because of the primary importance attached to obedience to God, rights seem to be secondary to duties. Rules of conduct were laid down by God via the prophet Muhammad; Muslims serve God by way of thorough obedience to these rules. If rights are thought of as 'freedoms', then in Islam 'true freedom consists in surrendering to the Divine will rather than in some artificial separation from the community of God . . . rights remain subordinate to and determined by duties' (Vincent 1986: 42).

Governments in Muslim countries everywhere claim divine sanction for their existence; their rule is God's will, and everything they do is sanctioned by him. This is, of course, a potential justification for harsh or arbitrary government, and has indeed been used to justify the denial of democracy, freedom of speech and harsh treatment of women by some of the region's rulers (Owen 1992). There is, however, an emergent trend among some educated Muslims and revisionist *ulama* (theological teachers) to question the current poor position of women and non-Muslim minorities in Muslim society, areas which have 'seemed for a long time to be outside the Islamic critical gaze'. Such revisionists feel that 'many Muslims confuse some inherited traditional cultural values with Islamic values' (Saif 1994: 63; An-Na'im 1992: 20–1).

Despite current concerns with the position of females and minorities, however, it seems unlikely that there will be a swift culture shift whereby individual rights take precedence over collective rights. There are several reasons for this. First, most societies are conservative, and Muslim societies are like others in this respect. Second, incumbent political elites do their best to ensure that the *status quo* continues. Since independence, political elites in the Middle East and North Africa, often in alliance with the military, have striven to modernize their political systems, while retaining a tight grip on power. The avowed aim in, e.g., Syria and Iraq was to build nation states along Western lines. As a result, the status of Islam was at least temporarily downplayed, and religious professionals were either incorporated into the state elite, or, if not, their power was neutralized. The result has been a modernist superstructure balanced uncomfortably atop a substructure deeply rooted in traditional beliefs, with Islam as the cement holding the social system together. Such governments have not always been noted for ruling either wisely or well. In some of the more traditional states, such as Saudi Arabia and Morocco, on the other hand, states have sought to deepen the Islamic credentials of their regimes and tried to limit the spread of Western ideas. The result has been that Islamic values have been strengthened and Western ideas regarded with suspicion by many Muslims.

South Asia

South Asia is an anomaly as far as the link between freedom and development is concerned. In terms of the PFI the states of the region achieve the best average score – 58.2 – of any Third World region so far surveyed; regarding the HDI, on the other hand, the region is the worst average performer – with an average score of 0.41. Within the South Asia region itself (see table 6.5), there are notable variations in HDI, between Sri Lanka (0.665) and the second best, Pakistan (0.393). The five countries of the region surveyed achieve fairly similar rankings in terms of the PFI: in the range 52–63, all have moderate political freedoms. It is worth noting, however, that, as in Latin America, democracy was only recently reintroduced in Bangladesh, Nepal and Pakistan, and may not endure. Nevertheless, Sri Lanka's good HDI performance and reasonably satisfactory democracy rating give support for the hypothesis that by developing human resources and by increasing per capita incomes the basis for democratic political systems are more likely to be secured.

Table 6.5 South Asia: human rights indicators, 1992–4

Country[b]	Population (millions, 1993)	Life expectancy (1992)	Adult literacy rate (%, 1992)	'Real' GDP per capita ($, 1993)	HDI[a] (1993)	Global HDI ranking out of 173 states	PFI (1994)
Sri Lanka	17.8	71.2	89.1	2650	0.665	90	52
Pakistan	122.4	58.3	36.4	1970	0.393	132	55
India	908	59.7	49.8	1150	0.382	135	63
Bangladesh	122.3	52.2	36.6	1160	0.309	146	59
Nepal	20.4	52.7	27.0	1130	0.276	149	62

[a] The constituents of the HDI are life expectancy, adult literacy rate and 'real' GDP per capita.
[b] Countries with over 10 million inhabitants only.

Sources: UNDP 1994: 129–31, table 1; 'Bite the Ballot' 1994

Both Bangladesh and Pakistan have large Muslim majorities, while Sri Lanka has a majority Buddhist population. As we saw above in relation to Islam, religion may impart certain characteristics to societies which affect how they perceive and relate to human rights. In relation to cultural factors, the region is noteworthy because of the influence of Hinduism. An estimated 82 per cent of India's more than 900 million people and 90 per cent of Nepal's population of 20 million are Hindus; in sum, over 60 per cent of people in the South Asia region follow the Hindu religion. Many Indian Hindu traditionalists argue that their country's secular constitution runs counter to their core values. Kane argues that 'the [Indian] constitution engenders a feeling among common people that they have rights and no obligations whatsoever' (quoted in Chiriyankandath 1993: 247). Traditionalists claim that the values of Hinduism are 'essentially derived from the social duties and status hierarchies based on *varna* (the classic all-India caste categories) and *jati* (the multiplicity of locally relevant castes' (ibid. 1993: 247). As a result, the rights and duties of Hindus are said to be determined by their position within an essentially hierarchical system of relationships constituting an 'all-embracing cosmology'. Such a view, Chiriyankandath argues, might imply the 'duty of any Hindu [state] ruler to recognize and [seek to] maintain the caste system . . . and consequently reject the primacy according to individual rights and the idea of human equality' (ibid.) which are the foundations of both the Universal Declaration of Human Rights, of which India is a signatory, and the Indian Constitution.

The fact is, however, that encounters with the West have helped to encourage non-hierarchical currents within Hinduism: the agnostic Jawaharlal Nehru, India's first Prime Minister and the chief drafter of the Constitution, was a modernizer who sought to reduce the influence of what he saw as an inappropriate Hindu traditionalism on the post-colonial state. There was, in other words, a concern to update traditional cultural norms both to take account of domestic change and to embed India more thoroughly within the emerging global consensus as to the appropriateness of fundamental, universal human rights. In India, as in the rest of South Asia and the Third World more generally, the controversy over human rights remains mixed up with problems of culture and religion, economic development and social change, and the problem of trying to build a nation-state from groups of often diverse peoples.

Table 6.6 Sub-Saharan Africa: human rights indicators, 1992–4

Country[b]	Population (millions, 1993)	Life expectancy (1992)	Adult literacy rate (%, 1992)	'Real' GDP per capita ($, 1993)	HDI[a] (1993)	Global HDI ranking out of 173 states	PFI (1994)
South Africa	42.5	62.2	80.0	3885	0.650	93	49
Zimbabwe	10.7	56.1	68.6	2160	0.474	121	68
Cameroon	12.9	55.3	56.5	2400	0.447	124	24
Kenya	27.9	58.6	70.5	1350	0.434	125	44
Madagascar	13.0	54.9	81.4	710	0.396	131	60
Ghana	16.7	55.4	63.1	930	0.382	134	70
Côte d'Ivoire	13.5	51.6	55.8	1510	0.370	136	41
Nigeria	112.1	51.9	52.0	1360	0.348	139	10[c]
Zaire	40.2	51.6	74.0	469	0.341	140	8
Tanzania	28.2	51.2	55.0	570	0.306	148	40
Sudan	29.2	51.2	28.2	1162	0.276	151	4
Uganda	19.0	42.6	50.5	1036	0.272	154	51
Angola	10.9	45.6	42.5	1036	0.271	155	11
Mozambique	16.6	46.5	33.5	921	0.252	159	22
Ethiopia	52.5	46.4	50.0	370	0.249	161	32

[a] The constituents of the HDI are life expectancy, adult literacy rate and 'real' GDP per capita.
[b] Countries with over 10 million inhabitants only.
[c] Author's estimate.

Sources: UNDP 1994: 129–31, table 1; 'Bite the Ballot' 1994

Sub-Saharan Africa

The states of Sub-Saharan Africa featured in table 6.6 score, on average, worst of all Third World regions in terms of HDI (0.36), but better than the Middle East and North Africa in relation to freedom, with 35.6 the average PFI. There are, however, wide variations in the latter between various countries: both Ghana and Zimbabwe achieve a 'high' PFI rating, while South Africa, Kenya, Madagascar, Uganda, Tanzania, Côte d'Ivoire and Ethiopia achieve only a 'moderate' score.

There does not appear to be a strong correlation between HDI and freedom in sub-Saharan Africa. Only South Africa is in the 'medium human development' category, while all the rest of the countries have a 'low' HDI rating. The situation in sub-Saharan Africa does not confirm the hypothesis relating to economic development and democracy; there is no apparent correlation between democratic performance and the delivery of 'human development'; on the other hand, nearly all improvements in the PFI in the region are very recent. As in Latin America and East and South-east Asia, there is no guarantee that this improvement will continue; democratic reversals are no doubt possible in the region.

There are of course many different cultures, traditions and religions in Africa, making it impossible to perceive a unitary 'African' culture (Haynes 1991, 1996). Despite this diversity, Africans, it is claimed, have traditionally been more prepared to accept authoritarian governments and are less concerned with political freedoms than many people elsewhere (Howard 1986). Like the Muslim, the 'African' conception of human rights is said to be characterized by societal concern with collective over individual rights. According to Bayart (1986: 109–10), individualistic conceptions of 'democracy and of human rights [in Africa] are the products of Western history'. In other words, it is claimed that individualistic values were not respected by pre-colonial societies in Africa, but were introduced into Africa in the wake of colonial rule. At the same time, however, 'Africans were [not] "traditionally" more tolerant of arbitrary power' (Bayart 1986: 110) . Events over the last few years, when large numbers of African countries democratized, cast serious doubt on the assumption that Africans are more tolerant of authoritarian government than other people. In fact, it seems highly likely that the generally poor performance of African governments in relation to both human development and democracy over time has been instrumental in stimulating challenges to their rule.

In this chapter we have explored human rights in the Third World in relation to economic development, freedom, and social and cultural factors. We discussed Mitchell and McCormick's (1988) contention that 'countries that enjoyed higher levels of economic well-being ha[ve] . . . better human rights records than those that d[o] not'. The conclusion is that in two regions – Latin America and the Caribbean and East and South-east Asia – there does seem to be reasonable evidence for the veracity of the hypothesis, while in the remaining three regions there appears to be little sign that economic development and political freedoms go hand in hand. At the same time we need to bear in mind that advances in the PFI in Third World regions – and especially the spread of democracy – are by no means entrenched everywhere; anti-democratic reversals are quite likely, particularly in sub-Saharan Africa and South Asia where the human development position is generally poor.

Regarding cultural factors, Huntington (1991) argues that Christianity is especially conducive to democracy, and indeed Latin America and the Caribbean, scoring an average of 54.5, is a heavily Christian area. On the other hand, the region which did best in terms of the PFI – South Asia, with 58.2 – is filled with Hindus, Muslims and Buddhists, with few Christians. The region with probably a slim majority of Christians over Muslims – sub-Saharan Africa – achieved a score of only 35.6 on the PFI, better, however, than the strongly Muslim Middle East and North Africa, with a score of 24 (Haynes 1996). Muslim and Hindu countries, Fukuyama (1992) maintains, are very likely to be non-democratic and poor respecters of human rights. Yet, *some* Muslim countries are democracies – e.g. Malaysia, Jordan and Lebanon – while India and Nepal, both predominantly Hindu countries, are also democratic. The conclusion must be that cultural factors cannot be taken in isolation from others. It seems reasonably clear that, usually, *whatever* a country's dominant culture, if it has a reasonably good HDI and has been a democracy for a reasonably long period, then it is likely to have a comparatively good human rights record.

One indicator of the extent to which human rights has become a legitimate concern of international society is the support which states give to various human rights conventions. For example, freedom from racial discrimination and slavery, refugees' rights, and the *political* rights of women are widely upheld in nearly all states (Vincent 1986: 99). As we noted in chapter 4, it is not necessarily the case that national minorities are in reality treated equitably by government. Additionally, it often seems that the rights of women begin and end with the right to vote. Just as we saw that there are cultural issues in relation to human rights in the Third World, so the position of women, as we shall see in the next chapter, is bound up with issues of culture, religion, traditionalism and modernization.

Notes

1 See Amnesty International's *Annual Reports*, published in London.
2 The depredations of the 'socialist' regime of Pol Pot in Cambodia and the state's treatment of dissidents in the Soviet Union finally put paid to such notions by the early 1980s.
3 For reasons of space it is impossible to present data on all 120 or more Third World countries. By using the criterion of size, it is possible to cover the 53 largest states (with the exception of the Caribbean) in the regional surveys. I am aware, however, that this method bars a great number of smaller countries which would no doubt throw up some interesting data.
4 HDI is ranked in three categories: 'high human development', 0.8 or greater; 'medium human development', 0.5–0.799; and 'low human development', up to 0.499.
5 The PFI is currently an imprecise measure. Apart from the subjectivity involved in calculating the degree of freedom in a country, there are also political considerations. Countries may not mind their low 'human development level' publicized, because they can blame the unfairness of the international economic system or the legacy of colonialism. Political freedoms, on the other hand, are clearly the responsibility of the government in power. As a result, there is no definitive PFI measurement of the world's countries currently available. PFI data used in the tables in this chapter are extracted from 'Bite the Ballot', 1994. The PFI score in the tables (out of 100) for the world's countries was devised by a 'panel of experts – academics, journalists and human rights campaigners' – according to four criteria: 'voting', 'participation', 'freedom' and 'rights'. Finland, with a score of 90, did best; Iraq, Afghanistan and East Timor, with a score of 3, did worst.
6 Unlike the HDI, with its division of countries into 'high', 'medium' and 'low' categories of human development, the PFI index does not categorize countries in this way. However, I deem it appropriate for purposes of analysis to divide the 1–100 ranking system, albeit

arbitrarily, into three divisions: 0–33, few political freedoms; 34–66, moderate political freedoms; 67–100, high levels of political freedom.

7 'Latin-Americanization' is a label that indicates a phenomenon that is not really fully understood. It implies not only that civil and political rights have been fragile in Argentina, Brazil, Chile and Peru, but also that civil administration is not easily maintained for long periods of time in these countries. It is not really known why some states that move towards democratization fail to achieve a stable political state.

7

Women and Power

In previous chapters we have been concerned with democracy, economic reform, religious and ethnic schisms, and human rights. These concerns attract sustained international attention in the 1990s, and are at or near the top of the political agenda in many parts of the Third World. In the current chapter the aim is to supplement the accounts given so far by focusing on social, political and economic issues in the Third World from the perspective of gender, a set of concerns which is often kept from domestic political agendas by those with power: men.

The gradual rise of the international women's movement from the early 1960s helped to change perspectives in the West about the political and economic roles of women. The position of women was put under the global spotlight at the fourth global women's conference held under United Nations auspices in Beijing in September 1995. The Beijing event followed not only three earlier UN conferences concerned with women's position, but also other conferences regarding human rights (Vienna, 1992), the natural environment (Rio de Janeiro, 1992), population (Cairo, 1994) and human development (Copenhagen, March 1995), of which each discussed the situation regarding women. The cumulative effect of these events was 'to shift the agenda from the relatively safe area of "women's issues" to focus the debate on mainstream political, economic, social, environmental and military issues' (Brittain 1995b).

I have decided to concentrate the material on gender in this book into one chapter, although there are references to women elsewhere. It is my belief that a chapter focused upon gender issues will help to clarify and further a comprehension of the topics already covered. A sustained focus upon gender relations is necessary for a comprehensive appreciation of the instruments which have been central to the dynamics of socio-political change and economic development in the contemporary Third World. It will hopefully become clear in the course of the chapter that there is a variety of gender-related social, economic and political issues of importance in this respect. One of the key issues is the impact of modernization upon Third World societies; another is the impact of economic crisis and structural adjustment. The evidence presented here suggests acute variations not only in the degree of women's autonomy but also in the extent of change from region to region.

After discussing the neglect of women in the traditional developmental paradigms in the first section of the chapter, we move in the second to an examination of three sets of issues which reflect not only women's subordinate position in the Third World, but also their increasing unwillingness to accept a permanently lowly role in society: (a) *social issues*: education, health and work; (b) *economic issues*: the effects of structural adjustment on women and girls; (c) *political issues*: women's responses to their lack of political power. In the third section we examine the range of women's experiences across the Third World, aiming to identify the dynamics of social, economic and political change.

Women and Development Theory

Until recently, theorizing about Third World development and politics tended to be situated either at the country level (developmental theory) or at the level of the international economy (dependency theory). Women, although comprising just over 50 per cent of the population of the Third World, were virtually ignored by many (male) scholars.

Recently, however, feminist debates on development have begun to focus on the roles and position of women in a sustained way, stimulated by the social and economic impact of structural adjustment and by the political impact of the growth of women's groups in the Third World. Feminist approaches to the role of women in development fall into two broad categories: the 'women *in* development' (WID) and the 'women *and* development' (WAD) schools of thought. In some respects, the WID 'school' is informed by the perceptions of developmental theory, while the WAD 'school' finds parallels with those of dependency analysis (Marchand 1994: 66).

'Women in Development' (WID)

The liberal WID school of thought appreciates that women tend to be negatively affected by development efforts in the Third World, especially as a result of the impact of attempts at structural adjustment. To deal with the situation, it is prescribed that women should attempt to involve themselves more thoroughly in the mainstream modernization process by securing better access to education, the job market and material resources. Yet, as we shall see, with the partial exception of employment, these are precisely the areas from which women find themselves excluded, especially at times of economic crisis. As a result, attempts by the mass of Third World women to improve their position by individual effort seem doomed to failure.

'Women and Development' (WAD)

The WAD analysis, by contrast, argues that the development of women only, small-scale economic projects would best free them from male domination, whether from external or local sources. Such projects would be advantageous in propelling women into positions of economic independence. As far as possible, rather than try to succeed in the male-dominated development process, women should set up their own projects outside the mainstream development processes (Marchand 1994: 66; Marchand and Parpart 1995). The problem with this is that while such projects would probably enhance women's economic position to a certain degree, little pressure would be applied at the level at which it is most necessary if wide-ranging change is to be achieved – i.e. the national level.

The Position of Women in the Third World

Social issues

From birth to school

Compared to males, 'females score poorly in every development indicator, including literacy, school enrolment, attendance at clinics, earnings per hour, access to land, access to credit, access to political power' (Brittain 1994).[1] Discrimination against women begins at birth. One of the indices which differs most between the Third World and the industrial democracies is that of maternal mortality. At the extremes are Norway and Bhutan. In the former, two women per 100,000 live births die; in the latter, 1,710 – i.e. 855 times more. The world average is 250, with several Third World countries, including Madagascar and Botswana, reaching this level (Hadjor 1993: 157). When girl children are born, their chances of survival partly depend upon the cultural view of females which pertains in their society. While no reliable estimates exist of the extent of female infanticide, it is reported from a number of countries such as China, which has had a single child policy for years, and India, where boys are valued much more highly than girls, that new-born females face a serious danger of death. Brittain (1995b) claims that over a million new-born girls are murdered or left to die every year. If they survive, girls up to the age of 5 years are more likely to die than boys in the Third World, because the latter will obtain the chief share of often scarce food supplies, reflecting the high value placed on boys' survival. During adolescence, millions of girls will endure genital mutilation; currently, over 90 million girls have undergone this (Brittain 1995b).

If girls in the Third World live to school age, they are much less likely than boys to attend educational establishments. In many cultures, access to education – particularly secondary education and above – is a crucial variable, essential to enhancing an individual's status in society, a fact which many men are aware of and which helps to explain why females are so disadvantaged in this respect. Discrimination appears to rise at each level of the educational ladder, with the most pronounced difference at the tertiary level. Looking at the Third World as a whole, only 80 per cent of girls compared to boys go to primary school (Hadjor 1993: 297).[2] At the secondary level, the proportion drops to 70 per cent; for the tertiary stage, 50 per cent. The general lack of education for girls in the Third World is reflected in one statistic: of the one billion illiterates in the world, two-thirds are females. The vast majority live in the Third World.

The world of work

Once girls become old enough to work, they face further discrimination: they will work longer hours than men in every part of the Third World, ranging from an estimated 35 per cent more in Kenya to 5 per cent more in Nepal. Overall, an estimated two-thirds of the world's work is done by slightly over half the world's population: women. Two-thirds of women's work (and a quarter of men's) is unpaid, amounting to 70 per cent of the world's annual global output of $23,000 billion (Brittain 1995a). Yet, women earn only 10 per cent of global income, and own less than 1 per cent of the world's property.

Much of women's work is connected with familial duties: cooking, cleaning, looking after children and relatives, including the sick and aged, farming for subsistence, and fetching wood for cooking and water for drinking, sometimes from long distances. Women's working hours in the Third World are indicated in table 7.1.

As table 7.1 indicates, in every Third World region women work on average much longer hours than men, ranging from 48 hours a week in Asia and the Pacific to 66 hours a week in Africa. Women in Africa work 18 hours a week more than their counterparts in Asia and the Pacific, because the latter, especially in the newly industrializing countries of East and South-east Asia, have better access to labour-saving devices and smaller numbers of children. The result is that, even though a relatively higher proportion of women in Asia work in paid labour or are self-employed, many work fewer hours a week than women in Africa or Latin America and the Caribbean.

There is no clear evidence that the overall position of women either improves or declines when they take paid work; the evidence points both ways. Take the example of garment workers in Bangladesh. Women comprise 5 million of the country's labour force of 33 million. Half a million women work in the garment

Table 7.1 Hours worked weekly by women and men in the Third World, 1976–88[a]

Region	Men	Women	Index (men's working time = 100)
Africa	54	66	122
Latin America and Caribbean	55	60	109
Asia and the Pacific	48	62	130

[a] Total working time, including unpaid housework.

Source: UNRISD 1995: 148

industry, where 90 per cent of workers are female. Sometimes women are forced to work for no pay, 'many' have been sexually assaulted at work. According to a report in the *Toronto Star* in July 1992, one-tenth of all female garment workers had been beaten or tortured by an employer; some were compelled to 'stand on their heads for extended periods as punishment for flaws in their work' (Human Rights Internet 1993a: 16). In a series of incidents in late 1991, many Bangladeshi garment workers were locked out from their jobs for taking to the streets to press for improvements in working conditions; 25, mostly female workers were injured.

While conditions in general seem poor, for many women a job means the difference between struggling to survive and the ability to afford a few luxuries. Mosammat Aleya is a 35-year-old worker in a garment factory in Dhaka. Because her husband's wage in another garment factory is inadequate to support the family, Aleya first began working in 1985. Then, she says, she faced criticism from her extended family, but lately economic pressures have altered the tradition of women staying at home to look after the children. Now, she says, 'lots of women go to work every day'. Relief from economic pressures for Aleya is counterbalanced to a certain extent by having to work an even longer day than formerly. She must get up at 4 a.m. to do her housework and prepare breakfast for her children and large extended family. After taking the children to school, she walks a few miles to work, beginning at 8 a.m. She arrives home after the two children, aged 11 and 5 years, get home from school. But she has been able to buy them a stereo and a television to offset her absence when they come home from school. Aleya practises contraception, and is determined to have no more children. She wants the best for her existing two, hoping that they will have the chance to achieve something in their lives (Braid 1995).

The benefit of paid work for Third World women must be offset against the costs: longer working day, less time with the family, often poor wages, and, at least initially, familial criticism for going against tradition by going out to work. Yet, despite such drawbacks, it is clear that increasing numbers of Third World women are choosing – or, to put it another way, are forced by economic pressures – to enter the world of paid work. Women comprise about 38 per cent of the labour force in East and South-east Asia, 35 per cent in sub-Saharan Africa, 31 per cent in South Asia, 29 per cent in Latin America and the Caribbean, and 16 per cent in the Middle East and North Africa excluding Israel (UNDP 1994: 146–7, table 9). Women currently make up more than 25 per cent of the manufacturing work-force in East and South-east Asia, a larger proportion of factory workers than anywhere else in the world (Cammack et al. 1993: 220). In many Third World countries, however, women are often employed in agricultural labour, yet they nearly always get paid proportionately less than men for the same work, as table 7.2 shows.

In conclusion, about 30 per cent of women in the Third World work outside the home, according to official statistics. This is almost certainly an understatement of the true proportion of women engaged in paid work, as many work in the informal sector unseen by the collectors of statistics. Generally, the aim is to bring in a second income, or perhaps the sole income, since women often obtain – and retain – employment more easily than males. As a result of the growing numbers of Third World women who go out to work, 'traditional values such as the importance of motherhood, the inadmissibility of women earning money, and other primordial core symbols are eroded as the general social and economic positions of women is [sic] somewhat ameliorated through industrialization' (Kamrava 1993: 115).

Table 7.2 Women's non-agricultural wage as percentage of men's in selected Third World countries in the 1990s

Region	Country	Percentage
Sub-Saharan Africa	Central African Republic	72.6
	Swaziland	73.0
	Zambia	78.0
	Kenya	84.7
	Tanzania	92.0
East and South-east Asia	Singapore	71.1
	Vietnam	91.5
South Asia	Sri Lanka	89.8
Middle East and North Africa	Egypt	79.5
	Turkey	84.5
Latin America and the Caribbean	Paraguay	76.0
	Colombia	84.7

Source: Brittain 1995a

Economic issues: women and structural adjustment

The main pressures compelling women into paid work in the Third World are economic crisis and the attempt to deal with it, structural adjustment. The cumulative effects of economic upheavals led to a 'feminization' of poverty, whereby women and girls suffer disproportionately. The numerous ways in which women absorbed the fall-out from economic crisis amount to what some feminist economists call the 'gender-related costs of invisible adjustment', reflected especially in the areas of work, health and social safety net programmes.

In relation to work, during structural adjustment wages are squeezed by government policy (ILO 1994: 108). Women, already receiving proportionately lower wages than men across the Third World, find that they can afford fewer processed foods than before. As a result, they must spend more time shopping for cheaper items and buying them in small quantities if they cannot, like most women in the Third World, afford a refrigerator. They will be forced by economic pressures to try to grow more of their own food. A study in Java found that women spent more time than before growing vegetables on family plots, both for home consumption and for outside sale. The female work burden is passed on to daughters: a study in Ecuador found that as mothers worked outside the home, so daughters had to spend more time on domestic work at the expense of their education (Sparr 1994: 26).

A second gender-related cost of adjustment is linked to declines in health care. Women are likely to suffer more from cuts in public services: as health services deteriorate, they are called upon to look after sick relatives, and when education cuts reduce school hours, they must spend more time supervising children (UNRISD 1995: 147). A recent Oxfam report entitled *Paying for Health* suggests that one effect of Zimbabwe's attempt at structural adjustment, which increased user fees for medical services, was that maternal deaths 'rose by 240 per cent between 1989 and 1991 . . . [while] maternal mortality rates doubled between 1991 and 1992 in the capital, Harare' (quoted in Brittain 1994).

A third impact of structural adjustment especially affecting women is related to social safety net programmes which normally have a pronounced male bias. Social safety net programmes were introduced in many parts of the Third World to provide employment opportunities to those worst affected by structural adjustment. As we have seen, women tend to suffer disproportionately during adjustment, yet social safety net programmes typically provide employment opportunities which are largely filled by men. In Bolivia, only 1 per cent of those employed in social programmes were women; in India the figure was 16 per cent; and in Honduras one-quarter of these 'social jobs' were held by females (UNRISD 1995: 53).

In conclusion, while the effects of economic crisis and structural adjustment in the Third World generally lead to increased poverty for the poor, women are particularly badly affected. This is manifested in three ways: they must work harder both in the home and outside to try to maintain income levels; they experience declining levels of health care; and they receive few benefits from job-creation schemes.

Political issues: women's responses to a deficiency of political power

Throughout the world the great majority of heads of state, presidents, prime ministers, and members of legislatures are men.[3] Generally, at the institutional level women are grossly under-represented in political life. Women are increasingly unwilling, however, to put up with the situation of political subordination. Their response is to form thousands of groups whose common objective is women's empowerment. The International Women's Tribune Center (IWTC) in New York is the contact and referral office for over 6,000 women's groups from more than 160 countries, i.e. an average of nearly 40 from each state. In addition, there are probably *tens of thousands* of women's groups in the Third World which are *not* registered with the IWTC. Durning (1989) reports, for example, that in rural Brazil the growth of women's groups in recent times has been explosive; virtually none of these bodies would be registered with the IWTC.

Women's groups can radically change the way that their members think about themselves and the way they act. There are thousands of women's groups known as 'Mothers' Clubs' in Latin America, South Korea and Indonesia. Initially, women were reluctant to join the clubs, for many were not sure what their objectives were. It soon became clear, however, that club membership would lead to material benefits. Clubs organized money-making activities – e.g.

food preparation for sale – and became actively involved in community activities, the work of local development associations and family planning campaigns. The popularity of mothers' clubs is linked to their cultural acceptability: they are not perceived as part of a radical, international feminist movement, which is regarded with suspicion. Nevertheless, as Fisher (1993: 100) notes, 'family issues for women soon evolve into political concerns.' Brazil's mothers' clubs, created by the Catholic Church in the 1960s, have become involved in both family planning and women's rights – i.e. they have become politicized. Such objectives are quite different from those envisaged by the Church, which were to strengthen the family as a unit.

Examination of the evolving objectives of the mothers' clubs serves to emphasize a wider point: existential concerns will often lead women – especially poor women, the vast majority of women in the Third World – to organize themselves for a wide range of both economic and social goals. While it is virtually impossible to categorize precisely the thousands of groups that currently exist, it is plausible to divide them into two broad types: grass-roots development groups and feminist organizations. The former are principally concerned with development goals, while the latter address the wider issue of women's position in society, although it is very difficult to draw a firm line dividing the concerns of each type of women's group.

Grass-roots development groups

Most women's groups in the Third World, like the mothers' clubs referred to above, are grass-roots development groups organized at the community level. While it is difficult to generalize, most are concerned with broadly developmental goals, such as job creation, trading, community solidarity, child care facilities and farming for profit. They are self-help groups, not relying upon state support. Some are centred on religious institutions, such as the church, temple or mosque.

In many of the groups, there is a progression from a traditional concern with 'women's projects', such as developing housekeeping skills and handicraft production, towards questioning women's position in society. By the 1990s, Fisher (1993: 100–1) notes, many grass-roots development groups realized that social and political progress for women depended on achieving sustained falls in infant mortality, social acceptance of family planning, and improved attempts at income generation. All these measures entailed educating and involving women to a greater extent than hitherto in their existential problems.

Feminist organizations

As a result of the growing politicization of the grass-roots groups, Fisher (1993: 103) argues that the 'distinction between feminist and [grass-roots development groups has] begun to blur in some Third World countries, as middle- and lower-class women define their common interests'. We need to bear in mind, however, that despite Fisher's optimism, class still divides great numbers of women in the Third World, just as it does elsewhere. Generally, poor, uneducated women cleave to grass-roots development groups, while their educated middle-class counterparts join feminist organizations.

Feminist organizations are concerned with the self-conscious expression of an outlook grounded in notions of women's rights, roles and power. Nearly always independent of government control, they seek to challenge the position of women as 'second class' citizens in relation to men. Frequently, however, they attract only small memberships, and enjoy rather limited political influence. The reason for this is not only that some poor, working-class women feel alienated because of the superior educational levels of members of feminist groups, but also because the former are not attracted by what they see as feminist ideas which may regard men as women's enemy (Ahmed 1992: 243–4).

Many women in the Third World fear that feminism may simply be another form of Western imperialism or neo-colonialism. Bethke Elshtain (1995: 544) argues that in Argentina and Israeli-occupied Palestine, where she conducted research, the attractiveness of what is regarded as 'American-style' feminism – i.e. a single-minded concern with the advocacy of women's rights and the advancement and emancipation of women more generally – depends on three factors: (a) the social status of the recipients of the message, (b) the degree to which the country is hostile or friendly to the United States and its cultural influences, and (c) whether the feminist message seems to 'connect' with the putative recipients' existential concerns. As far as Palestinian women were concerned, American-style feminism was associated with irreligiosity and a misunderstanding of Palestinian and Islamic culture. When a number were asked by Elshtain about their political aspirations and what they would like to say to American feminists, the reply was: 'If the Americans love freedom so much, why don't they help us to get our land back?' It would seem from such a response that Palestinian women were uninterested in feminist projects, perhaps because they were chiefly concerned with the pursuit of a collective political goal: regaining control of their land.

In sum, material and existential concerns often lead women – especially poor women, the vast majority of women in the Third World – to organize themselves for a wide range of both economic and social goals. When it comes to the political organization of women *qua* women – i.e. a feminization of politics – there is a different situation. Class divides women in the Third World just as elsewhere: the ideal of 'women's solidarity against men' turns out for the most part to be a chimera, while foreign feminism is often regarded with suspicion.

We have examined and discussed social, economic and political aspects of women's subordination in the Third World. While there is undoubtedly progress in a number of areas – such as a growth of women's solidarity, especially at the grass-roots level – there is still a long way to go before women can perceive that they have equal opportunities.

The questioning of women's traditional role as only wives and mothers in domestic contexts has been augmented by international pressure. The United Nations Development Programme (UNDP) suggests concrete steps to improve the position of women in the Third World. It put forward the idea of the creation of a 'global compact' of donor countries to increase the proportion of aid devoted to women, education and health, from 7 to 20 per cent. Recipient countries, for their part, would agree to increase their social spending to one-fifth of their budgets by cutting military expenditure and spending on prestige projects, like huge dams for hydroelectric power generation. The estimated $30–40 billion which the scheme might raise would, UNDP economists calculate, have a dramatic impact on world poverty, particularly as it affects women, within a decade of its inception (Brittain 1994).

Despite expected improvements in social welfare, especially for women and girls, the UNDP proposal was turned down by many putative donor and recipient governments. The former were unwilling to commit large sums of new aid, while many Third World governments were not inclined to alter current spending patterns, for two reasons. First, it was, no doubt, more important for many to ensure a tight grasp on power by spending money on, and thus placating, traditionally powerful male interests such as the military. This would not be achieved by raising the position and prosperity of women, which would antagonize many men. Second, many of the traditionally powerful elements in Third World societies – such as religious figures – are deeply conservative. Dedicating new funds to improvement of the position of women would incur the displeasure of many religious leaders. An example of the suspicion which many feel on the issue of improvement of women's material well-being was provided in mid-1995. The draft declaration of that year's United Nations conference on women, stressing the globally subordinate position of women, was attacked vituperatively by influential religious figures at Egypt's Al-Azhar University, a 1,000-year-old institution of Sunni Muslim orthodoxy. They complained that the conference declaration 'contradicted religion', seeking to destroy the family and aiming to create 'a new kind of life which is against religious values and destroys moral barriers' which protect 'peoples and nations from falling into the abyss of sexual corruption, psychological disturbance and the swamps of moral disintegration' (Reuter 1995).

It is clear from the discussion so far that the economic, social and political position of women in the Third World is subordinate to that of men. The vast majority of women are excluded from positions of power. Traditional (male) elites, such as religious figures, are determined to keep things as they are. As a result of the lack of power, millions of Third World women seek to empower themselves by organizing themselves to enhance their economic, social and political positions. Women's groups are not only the most common type of categorical interest group in the world, they are also probably the most rapidly proliferating type of grass-roots organization in the Third World.

A Woman's Place: Regional Analysis

The final section of the chapter examines a range of women's political experiences across the regions of the Third World. It aims to identify specific dynamics of change from region to region. In analyses of Latin America and the Caribbean, East and South-east Asia, and sub-Saharan Africa the focus is on women's political participation during modernization and democratization, while in relation to the Middle East and North Africa and South Asia we examine the relationship of religion – Islam and Hinduism – to the socio-political position of women.

Latin America and the Caribbean

The recent history of Latin America is characterized by a distinctive process of modernization which, proceeding from export-led development to limited industrialization, had a marked effect on the status of women in society. The lack of political participation, until recently, was in line with the virtually universal pattern of subordination and relative exclusion, underpinned by the influence of traditional Catholic ideas of female subservience. Over the last few years, however, a combination of social responses to deep economic crisis, widespread challenge to dictatorial rule, and the dissemination of feminist ideas has resulted in a pronounced shift in the nature and scope of women's political activity.

Regarding the Caribbean, the extent of women's political participation is also moulded by the experiences of the past. The islands of the area have a shared history of colonialism, slavery and racism, shaping the social, cultural, economic and political foundations of local societies. Enslaved Africans were first brought to Jamaica, Trinidad and Tobago, and other Caribbean islands by the British for the production of sugar. Once slavery was abolished in the 1830s, sugar production came to rely heavily on the importation of indentured labour from India. Indian women, both Hindu and Muslim, were among those recruited in Calcutta and Madras to work on the sugar plantations. The descendants of these Africans and East Indians now comprise the two dominant ethnic groups in the Caribbean (Human Rights Internet 1993b: 3).

Several of the Caribbean islands, such as Trinidad and Tobago, have a tradition of women's organizations dating back to the 1930s. In the 1970s and 1980s women in the islands of the Caribbean began to organize around the issue of male violence against women, including rape and domestic violence. A large array of grass-roots-level organizations also developed during these decades, providing day-care centres and hostels for young working women, which complemented the efforts of the state.

Although women are relatively well represented in political life in a few Caribbean islands, such as Trinidad and Tobago, generally the situation in Latin America and the Caribbean follows the common Third World pattern of under-representation (Human Rights Internet 1993b: 3). The low participation of women in the national politics of many Latin American countries is a result, according to Waylen (1993: 573), of the way in which 'political parties are structured and to the fact that women are not taken seriously in this field'.

During the 1970s and early 1980s, years of dictatorship in Latin America, a great number of women's groups emerged in response to the effects and social conditions of military dictatorship. Most, however, did not manage to convert political mobilization into institutional representation after pluralist politics revived (Safa 1990). This was despite the fact that during the years of dictatorship, politicization of women's groups grew immensely, a result of the banning of customary public political activity. The paradoxical result of the ban on conventional party politics was to improve the availability of political space to women by affording them greater visibility and prominence. A large number had leadership roles in human rights and other campaigns (Waylen 1993: 576). In sum, the suppression of formal democracy in Latin America actually served to empower many women.

Once it emerged that normal party politics was re-establishing itself, groups operating outside this arena, including women's organizations, were confronted by an often difficult choice, that of 'liberty or association'. In other words, should they continue operating outside the party political arena or not? If they chose the former path, they risked political marginalization and a loss of influence; if the latter, how were they to prevent their co-optation and subsequent loss of autonomy by male-dominated political parties? Evidence points to the apparent preference of many women's groups for 'liberty' – i.e. for remaining outside the confines of party politics so as to retain independence and freedom of action.

In conclusion, redemocratization in Latin America did not destroy the networks of women's groups which grew up during the period of dictatorship. Rather, there are two systems of political activity in operation: on the one hand, there are the male-dominated legislatures and political parties; on the other, thousands of women's groups which have political, economic and social concerns which they pursue by their own efforts.

South Asia

As in Latin America, where women do not appear to be inhibited from organizing their own groups by their Catholic background and traditions, so in India, with a strong cultural background of Hinduism, women have also organized themselves into thousands of different groups. In Bangladesh and Pakistan, on the other hand, women are inhibited, for the most part, by the dominant religion, Islam. Despite cultural differences, however, in the South Asia region generally, as elsewhere in the Third World, the goal for women is increased empowerment, facilitating greater access to decision-making and to resources.

The position of women in India is a result not only of cultural factors, including Hinduism and the caste system, but also of the fact that the country has been a democracy for nearly 50 years. During much of this time Congress has been the dominant political party. Despite the long period of democracy, however, there is a long tradition of women's political activism at grass-roots level, which suggests that, as in Latin America, many women are sceptical about the efficacy of the party system to allow them a meaningful political voice. While the failure of the Congress Party to allow women a say in party decision-making was a factor in the founding of thousands of women's groups, the insistence of more radical rivals, such as the Communist Party of India (Marxist) upon democratic centralism, meant that its women's wing got little autonomous space within which to function, especially when its radicalism might be seen as dangerous to building cross-class/caste alliances in the electoral field (Omvedt 1994: 37). On the other hand, a non-party women's organization like *Sangathana*, while free from the constraints of electoral politics, is marginalized in the political arena because of its decision to maintain its ideological 'purity' by not participating in the institutionalized democracy that the Indian political system maintains through its electoral system (Rai 1994: 534). As in Latin America, it seems that the choices women face in India are ' liberty or association'; each, it appears, leads to political marginalization.

The position of women in predominantly Muslim Bangladesh – more than 80 per cent of the population is Muslim – has become an issue of discussion in the more than 20 years since the country gained its independence from Pakistan. Bangladesh is one of the poorest and most densely populated countries in the world; women suffer disproportionately more from poverty than men (World Bank 1990: 7–9). Violence and discrimination against women remain common features of Bangladeshi society, even though the 1972 Constitution established equal rights for men and women in 'all spheres of the State and public life' (Blaustein and Flanz 1993: 41). Many Bangladeshi women live in a state of dependency on men as a result of poverty and lack of education, employment and training opportunities (Khan 1988: 1). Perhaps unsurprisingly, women's political position is generally under-developed, partly because of cultural factors.

In accordance with the traditional Muslim practice of *purdah* – i.e. the seclusion or veiling of women – a woman is expected to stay within her *bari* or homestead, discouraged from contact with anyone outside her close family (Human Rights Internet 1993b: 1). This practice limits the social and educational development of most Bangladeshi women, and also restricts access to employment opportunities. Although the institution of seclusion is being challenged as poverty forces increasing numbers to seek paid employment outside the home, the ideals of *purdah* – modesty, humility, domesticity and non-involvement in public life – are still strong, even if physical seclusion is less commonly practised. International aid programmes tend to reinforce rather than diminish disparities between men and women, because they usually work within established distribution systems, placing the 'target population . . . in the passive position of recipients rather than participants' (Tomasevski 1988: 5).

In conclusion, in recent years a number of women's organizations have been formed for the purpose of raising public awareness about women's issues and to lobby government to improve their social, economic and legal position in both India and Bangladesh. Nevertheless, women in both countries still appear to be politically marginalized.

East and South-east Asia

Women in both Latin America and the Caribbean and South Asia pursued political goals of empowerment, while playing a vital role in bringing an end to military dictatorships. In East Asia, by contrast, while both South Korea and Taiwan are democratic, women's social, economic and political position remains lowly.

Young women have been entering factory work in the states of the region since the late 1960s. This does not, however, appear to have made dramatic changes in the character and extent of their political activity. This is probably partly a consequence of the fact that in many states of the region political activity by any group was, until recently, discouraged, and partly a result of the close connections between 'family structure, family employment strategies, and women's entry to paid employment' (Cammack et al. 1993: 220). The relationship between work experience and gender politics is influenced not only by patriarchal traditions, but also by the interaction of these traditions with national economic structures and social and political factors. Governments and employers oppose the organization of workers, whether men or women, in vigorous trade unions, as part of a general strategy of maintenance of a low wage economy (ibid.: 222).

In conclusion, there are generally weak labour unions and often a paucity of democratic institutions in many countries in East and South-east Asia. Yet, as the region's economies advanced over the last two decades, increasing numbers of women joined the formal work-force. This has not been sufficient, however, to advance the general position of women to any great degree. Unlike Latin America and the Caribbean and South Asia, there are relatively few women's organizations in the region, serving to diminish further the impact of women on politics.

The Middle East and North Africa

As in East and South-east Asia there are important cultural and political factors which combine to inhibit women from organizing themselves to pursue goals of empowerment. Very few of the countries of the Middle East and North Africa are fully functioning democracies, and, except for Israel, all countries of the region are predominantly Muslim. Islam is highly influential regarding the political position of women, although the link between the inferior status of women and Islam is actually complex and varied. This is not only because factors including regime ideology, power relations within the family, low literacy rates and employment opportunities have an important role, but also because the faith itself and interpretations of Islam vary from country to country.

Nevertheless, in many of the Muslim societies of the Middle East and North Africa, as in Bangladesh, women are usually expected to

Table 7.3 Women as a percentage of the labour force in the Middle East and North Africa, 1992

Less than 10%	10–15%	16–20%	Over 20%
Algeria	Egypt	Iran	Turkey
Iraq	Jordan	Morocco	
Libya	Kuwait		
Oman	Syria		
Saudi Arabia	Tunisia		
UAE	Yemen		

Source: UNDP 1994: 146–7

remain at home to look after their children, rather than to seek a wider role in society. The result is that, for the most part, a relatively small proportion of women in Muslim countries work outside the home. As table 7.3 shows, in many countries of the region 80 or even 90 per cent of women do not have jobs outside the home. The influence of the cultural norms of Islam is responsible, as they constrain 'female economic and political activities through purdah or ritual seclusion' (Parpart 1988: 209). In addition, women rarely hold public positions of authority, and are prohibited from holding religious offices. The result is that in many Muslim societies, women constitute a 'subordinated group' (Reveyrand-Coulon 1993: 97).

Several examples will illustrate the degree of women's social and political subordination. In Iraq a 1990 proclamation of the ruling Revolutionary Command Council announced: 'Any Iraqi (male) who kills *even with pre-meditation* his own mother, daughter, sister, niece, or cousin for adultery will not be brought to justice'; while in Pakistan the Hudood Ordinance promulgated in 1979 resulted in raped women being whipped and imprisoned (Ekins 1992: 76, emphasis added). In Jordan, an Islamic kingdom torn between strict ethnic traditions and swift modernization, at least a quarter of all premeditated murders in 1994 were so-called honour killings: women were killed by male relatives for a variety of allegedly 'immoral' types of behaviour, from 'flirting' to losing their virginity before marriage (Sabbagh 1994). Finally, in Iran, women's subordination is not 'just' a question of inter-family issues and concerns; it is also an integral facet of societal control. An all-party British Parliamentary Human Rights Group reported in 1994 a catalogue of state-sanctioned crimes against women, including mutilation, execution, disfiguring women's faces with acid for not wearing the veil and raping women detainees (Coles 1994).

As Saif (1994: 63) argues, and as the above examples suggest, some Muslim societies have 'not always complied with principles of Islam . . . [T]his certainly applies to the issues of human rights . . . [and] the status of women.' The status of women, Saif asserts, has 'changed in the course of Muslim history and has been influenced by a male dominated society and culture', resulting in 'many Muslims confusing some inherited traditional cultural values with Islamic values' (ibid.). The result has been that, in many cases, women have been marginalized politically and socially, having few avenues to express their concerns and difficulty in pursuing goals of empowerment.

Sub-Saharan Africa

As Cammack et al. (1993: 211) note, 'in pre-colonial African societies, great variations existed in the social and economic positions of women.' It is pertinent to note, however, that, during the first 50 years of the twentieth century, sub-Saharan Africa underwent a period of quite unprecedented modernization, almost revolutionary in its medium- and long-term effects. Urbanization was an important effect of this process, leading to mass migrations and patchy and slow industrialization. Pre-existing towns expanded, and new urban centres grew, following the formal establishment of colonial rule. The European colonial rulers brought with them their own conceptions of gender relations and responsibilities, which, in the case of Britain, had been formed by the mores and morals of Victorian society. Colonial rulers assumed that men's domination of women was universal, a God-given fact. Colonial officials accepted Western gender stereotypes which assigned women to the domestic domain, leaving economic and political matters to men. As a result of these factors – modernization, Western conceptions of women's role and position in society, and improvements in men's social standing – the status of women in sub-Saharan Africa generally worsened during the colonial era. For many African women the colonial period was characterized by significant losses in both power and authority (Parpart 1988: 210).

During the period of agitation against European rule in the 1950s and 1960s, women's participation was usually welcomed by men; often women were promised (and expected) economic and political benefits from independence. These promises, for the most part, failed to materialize (Parpart 1988: 215). Although since independence some attempts have been made to involve women in state-linked activities, as a group, females are systematically neglected and under-represented in central institutions. Generally, the post-colonial state in Africa is a male preserve. The comments of a (male) Tanzanian MP may not be atypical of men's attitudes: women, he proclaimed, 'were meant to serve men and they can never be equal to men' (quoted in ibid.: 216).

Unlike in Latin America or India, the political marginalization of women in sub-Saharan Africa does not often lead to attempts to build solidarity, because class, ethnic and religious divisions are often pronounced. Nevertheless, *some* women as individuals have done very well out of the existing arrangements. Politicians' and other important men's wives and relations have benefited from a traditional strategy for increasing their economic and social leverage: viz. a strategy of aligning themselves with powerful men.

In conclusion, in the post-colonial era in sub-Saharan Africa the position of women did not generally or markedly improve from the time of European rule. African men enthusiastically continued the stratification of society based on their dominance. African women were – and are – restrained from developing their full potential, not only by men's resistance, but also by social and cultural fragmentation.

This chapter has sought to highlight the social, economic and political position of women in the Third World. The intention has not been to depict women universally as *passive* victims, but to highlight how millions of women are not only increasingly aware of discrimination, but also joining together to fight it.

The account also sought to explain how the situation of women across the Third World differs greatly in the contemporary era, having become more varied over the last few decades as a result of different patterns and rates of development. One conclusion which emerges is that it is quite difficult to relate supposed shared characteristics of generic 'Third World' women. Rather, the comparative material presented here indicates that more is explained by the combinations of circumstances in particular cases. It was also explained how there are powerful global factors at work, including the effects of colonialism, modernization and economic pressures arising from structural adjustment, affecting the position of women.

Their impact varies from region to region, depending upon the differential effect of their interaction upon local social, economic and political patterns.

The effects of modernization, such as paid employment in factories, serves both to improve and to worsen the position of women who work in such places. It improves their position to the extent that they are paid, which helps them to support their families, especially when husbands and partners are unemployed; at the same time, their position is worsened when (usually male) factory-owners and employers beat, torture or rape them, as in Bangladesh.

On the other hand, the development of women's groups, as we saw in Latin America and the Caribbean and India, helps to build an enhanced socio-economic role for women. In our final chapter, we move to an issue – the natural environment – which also engages the interest of hundreds of thousands of women in the Third World who see their livelihoods, homes and families threatened by the destruction and degradation of their surroundings.

Notes

1 As Hadjor (1993: 297) notes, 'many indicators of development and underdevelopment tell a very different story if we look at gender differences rather than at aggregated statistics.'
2 Over 60 per cent of those deprived of primary education in the Third World – 80 million out of 130 million – are girls.
3 Globally, less than 10 per cent of seats in national legislatures and under 5 per cent of cabinet posts are occupied by women (Braid 1995). Female heads of state can be counted on the fingers of both hands. Not all the industrial democracies by any means do well compared to their Third World counterparts. Britain is nineteenth in the 1995 *Human Development Report*'s 'league table' of female participation in politics and business, behind Cuba, Barbados, the Bahamas, and Trinidad and Tobago. In Britain less than 7.5 per cent of parliamentary seats are held by women, the same proportion as in India. By contrast, 50 per cent of Sweden's cabinet seats are held by women (Brittain 1995a).

8

The Politics of the Natural Environment

In chapter 8 we examine the issue of politics and the natural environment in the Third World. During the 1980s, rising levels of pollution and environmental destruction led to growing international concern about the viability of current economic development policies, not only in the Third World but also elsewhere. The 1992 Rio de Janeiro United Nations conference on the Environment and Development, known as 'the Earth Summit', was a concrete symptom of widespread concern.

The global environmental crisis is a function of several developments. On the one hand, there is the wasteful, polluting, resource-intensive consumption pattern characteristic of the rich countries and of Third World elites, responsible for the bulk of global warming, production of chlorofluorocarbon (CFC) gases, depletion of the ozone layer, and acid rain. On the other hand, there are the environmentally destructive practices of the Third World poor which lead to desertification, deforestation and soil erosion. In addition, in some parts of the Third World industrial pollution is a serious problem, a result of rapid, poorly controlled economic growth.

There is a wide range of issues involved in analysis of the natural environment and politics in the Third World. We shall examine some of them in this chapter. Its structure is as follows. First, we discuss the importance of the 1992 Earth Summit, in order to locate growing concern with the environment in a Third World and international context. Second, we emphasize the recent nature of this concern by noting how the traditional development paradigms afford little importance to environmental issues. Third, rather than a regional breakdown of environmental problems, we explore the social, political and economic aspects of four issues common throughout the Third World: (a) *desertification and deforestation*, which affect nearly all parts of the Third World, especially Africa, Latin America, and East and South-east Asia; (b) *rural poverty*, a result of skewed land-use patterns, which leads to serious environmental degradation, with examples from Costa Rica and Nepal; (c) *large hydroelectric dams*, resulting in massive displacement of peoples, with illustrations from India and Nepal; and (d) *the environmental destructiveness of structural adjustment and swift economic growth*, the latter exemplified by what has occurred in South Korea and Taiwan. Finally, we address the issue of 'sustainable development' in the Third World, a broad strategy for economic growth coupled with environmental protection.

The 'Earth Summit' of 1992

Increasing global environmental concern led the 1980s to be labelled the 'decade of the discovery of the environment' (Hadjor 1993: 105). This was because the issue of the relationship between people's social and economic demands and the natural environment began to be discussed, for the first time, in a scientific way. The most tangible sign of concern was the Earth Summit held in Brazil in 1992. More than 100 heads of state and 30,000 bureaucrats and representatives of non-governmental organizations met to discuss 24 *million* pages of preparatory documents and to make wide-ranging decisions regarding the future of the global environment.

The Earth Summit was called in order to confront two of the world's most pressing, interlinked problems: environmental degradation and poverty and underdevelopment. There was widespread hope that relaxation of Cold War tensions, juxtaposed with a new awareness of environmental matters, would be a conducive background to real progress. The conclusion of the Earth Summit was marked by the signing by representatives of all the countries present of a document known as 'Agenda 21', trumpeted as 'a plan of action to save the planet'.

Despite high hopes, however, the immediate outcome of the

Summit was less than many environmentalists expected. Governmental representatives from Western industrialized countries sought to proclaim fine principles of wide-ranging environmental concern, yet without agreeing to do anything very concrete to implement them. For their part, many Third World governments expressed ambivalent feelings about environmental protection, as it was generally agreed that the West's industrial development had come about only through exploiting its own environment as well as those of its colonies. The situation was made more complex in that the Earth Summit coincided with the middle of a serious global economic recession. This led to a widespread focus, which some environmentalists regard as short-sighted, on how to restart economic development and reduce unemployment, while leaving relatively little time for serious discussion of how 'to save the world' environmentally.

Agenda 21 was a compromise between the advocates of environmental conservation (most Western states) and those of more or less unbridled growth with scant regard for the environment (many Third World governments). It was an aspirational response to public concern, rather than a document encompassing a variety of concrete measures. It is important to note, however, that during the 1980s international political responses to environmental issues resulted in several agreements – concerning the oceans, the deep sea-bed, the atmosphere and outer space – which amounted to a sustained international co-ordination of responses heralding a new era of state–state environmental co-operation. As Vogler (1992: 118) explains, such agreements are necessary, because environmental issues 'cannot be parcelled up and placed under the sovereign control of nation-states'.

Despite the lack of concrete measures, the most important thing is that the Earth Summit happened at all, thereby reflecting the fact that the global environment is higher than ever before on the international political agenda. Having such a meeting was an essential step to the eventual forging of a global imperative to tackle pressing issues of development and environmental sustainability, especially global warming, forest conservation, and protection of biological diversity ('bio-diversity'). It would be wrong to infer from what I have written that there were *no* tangible results. First, there was the Climate Convention, signed by all the world's big polluters, aimed at slowing down global warming. A second was an agreement on bio-diversity, whereby every country represented at the Earth Summit was to produce a plan to protect its own flora and fauna and animals. A third tangible result was three follow-up UN conferences: on population (Cairo, 1994), social development (Copenhagen, March 1995) and women (Beijing, September 1995), all of which had environmental concerns on their agendas (Brown 1995).

As noted above, the environment is a sensitive issue for many Third World governments, like democracy, economic development, human and women's rights, and the position of ethnic and religious minorities. Most feel that the West's development was strongly facilitated by exploiting its colonies, with little or no concern with the environmental impact of their policies. Why, they ask, should the Third World be any different? In addition, many Third World governments are irritated by the West's attempts to lay down universal standards in relation to the environment. Annoyance is furthered by two specific issues: first, by what is perceived as the industrial democracies' sudden concern with protection of the environment when they themselves have for centuries pursued – and continue for the most part to adopt – practices which contribute far more to the degradation of the natural environment than does deforestation, the main environmental 'sin' in the Third World. Second, while deploring environmentally harmful policies in the Third World, Western governments and agencies like the IMF and the World Bank simultaneously urge them to 'open up' their economies to foreign investment and to develop their export capacity, leading to greater environmental degradation.

The ambivalence reflected in the ways that governments in both the Third World and the West perceive environmental protection in the context of economic growth, was also manifested in the attitude of the traditional development paradigms. Until recently, neither paid much attention to the natural environment, often seeming to regard environmental degradation as a necessary price for economic growth.

The Natural Environment and Development Theory

Developmental theory

Until recently, the political and social ramifications of the degradation of the natural environment in the Third World were either ignored or only sketchily – and often optimistically – addressed. A disciple of the developmental approach, Francis Fukuyama (1992), has very little to say about the potential environmental consequences of massive increases in consumption and industrialization in the Third World, despite a focus on international change after the Cold War. This is not because he thinks environmental issues are insignificant or unimportant, but, on the contrary, because he does not think that they pose insurmountable problems. For Fukuyama (1992: 114–15), 'what is most effective in protecting the environment is neither capitalism nor socialism, but democracy'.

Fukuyama believes that once Third World countries democratize, they will then deal with the environmental consequences of industrialization. His equanimity indicates strong belief in the idea that democratic control of a state will *necessarily* lead to a strengthening of environmental policies and safeguards. Contrary to Fukuyama's optimism, however, there seems to be no clear proof that Third World democracies always keep a better check on environmental destruction than non-democracies. For example, while Communist China's lack of controls on industrial pollution is a cause for concern, it is no probably no worse than that of democratic South Korea or Taiwan, which, as we shall see below, have laws on the control of industrial pollutants, but whose governments often *choose to ignore them*. In addition, Costa Rica, a democracy for nearly 50 years, has shown little concern or ability to deal with environmental degradation caused by extensive cattle ranching. For countries subject to the rigours of structural adjustment, on the other hand, it appears to matter little whether they are democratic or not. The aim is growth at virtually any cost; the issue is 'jobs versus the environment', and almost inevitably, it seems, the latter loses out to the former. In conclusion, the developmental view is unwarrantedly optimistic that democracy will protect the natural environment. Structural adjustment and economic growth generally take precedence, often regardless of what kind of political system is in place.

Dependency theory

When Western industrial democracies seek to control environmental pollution – as in the location of a chemical-producing factory plant or getting rid of toxic waste, a by-product of industrial production – it is likely that the problem will be exported, usually to the Third

World. Evidence suggests that the best politically and economically cost-effective way that Western democracies have devised to deal with environmental problems is to pass them on to someone else if they can (Miller 1995: 87–108). Such practices are consistent with the view of dependency theory, which, it will be recalled, understands the development and wealth of the Western industrial democracies and the concomitant underdevelopment of the Third World as functions of each other. Export of environmental problems to the Third World is seen as entirely logical, given the structure of the world economy in favour of the rich countries of the West.

Within the Third World, the dependency approach advocates enabling local people to manage their own environment in a sustainable fashion (Fairhead and Leach 1994: 481–5; Miller 1995: 22, 24). It focuses on the desirability of the *withdrawal of communities from the power of the state and of the international economic system*, also noted in relation to women in chapter 7. In respect of the natural environment, the dependency approach stresses not only community empowerment, but also the need for environmental protection measures to help establish sustainable livelihoods for the rural poor, in order to reduce their dependency on government. This approach requires community level organization and collective action to undertake environmental projects. However, the institutional changes brought about by structural adjustment measures often undermine the potential for community-based action, while weakening the capacity of communities to adapt to changing ecological conditions. At the present time, much of the Third World remains firmly in an environmental crisis which seems to be worsening.

The Environmental Crisis in the Third World

The 1980s was a decade of environmental crisis for the Third World, affecting millions of mainly poor people. Internationally, developments in the global economy served to widen further the gulf between rich and poor: prices for poor states' exports generally fell, and growing international indebtedness led to an increasing share of poor people's incomes falling into the hands of foreign financiers and banks. Domestically, swift population growth in all parts of the Third World hastened environmental decline by putting increasing pressure on the natural environment, which in turn helped to drag down living standards. Given pressures of poverty and population growth, many Third World governments appear to believe that environmental concerns are 'anti-development', 'a luxury for the middle classes of the rich countries, of little relevance for countries that desperately needed to develop' (Hadjor 1993: 106). Local environmentalists in the Third World are often regarded by their governments as subversives, perceived as both 'anti-nation' and 'anti-people', agents of Western imperialism wedded to blocking the necessary development of industry.

Third World peoples are fighting back, however. Although many of their governments flagrantly ignore environmental safeguards, ordinary people are struggling to defend their local environments from destruction. In this section, we examine four of the most pressing environmental concerns affecting the Third World. With regard to each issue, ordinary people are demanding, sometimes with success, that governments change environmental policy in their favour.

Desertification and deforestation

'Desertification' refers either to invasion of arable land by sand or to irreversible damage to vegetative cover. The United Nations Environmental Programme (UNEP) estimates that about 1.2 billion hectares – i.e. about 10 per cent of the earth's vegetated surface – underwent moderate or severe soil degradation between 1945 and 1990. UNEP calculates that an area equivalent in size to North and Latin America combined is threatened by imminent desertification. It is a process which affects all parts of the world, although dry tropical soils are particularly vulnerable. At particular risk are large swathes of the Middle East and North Africa, Asia and Latin America, where rainfall is low.

Two theories compete to explain desertification. The first blames smallholder agriculture and nomadic pastoralism, a combination of so-called 'primitive' farming measures and population pressures, which allegedly results in famine and hunger. The second argues that over-intensive mechanized agriculture and large-scale raising of cows, sheep and other animals, often run by modern, capitalist enterprises, is the main cause of the phenomenon. The real answer probably lies in a combination of the two. Desertification may certainly contribute to both hunger and famine, although evidence suggests that neither smallholder agriculture nor nomadic pastoralism leads to desertification *providing* there is sufficient land available for all, so that land is allowed to recover for several years before being reused (Harrison 1987). In sum, desertification is a symptom of several social and economic factors, like changing land use and land-holding patterns, which combine to deprive the poor of the use of adequate land.

'Deforestation', on the other hand, refers to massive, often irreversible destruction of forests. Tropical moist forests, usually referred to as 'rain' forests, cover an area of 1.5 billion hectares globally. Two-thirds are in Latin America, with the rest divided between sub-Saharan Africa and East and South-east Asia. Rain forests are the 'richest ecosystems in biomass and biodiversity on land', yet in the 1990s alone, around 20 million hectares were destroyed *each year* (Thomas et al. 1994: 62). At current rates of destruction, there will be *no* rain forests left in 75 years' time.

Millions of hectares of tropical rainforest are destroyed each year for a variety of reasons. In Brazil, e.g., 167 million cubic metres (m m^3) of rainforest were destroyed in 1987; over three-quarters (128 m m^3) were consumed by fire in order for the land to be farmed, often a consequence of widespread poverty and landlessness; less than 1 m m^3 of timber was exported. By contrast, Malaysia produced 42 m m^3 of timber in 1987, of which 36 m m^3 – i.e. 88 per cent – was for export. Table 8.1 shows the contrast between the two countries.

Whether largely for farming, as in Brazil, or mostly for export, as in Malaysia, the result of deforestation has negative consequences at local, regional and global levels. Locally, it threatens or destroys the lifestyles of forest-dwelling peoples; regionally, it provokes the leaching and erosion of soils, flash-flooding and desertification; and globally it leads to reduced biomass stocks and species diversity, changing patterns of rainfall, and long-term climate change.

Table 8.1 Production of tropical timber in Brazil and Malaysia, 1987 (million m^3)

Country	Non-fuel wood	Non-fuel wood exports	Fuel wood	Total
Brazil	39	0.8	128	167
Malaysia	36	27	6	42

Source: Thomas et al. 1994: 62

Struggles against deforestation and accompanying loss of people's livelihood emerged in the 1980s as important rallying points for popular movements in the Third World. Chipko (India), Green Belt (Kenya), SAM (Malaysia), WALHI (Indonesia) and National Council of Rubber Tappers (Brazil) were all influential (Ekins 1992: 139, 143ff.). In Brazil, Projeto Seringueiro, organized by the National Council of Rubber Tappers, 'aims to encourage the rubber tappers to identify more closely with the forest, to understand it, to learn more about it and defend it' (Breyman 1993: 129). Conflicts, in Brazil between rubber-tappers, loggers and farmers, in Sarawak between loggers and the indigenous Penan people, and in India between members of the Chipko movement and tree-fellers, are indicative of the opposing interests involved in exploitation and conservation of forest resources. As these examples indicate, the use by subsistence-based people of forest resources for their survival is often in conflict with their use for industrial or cash-crop purposes.

Poverty and land-use patterns

Environmentally negative effects of desertification and deforestation are exacerbated by national development patterns and pro- grammes that take natural resources away from the poor, who tend to use them sustainably, and instead hand them over to the relatively rich, who usually exploit them unsustainably. In the Third World, lack of secure control over resources, population growth, inequity and misguided policies form the common backdrop of the environmental context of poverty, responsible for the deterioration of both agricultural and non-agricultural land. Leonard et al. (1989) calculate that more than 350 million of the 800 million poorest people in the Third World live on marginal or fragile lands where environmental degradation is a virtual certainty. Whether poor people are subject to displacement by influential individuals who wish to use their land for cash-cropping (e.g. plantations and ranches) or by government policy (e.g. the Brazilian government's plan to populate the Amazon basin), the result is the same: the struggle for survival will impinge negatively on the marginal or unsuitable forest land where such people are forced to seek their livelihoods (Peluso 1993).

Poverty can drive environmental deterioration when desperate people over-exploit their resource base, sacrificing the future to try to salvage the present. It is the logic of short-term needs which virtually compels poor, landless families to burn sections of rain-forest or to put hardly viable land – such as mountain slopes – to the plough. The most impoverished, most overcrowded regions suffer the worst ecological damage. For example, in South Asia millions of poor people inhabit environmentally degraded regions such as the crowded hill country surrounding the Himalayas. In China, poverty is particularly concentrated on the Loess Plateau, where soil is swiftly eroding. In the Philippines, the north-east of Thailand, the Amazon basin of Brazil, and the countries of the Congo basin in West Africa, poor farmers carve out a precarious living on plots reclaimed from the forest. In parts of East and southern Africa, on the other hand, poor people try to exist on already deforested land, which, as a result, is turning into desert (Durning 1989: 44–5).

Generally, the poor knowingly harm their environment only when under severe duress. Pushed to the brink of starvation, often evicted from familiar land by big commercial interests, they will lack access to adequate amounts of land, water or capital to provide themselves with a sustainable livelihood. Two of the most common sequences by which poor people get themselves into a downward spiral of environmental degradation are illustrated by the contrasting examples of Nepal and Costa Rica. In Nepal, it is growth in human numbers which threatens the viability of the environment, while in Costa Rica it is the ousting of smallholders from their land by large commercial interests. The result in both cases is that ever larger areas of marginal land are rendered unsuitable for farming, while the rural poor are increasingly disadvantaged.

Nepal: population pressures and environmental damage

The situation in Nepal exemplifies how unremitting growth of human numbers feeds the poverty and environmental degradation spiral – i.e. when human practices at a given level of technology exceed the carrying capacity of local environments. As population swells and forests are destroyed, people living in highland valleys are forced to expand their plots onto steep forested hillsides, extending the distance women must walk to gather fuel and fodder (Durning 1989: 42). Short of time, their workday in the fields shortens, family income falls, and they have less food to cook. Daily food consumption in the area fell by about 100 calories per person on average in the 1980s. As Durning (1989: 42–3) notes, 'childhood malnutrition rates and deforestation rates are closely' linked.

Costa Rica: development patterns which disadvantage the rural poor

Costa Rica is one of the few Latin American countries which has enjoyed a long period of continuous democracy. Development indicators are generally good; e.g. life expectancy is 76 years (on a par with that in Western Europe), while 93 per cent of the population is literate, a proportion that compares well with Greece (94 per cent), Portugal (86 per cent) and virtually all Eastern European countries (UNDP 1994: 129–31, table 1). Sustained economic growth, while falling to 0.7 per cent a year in the 1980s, well below population growth levels of 2.7 per cent, provided the resources to buy off discontent through expansion of the social welfare system and public sector employment, particularly helping the urban middle and working classes. Little progress was made, however, on reforms affecting private property. The Costa Rican cattle-ranching elites learned how to protect their interests through the political party system. The landless rural population, poorly organized, remains a severely disadvantaged group (Rueschemeyer et al. 1992: 249).

Average population density in Costa Rica is much less than in Nepal: 61 people per square kilometre compared with 147 (Thomas et al. 1994: 74). Despite this, distorted land ownership patterns in Costa Rica have a similar effect of diminishing the amount of arable land available for each poor family. Many of the poor were driven from their land by a cattle boom that began in the early 1960s. Large landowners took the lion's share of the best land, small-holdings were overburdened, and millions were left landless. The dispossessed had to make use of whatever land was still available, extracting as much out of it as possible (Rueschemeyer et al. 1992: 236–9). The result was swift deforestation.

Until the 1940s, Costa Rica was almost completely covered in rainforest. What little now remains is seriously degraded. By 1983, after 20 years of growth of the cattle industry, pastures accounted for about half of the arable land; less than 20 per cent of the original forest remained; and soil erosion was a growing problem. While Costa Rica's economic prosperity no doubt depends on developing a viable export sector, the distribution of power, heavily weighted in the hands of a tiny elite despite the democratic status which the country has enjoyed for nearly 50 years, means that the cattle boom was 'driven not so much by market forces as by heavy flows of international capital to, and special treatment for, the 2,000 politically powerful ranching families who control the industry' (Sheldon Annis, quoted in Durning 1989: 42). During the 1970s and 1980s, such cattle-ranchers received around 40 per cent of all agricultural credit, although producing a mere 10 per cent of agricultural output.

The Costa Rican poor did not by and large benefit from the deal, as many smallholders were pushed from their land to make way for cattle. Rural employment opportunities diminished, as cattle ranching requires little labour. The rising tide of landlessness spilled over into the country's cities and into the shrinking forests, where families were left with little viable alternative but to increase the speed of deforestation.

The conclusion to be drawn from these accounts of Nepal and Costa Rica is that, despite differences in national political systems – monarchical Nepal[1] and liberal democratic Costa Rica – it is the rural poor who are particularly disadvantaged in the political and economic stakes; it is they who suffer most from the socio-economic effects of environmental degradation. Democracy does very little for the rural poor when it comes to protecting their economic position. The poverty trap patterns evident in Nepal and Costa Rica – population growth and unequal control over resources, reinforced by counterproductive development policies – reappear in infinite variations around the Third World. The net effect is the same nearly everywhere: the rural poor are increasingly concentrated in fragile regions where land is least productive and tenure least secure – arid and semi-arid lands, mountain slopes, tropical forests and sprawling shanty towns around overcrowded urban centres.

The lack of empowerment of the rural poor in the Third World can be illustrated in another way. Like the drive to large-scale cattle ranching in Costa Rica, the construction of large dams for hydro-electricity and for irrigation purposes is also pursued in the name of development. While the result is that the rural poor do not benefit, while large landowners gain, opposition to large dams has galvanized opposition which is increasingly successful in preventing the com-pletion of large dam projects.

Large dams for hydroelectric power and irrigation

The building of large-scale dams for irrigation and hydroelectric power in the Third World was widely regarded until recently as a spectacular symbol of development. In many governments' view, massive dam projects can be an important component of building a modern developed economy by the provision of cheap, hydro-electric power. Such dams were thought to justify both huge investments of capital and severe disruptions of the affected people who are forced to leave their homes and livelihoods by rising water levels. Now, however, large dams increasingly encounter dwindling acceptance or militant resistance from those affected (Stiefel and Wolfe 1994: 180). Like cattle ranching, the development of large dams in the Third World is related to issues of economic and political power (Rich 1990; Stiefel and Wolfe 1994: 171, 180; Tran 1994).

In one sense, large dams are a 'good thing', as they provide energy without atmospheric pollution. On the other hand, they also arouse violent hostility from local people and environmentalists. Timberlake (1985) explains why: they cause 'the displacement of people, saliniza-tion of land, water-borne diseases, increasingly unequal distribution of wealth, disruptions to fisheries, loss of forests and wildlife, siltation due to erosion, excessive water losses due to evaporation and even an increase in earth tremors'. By the end of the 1980s, as Harrison (1993: 281) explains, the world was using 40 per cent of the estimated hydro-power potential. Yet, because they were silting up at an average rate of about 1 per cent a year, large dams can be considered only as a 'short-term, unrepeatable stopgap that will within a century or so convert all suitable valleys into alluvial farmland'.

Despite such drawbacks, big dams have long been a prestige symbol of industrialization and development, perhaps nowhere more so than in parts of South Asia. India's first post-independence Prime Minister, Nehru, called large dams the new ' "temples" of a modernising India' (Ekins 1992: 88). Over time, however, the developmental credentials of big dams have been increasingly questioned. Two examples – the first from India, the second from Nepal – will illustrate why.

India's Narmada scheme

The Narmada is India's largest western-flowing river and its fifth largest overall, with a length of 1,312 kilometres. More than 20 million people, including many minority tribal peoples, live in its basins, using the river as an important economic and ecological resource. According to the World Bank, however, the Narmada river 'is one of [India's] least used – water utilization is currently about 4 per cent and tons of water effectively are wasted every day when it could be put to use for the benefit of the region' (quoted in Ekins 1992: 89). The Narmada Valley Project (NVP) was to be the solution to this 'under-use': the biggest river project in the world. It was to comprise two very large dams – the Sardar Sarovar Project (SSP) and the Narmada Sagar Project (NSP) – and 28 other dams and about 3,000 other water projects. The planned benefits, according to the Bank, included irrigation of 2.27 million hectares of land in Madhya Pradesh, Gujarat and Rajasthan states, pisciculture, drinking water and electric power. The two main dams would also be designed to moderate floods. The World Bank agreed a $450 million loan for SSP and was considering support for NSP until its backing for the project came to an end in 1994 (Tran 1994).

Despite these expected benefits, a vociferous campaign against the NVP developed when it became clear that the dams would entail massive displacement of local people. Anti-dam activists – including about a million potential 'oustees' from more than 150,000 families, voluntary social groups, local and foreign environmentalists, and local and foreign non-governmental organizations[2] – were pitted against an opposing coalition made up of the state governments of Madhya Pradesh, Gujarat and Rajasthan states, the World Bank, and rich landowners. The latter saw a potential in the scheme for a major boost to irrigation and supply of electrical power; local construction firms foresaw a bonanza; while many ordinary citizens believed that the benefits of the scheme would lead to an all-round growth in prosperity 'through flood control, increased drinking-water supply, new jobs through a spurt in industry and allied activities' (Sethi 1993: 133). In sum, struggles at several levels – grass roots, provincial, national and global – focused not only on the pros and cons of the NVP itself, but also expanded to include the benefits and drawbacks of large 'development' projects more generally. In the end, such was the furore over the apparent inadequacies of the resettlement project, that the World Bank felt obliged to pull out of funding the Narmada dam project in late 1994, thus placing the entire project's completion in grave jeopardy (Tran 1994).

Nepal's Arun 3

Despite the adverse publicity of the Namarda débâcle, the World Bank gave its support to another very large dam proposal in South Asia, the Arun 3 dam in Nepal. As with Narmada, however, the Bank later withdrew its funding, in August 1995 (Vidal 1995). Prior to this, the Bank's vice-president for South Asia, Joseph Wood, stated that, in the wake of the Narmada reverse, if the Bank failed to win approval for the Arun 3 project, it would indicate that the Bank lacked both domestic and international 'credibility as a financing partner for controversial power and infrastructural projects' (Tran 1994). At a cost of about $1 billion, the Arun project would provide more than 200 megawatts of much-needed electricity. Currently, Nepal has only 241 megawatts of hydroelectricity available, which only 10 per cent of the population enjoy. The Bank was to provide $140 million through its soft loan arm, the International Development Association. Japan and France were jointly to contribute $473 million, with Nepal supplying the same amount.

The problem with Arun 3 was not that it would displace hundreds of thousands of people: unlike Narmada, where over 150,000 families would have had to be resettled, only one-thousandth as many people – 150 families – would be touched by the Arun project. The problem with Arun 3 was its impact upon wildlife and its cost to Nepal's treasury. The Arun valley, 200 kilometres east of Kathmandu, is the home of the endangered Asiatic black bear, the clouded leopard and the Annamese macaque. The dam would certainly have led to disruption – perhaps near-extinction for some of these animals. In addition, the project was criticized by a coalition of local and international groups as unnecessarily large and expensive, diverting resources away from small-scale health and education programmes. The coalition instead favoured small- and medium-scale projects that would not use such a large proportion of Nepal's development budget (Miller 1995: 140). Eventually, the Bank bowed to pressure, and withdrew its funding. The effect was to place the dam's entire viability in grave doubt. As Lori Udall of the Washington-based International Rivers Network explained, the cancellation 'sends a strong signal to international donors that large dams are risky, expensive and destructive investments and that they should support smaller, more flexible projects' (Vidal 1995).

The role of the World Bank in funding both the Narmada and

the Arun 3 dams raises the wider issue of the part played by the international funding agencies in environmental degradation in the Third World as well as the relationship between economic development and the environment more generally. There is of course an inherent tension between the idea of economic development and simultaneous protection of the environment. Next, we turn to look at some of the environmental costs of both economic development and structural adjustment in the Third World, before assessing the viability of the alternative: 'sustainable' development.

Development and the environment: the impact of economic growth and structural adjustment

Structural adjustment

A World Bank vice-president, Armeane Chokski, suggested at the time of the UN 'social summit' at Copenhagen in March 1995 that no country has reduced poverty 'without economic growth . . . [T]he way to growth is through market reform.' Chokski added that too much attention is focused by 'advocacy groups' on the negative effects of structural adjustment programmes (SAPs), such as the removal of safety nets, user fees for basic services, and 'necessary' environmental damage as a result of economic growth (Black 1995).

Because there are multiple, complex linkages between economic policies, social forces, natural resource management practices and environmental degradation, it is not really possible to determine *direct* causal connections between structural adjustment policies and the state of the environment. In other words, it is very difficult to distinguish between the effects of structural adjustment and those associated with 'normal' economic growth. Nevertheless, it is widely believed that SAPs have contributed to (a) general damage to the natural environment, (b) a failure to push through laws protecting the environment, (c) pressure on the environment by redundant former government employees who take up farming once they lose their jobs.

First, the importance of increasing exports to earn foreign exchange can result in serious damage to forests, wetlands, mangroves and other natural resources, while swift development of ecologically damaging industries such as mining adds to pollution levels (Miller 1995: 31). Many Third World 'governments desperate for foreign exchange tolerate uncontrolled exploitation of forests and mineral resources and ecologically dangerous practices of commercial agri-

culture' (Fisher 1993: 31). Second, the pressure on adjusting countries
to reduce governmental expenditures may cause the removal or
postponement of various measures, including enforcement of
environmental laws. A third environmental impact associated with
SAPs is that redundant government employees, often unable to find
employment in an urban centre, may, as a result of no other form of
job being available, be virtually impelled to take up slash-and-burn
agriculture in forests or on marginal lands like mountain slopes. In
sum, the environmental effects of attempts at structural adjustment in
the Third World seem uniformly negative.

*Newly industrializing countries: economic growth and the
natural environment*

As we have already noted, not all Third World countries are economically unsound. The newly industrializing countries (NICs) of East
Asia, in particular, have been notable for extremely swift economic
growth over the last 20 years or so. They have certainly *not* been
compelled to follow structural adjustment, yet their pursuit of
economic development has still had deleterious effects upon the
natural environments. The cases of two of the most economically
successful Third World countries, South Korea and Taiwan, illustrate
the environmental costs of economic growth: large-scale destruction
of forests, highly intensive use of agricultural fertilizers and pesticides,
dumping of industrial waste in rivers and the sea, and seemingly
uncontrolled air pollution (Cammack et al. 1993: 312).

   We noted earlier that Fukuyama suggested that once a country
democratizes, then more concern will be devoted to environmental
protection. Our case-studies give only limited support for Fukuyama's
hypothesis. In South Korea, even when the government democratized, it was still able to pursue environmentally damaging policies
because, it argued, the alternative was less growth and therefore
less prosperity. Faced with such a choice, many Koreans seemed
prepared to put up with fast-declining environments as a necessary
price of economic success. In Taiwan, on the other hand, a national
environmental movement developed in the mid-1980s which had
some success in curtailing the appalling pollution levels in the country.
The evidence from Taiwan is that there are limits to the capacity
of authoritarian governments to compel their citizens to act in certain ways, particularly as the non-democratic state's grip begins to
weaken.

   It is not that there is no legislation to control pollution in South

Korea: the country has had environmental impact assessment legislation in place since 1982. The problem is that it is not enforced. Shin Chang Hyun, the director of Seoul's independent Environment Policy Research Institute, comments that 'Laws and regulations are all there, but the government will to enforce them is simply missing' (Cammack et al. 1993: 317). There is very little public pressure on the government to enforce its own laws. The almost non-existent environmental lobby has had no success in galvanizing mass opinion to its point of view (Gills et al. 1993: 251). The environmental impact of democratization after 1988 was very limited: the South Korean government promised to implement new and tougher measures to control pollution and to protect the environment, but to date there is very little concrete evidence of a change of environmental emphasis.

Like South Korea, Taiwan is a fast-growing industrial country, the fourteenth largest trading nation in the world, with an annual economic growth rate in double digits for most of the last two decades (King 1993: 139–40). The price of economic success, however, has been serious environmental problems, which are compounded by the fourth highest population density in the world, behind Singapore, Hong Kong and Mauritius. In Taiwan, 20 million people are crammed into an island twice the size of Wales.

Dr Y. F. Liang of the government's Environmental Protection Administration considers that the capital, Taipei's, 'air quality is perhaps the worst in the world. . . . Ninety per cent of the pollution comes from cars' (quoted in Bunting 1995). There are currently 5 million cars on the island, and they are increasing by 10 per cent a year. In the countryside, development of the mountainous interior for quarrying, cement making, house building and golf courses destroys the forests. Heavy rains trigger landslides, soil erosion and floods. Industries often seek to evade environmental legislation, threatening to relocate to China if enforcement is implemented (Bunting 1995; Cammack et al. 1993: 317).

There is collusion between wealthy business people and politicians: Land is bought cheaply by wealthy people, who then get it 'upgraded' to commercial use through manipulation of political connections. The media are controlled by government or powerful business people, so the situation is rarely exposed. Unlike in South Korea, however, there are several groups devoted to environmental protection, including the Taiwan Environmental Protection Union (TEPU) and the women-dominated Homemakers' Union (HU), which emerged in the mid-1980s. Their achievements include winning the suspension – although not the abandonment – of plans for a fourth nuclear power plant, the closing of a petrochemical plant whose discharged waste was claimed to be killing fish stocks, and preventing the building of a huge titanium dioxide plant by DuPont, the US chemicals conglomerate (Cammack et al. 1993: 317).

Despite such successes, however, no mass movement along the lines of Greenpeace or Friends of the Earth has yet developed in Taiwan. One of the main impediments to the growth of such a movement is that after 40 years of military dictatorship, 'there is no tradition of collective action or civic culture' (Bunting 1995). Ling Cheng Hsiou, vice-president of the TEPU, argues that there is a fear of public protest dating back to 1947, when thousands of opponents of the dictator, Chiang Kai-Shek, were murdered. Shiolin Wong of the HU sees the problem as a hangover from the military dictatorship 'when it was not possible to organize' (Bunting 1995). There may also be a further element: the result of forcing some multinational companies to curtail the pollution they create led to many relocating to China, South Korea or the Philippines. Many ordinary Taiwanese would have made the connection between environmental protection and job losses and chosen not to join a movement whose very success may be linked in many people's minds to the loss of employment.

In conclusion, although many Third World governments either fail to create or ignore environmental safeguards, citizens are struggling to defend their local environments from destruction. We saw how people in the Third World are defending their forests and fighting the building of large-scale dams, although in some cases the lack of organization of the rural poor prevents their gaining victories against much more organized landowners and governments. Democratization coupled with swift economic growth *may*, as in Taiwan, lead to growing environmental movements with teeth, although the same series of developments in South Korea led to a different outcome. There are indications, however, that popular pressure is making itself felt – though there is no certainty that such pressure will compel governments to change their environmental policies. Without concern for *sustainable* development, however, there is every indication that environmental disaster is on the horizon. In the last section of the chapter we turn to a discussion of the concept of 'sustainable development'.

Sustainable Development

Discussions at the 1992 Earth Summit encompassed a number of issues, one of which was the concept, desirability and obtainability of what is known as 'sustainable development' (Miller 1995: 143–52). As the industrialized countries found out decades ago, a downside of industrialization is degradation of the natural environment. Widespread, environmentally non-sustainable industrialization in the Third World would be a global disaster, because, as Hadjor (1993: 280–1) explains, there is a limit 'to the amount of pollution which can be produced and the quantity of resources which can be used without human life destroying its own physical environmental base'. Sustainable development was defined in the 1987 report of the UN World Commission on Environment and Development[3] as 'development which meets the needs of the present without compromising the ability of future generations to meet their own needs' (Thomas et al. 1994: 62).

The core of the concept of sustainable development is the use of renewable resources, such as solar power, waste reduction and recycling, as well as the design and implementation of new technologies and changes in consumption by those in the West and the rich in the Third World. The aim of sustainable development is to forge a form of development which maintains an appropriate balance, one which is environmentally tolerable over a long period. By its very nature, it is a global concept which would need to be put into practice by very many countries, both industrialized and industrializing. So far, however, there are few concrete signs of the necessary culture shift to counterbalance the inclination of the world economy to work against environmental concerns.

Most movement towards sustainable development would have to come from the existing industrial countries, few of which are in the Third World. With about 20 per cent of the global population, the industrial countries of the West and Eastern Europe together discharge about two-thirds of the gases that add to global warming (the greenhouse effect), most of the sulphur dioxide and nitrogen oxide emissions that cause acid rain, as well as over 85 per cent of the chlorofluorocarbon (CFC) gases which are responsible for the depletion of the ozone layer. Table 8.2 shows a regional breakdown of the emission of CFCs in 1984.

The Montreal Protocol, which came into force in 1992, aims to

Table 8.2 Production of CFC gases by region, 1984 (tonnes)

Region or country	Amount (1,000s of tonnes)	Percentage of global output
Western Europe	440	36.5
United States	455	37.5
Japan	150	12
Former Socialist countries	120	10
Third World	50	4
Total	1215	100

Source: compiled from data in Thomas et al. 1994: 62

eliminate CFC manufacture by the year 2000. There are signs that the industrial countries are taking seriously their commitment to cease use of CFCs, although Third World countries have been slower to commit themselves to phasing them out (Miller 1995: 81–2). Third World states often see the endeavour to curtail use of chemicals like CFCs as a *de facto* attempt by the West to slow down Third World development. Yet, without the development of policies of sustainable development, industrialization in the Third World will inevitably lead to increasing environmental degradation, more deforestation and desertification, and increasingly serious industrial pollution levels. This can be in nobody's long-term interest. For rational implementation, however, sustainable development requires a global decision-making process, which at present shows little sign of emerging.

For many people, the real importance of the Earth Summit was reflected in the growth in awareness of, and disquiet over, the emission of 'greenhouse' gases, global warming,[4] and the thinning of the ozone layer.[5] Such concerns combine to highlight the global implications of energy-intensive development policies pursued most destructively by the industrially developed countries and, encouraged by the IMF and the World Bank, also embraced with enthusiasm in the Third World. Sustained, widespread, environmentally destructive economic development in the Third World would greatly add to atmospheric pollution. At the current time, however, the most important forms of environmental degradation in much of the Third World are a function of primary commodity production. Such production, whether for export or local needs, leads to desertification, deforestation, the over-exploitation of natural resources and a loss of arable land.

Awareness of such issues led to a concern with the idea of sustainable development involving regeneration of the natural resource base (especially forests) and reform of Western-style production and consumption. While global compacts to control pollution are slow to emerge, many people feel that, rather than relying on governments to lead the way towards sustainable development, most progress will be made by increases in popular participation and community organization to pressurize them into taking substantive action (Miller 1995: 143–52). In short, the groundwork for sustainable development, for increased human and women's rights, democracy and economic justice, depends on people's ability to organize themselves to deal with both poverty and environmental degradation. Durning (1989: 55) calculates that 'grassroots environmental and antipoverty groups probably number in the hundreds of thousands, and their collective membership in the hundreds of millions'. As growing numbers of countries in the Third World democratize, it gives hope to the notion that genuinely self-sustaining development will be a wide-spread feature of the twenty-first century.

Notes

1 Nepal recently democratized, although much power resides in the hands of King Birendra.
2 It is estimated that nearly 350,000 hectares of forest land and 200,000 hectares of cultivated land would have been submerged if the dams had gone ahead. Western non-governmental organizations (NGOs) launched major campaigns in their own countries against finance being made available for the projects, while in India a new co-ordinating NGO, the National Campaign Against Big Dams, a coalition of about 100 groups from across the country, campaigned against the Narmada project (Sethi 1993: 133).
3 Known as the Brundtland Commission in honour of its leader, then Prime Minister of Norway, Mrs Brundtland.
4 Some of the islands in the 36-member Alliance of Small Island States (Aosis) are so low-lying that they could be inundated in the next century by a rise in sea-level and increased storms. Others, among them some of the world's most popular tourist spots, will lose valuable coastal land, and main centres of population will be drowned.
5 The thinning of the ozone layer will result, it is estimated, in greatly increased rates of skin cancer over the next few decades.

9

Conclusion

In concentrating on the state, and on its relationship with its citizens, I have endeavoured in this book to explore the main difficulties of governments and of those who must live under their auspices. My chief concern has not been with the day-to-day business of how the state conducts its affairs, but rather with a series of issues which relate to two general questions: first, what do states actually *do* for their citizens? Second, why are their efforts often unsatisfactory in the eyes of many of their people?

In raising these concerns, I do not simply mean that citizens, wherever they live under whatever state's auspices, often feel frustrated and disappointed with their government's efforts. What I am getting at is an issue which relates to the *degree* of a state's unacceptability or, if preferred, unpopularity. In all Western countries citizens enjoy a number of what seem to them fundamental rights: to vote, regularly; a variety of basic and not so basic human rights; not to face discrimination because of race, culture or religion; to expect governments to protect the natural environment, and so on. I do not mean by this that *every* Western government protects all its citizens all the time in relation to all these issues. What I am claiming is that in theory – and sometimes in practice – all governments claim to *endeavour* to do the best they can for their citizens across a range of issues. In the West, discontent with governments is usually kept within reasonable bounds. Criticism is, of course, often forthright and condemnatory; yet, unlike in the Third World, *coup d'états*, revolutions, rebellions and insurrections are very uncommon indeed.

This is not to suggest that politics in the Third World is intrinsically different from politics everywhere else. At the root of politics in whatever national context is the interactive relationship of the state to its people, and vice versa. In the Third World, however, in contrast to the West, very often the state fundamentally disappoints those on the receiving end of its policies and programmes. This is because, whereas all states have two basic purposes, to maintain or enhance their citizens' security and to allow them opportunities to increase their own well-being, in neither of these respects is the record of many Third World states a good one. Because of this, the perception of the legitimacy which most citizens have of governments in the Third World is, it appears, rather low.

The legitimacy and authority of many Third World states has declined over time. While virtually all have at least one great success to their credit – the achievement of national independence from colonial rule – as an enduring vehicle for expressing the aspirations of their people, many are widely perceived as resounding failures. The ramifications of a widespread sense of disappointment and frustration in the ability of the state are expressed in the issues which we have explored in this book, including democracy, economic growth and development, human and women's rights, religious and ethnic identity, and protection of the natural environment.

At independence, most citizens of colonies believed that freedom from colonial rule would lead to greater political, economic and social justice, for the simple reason that henceforward they would no longer be ruled by an alien government, but instead by leaders and bureaucratic personnel drawn from among their own people. In the event, however, popular aspirations were very often much greater than states' ability to deliver. Many apparently entrenched state structures, controlled by a united and established civilian or military elite group, were extremely hard to dislodge. Very few – less than a dozen – Third World countries have been able to maintain long-term, competitive electoral and party systems, in which the accountability of the government to its people is a live issue.

One of the results of the entrenchment in power of increasingly unelected elites has been that, for many people, the optimism of independence soon waned. The state was increasingly regarded not as a champion of popular interests at home and in relation to external actors and forces, but as a group of people driven by a primary desire to enrich themselves illegally from national resources. This might not have been so bad, perhaps, if states had been able to provide a *quid pro quo*: to protect their citizens from crime, terrorism, job losses, inflation and natural disasters; yet few could consistently do (m)any of these things. Why, then, should citizens respect and support those in power? As conditions worsened during the 1970s and 1980s as a result of widespread economic downturns, the gradual loss of respect of governed for governments developed into increasingly outspoken demands – encouraged by international developments, particularly the end of the Cold War and the astonishingly rapid demise of the East European Communist systems – for fundamental changes: for democracy, economic reforms and enhanced human rights.

The 'third wave' of democracy began in the mid-1970s in southern Europe, spreading first to Latin America and then to Asia and Africa, but failing to make much impact in the Middle East. While the number of democratic governments increased greatly over the 20 years from the mid-1970s, however, significant numbers of personalist dictatorships, one-party states and military regimes remain. Non-democratic regimes almost invariably deny a range of rights and benefits to most of their citizens: in particular, human rights are ignored or flouted; woman's demands are belittled; environmental safeguards – if they exist – are ignored; and ethnic and religious minorities are denied freedom of expression. When, on the other hand, a state's government is democratically accountable, such issues are at least contested ground: i.e. they appear on the political agenda, and differing viewpoints are expressed, debated and contested. Democracy, then, is the key to improvements in relation to a range of issues: an essential step, the first stepping-stone, to wider and deeper social, political and economic reform.

Democratic control of government also affects a state's economic direction. The widespread absence of democracy in the Third World until recently was paralleled by a general shortfall in economic growth and development. While some regions, especially East and South-east Asia, did consistently well in this respect, many others did badly, for two main reasons. First, there was a common inability to build on countries' pre-existing economic strengths. Many governments were overly concerned with ideologically driven, grandiose development plans which had little plausible hope, however, especially in hindsight, of being realized. Second, *all* Third World countries must deal with an international economic system which is not of their making and which they cannot control. There is little to be gained, however, from attempting a policy of autarchy or economic self-sufficiency, attractive though the 'go it alone' scenario may sometimes appear. This is because few states have either the technical expertise or the natural resources to make a success of it; in addition, a high degree of authoritarianism will be necessary to quell popular disquiet as the supply of imports dries up.

For a country to become economically prosperous, it will, of necessity, cultivate a strong export sector, using the proceeds to buy in essential imports to develop, in turn, a thriving export sector, so that an expanding array of goods can be dispatched overseas. It is no good relying on exports of primary products alone, however; over the last 15 years or so, world prices of most primary goods have declined or at best stagnated in relation to imported manufactured goods, which have risen steadily in price. A result of widespread trade imbalances has been that many Third World countries, especially in Latin America and sub-Saharan Africa, have experienced a steady rise in international indebtedness.

Gradually, so as not to put all the 'export eggs' in one basket, the cultivation of primary products for exports should be supplemented by selective industrialization. The result of a careful, yet imaginative, policy of building on one's strengths is well illustrated by the economic successes of Taiwan and South Korea. Both, 30 or 40 years ago, were on a developmental par with India, Kenya and Nigeria, but are now at the level of some of Western Europe's poorer countries, with every expectation of joining the developmental elite of the West in the next few years.

Shortfalls in democracy and economic growth and development led to a further area of conflict between states and societies: the striving by various groups for ethnic and/or religious identity in the context of attempts by governments to build nation-states. Measured by the types of state–society conflicts most common in the Third World in the 1980s and 1990s, many people's core values seem to be based on religion, ethnicity or an assumed common culture, rather than class. In chapter 5, we saw how governments throughout the Third World are challenged by religio-ethnic groups which have their own notions of solidarity and development. The point is that such conflicts are themselves a result of wider strains in the fabric of state–society relations. It is no coincidence that demands for greater ethnic and/or religious autonomy emerged during a time of widespread political and economic upheaval.

The issue of religio-ethnic identity is often linked with another concern which is redolent of people's desire to have a greater say in the direction and content of their lives: human rights. Demands centred on the right to choose one's government, the direction of economic policy, and enhanced freedoms for minority religio-ethnic groups are all human rights issues. Yet, while virtually all states in the Third World are signatories of the 1948 Universal Declaration of Human Rights, as well as of other human rights agreements, there is much evidence of widespread recourse to torture and unjust and illegal imprisonment throughout the Third World. Some governments seek refuge in claims of their society's cultural singularity which would allow them to adopt different human rights standards than elsewhere. We noted, however, that such claims are nearly always spurious, put forward by states claiming to rule in line with the human rights norms of their societies, but in fact using methods of rule which are unequivocally opposed to their citizens fundamental human rights.

One indicator of the extent to which human rights has become a legitimate concern of international society is the support which states give to various human rights conventions. Freedom from racial discrimination and slavery, refugees' rights, and the *political* rights of women are widely upheld in nearly all states. Yet, too often the rights of women begin and end with the right to vote. Just as we saw that there are cultural issues in relation to human rights concerns in the Third World, so the position of women is bound up with issues of culture, religion, traditionalism and modernization.

Nearly 50 years after the Universal Declaration of Human Rights pronounced that males and females have identical rights, serious gender inequalities remain in most Third World countries. The poor position of females in many parts of the Third World was one of the areas under discussion at the Fourth United Nations conference on women held in Beijing in September 1995. Three issues were especially controversial: women's physical well-being, women and work, and women and education. In most Third World countries women are less healthy than men, live shorter lives than men, get less education than men, and have less skilled jobs with lower rates of pay than men.

The impact of modernization, including paid work, both improve and worsen the position of women. It improves it to the extent that they have an income to help support their families; at the same time, their position may deteriorate when (usually male) factory-owners and employers mistreat them. The development of women's groups, on the other hand, as we saw in chapter 7 in relation to Latin America and the Caribbean and India, helps to build enhanced socio-economic – and sometimes political – roles for women.

One area where the importance of women's efforts is especially clear was noted in chapter 8, concerned with the politics of the natural environment. Because millions of women in the Third World see their livelihoods, homes and families threatened by the destruction and degradation of their natural environments, they have been influential in the environmental protection groups which have emerged in their thousands in recent times. A series of environmental catastrophes in the 1980s – including the burning of the Amazonian rainforest, the Union Carbide disaster at Bhopal, India, the nuclear accident at Chernobyl, acid rain, and holes in the ozone layer – provided the catalyst for the politicization of environmental concerns. Following the 1992 Earth Summit at Rio de Janeiro, the extent of public concern over damage to the environment was further demonstrated by the unprecedented world-wide protests at the French nuclear weapons testing at Muroroa Atoll in late 1995.

In conclusion, the concerns of the chapters of this book suggest strongly that in order to analyse and understand Third World politics in the contemporary era, we must take into account a wide array of actors, factors and developments. We have seen that international trends have been important in propelling many issues onto domestic political agendas in the Third World. On the other hand, the ability of some governments *not* to allow democracy, *not* to undertake meaningful economic and human rights reforms, *not* to make serious attempts to protect the natural environment, and so on indicates that while international trends encourage domestic groups to double and then redouble their efforts to compel governments to begin reform processes, they are, on their own, insufficient. There must be sufficiently strong local groups to build upon the pressures which develop at the international level.

Notwithstanding the increasing international concern with the issues which we have been concerned with in this book, if the state is regarded as providing the unavoidable structure within which politics is played out, then the way out of what often becomes a vicious circle of irresponsibility, illegitimacy and ineffectualness is to be found via the acceptance by governing elites of a group of common values acknowledging their accountability to their electorate. Accountability implies widespread approval of values like honesty and efficiency, which governments must develop to win the trust of their citizens. Much more effective institutions, capable of achieving more democracy, economic development and enhanced human and women's rights, are essential. At the present time, many Third World states are at a crossroads: the gradual entrenchment of democratic governments may lead to further social, political and economic reforms which collectively gain the accolade of popular legitimacy. Or, on the other hand, only lip-service may be paid to popular aspirations. Some countries, probably those with reasonable levels of economic growth and social homogeneity will do best; others, with apparently poor prospects of achieving sustained economic improvements and often riven by increasingly dichotomous religious and ethnic discord, will do less well.

Bibliography

Ahmed, L. 1992. *Women and Gender in Islam*, New Haven, Yale University Press.

Ajami, F. 1978. *Human Rights and World Order*, New York, Institute for World Order.

Almond, G. 1970. *Political Development: Essays in Heuristic Theory*, Boston, Little, Brown.

Amin, S. 1987. 'Democracy and National Strategy in the Periphery', *Third World Quarterly*, 9/4, 1129–56.

—— 1993. 'Social Movements at the Periphery' in P. Wignaraja (ed.), *New Social Movements in the South*, London, Zed Books, 76–100.

Anderson, B. 1991. *Imagined Communities. Reflections of the Origin and Spread of Nationalism*, 2nd edn, London, Verso.

An-Na'im, A. 1992. 'Islam and National Integration in the Sudan', in J. Hunwick (ed.), *Religion and National Integration in Africa*, Evanston, Ill., Northwestern University Press, 11–37.

Auda, G. 1993. 'The Islamic Movement and Resource Mobilization in Egypt: A Political Culture Perspective', in L. Diamond (ed.), *Political Culture and Democracy in Developing Countries*, Boulder, Colo., Lynne Rienner, 379–407.

Ayoade, J. A. 1988. 'States without Citizens: An Emerging African Phenomenon', in D. Rothchild and N. Chazan (eds), *The Precarious Balance. State and Society in Africa*, Boulder, Colo., Lynne Rienner, 100–18.

Ayoob, M. 1995. 'The New-Old Disorder in the Third World', *Global Governance*, 1/1, 59–78.

Ayubi, N. 1991. *Political Islam. Religion and Politics in the Arab World*, London, Routledge.

Balls, E. 1995. 'Learning Hard Lessons from Mexico's Crisis', *Guardian*, 10 July.

Bangura, Y. 1994. *The Search for Identity: Ethnicity, Religion and Political Violence*, Geneva, United Nations Research Institute for Social Development, Occasional Paper no. 6.

Barrow, G. 1995. 'Ethnic Riots Leave Five Kenyans Dead', *Guardian*, 18 Oct.

Bayart, J.-F. 1986. 'Civil Society in Africa', in P. Chabal (ed.), *Political Domination in Africa*, Cambridge, Cambridge University Press, 109–25.

—— 1991. 'Finishing with the Idea of the Third World: The Concept of the Political Trajectory', in J. Manor (ed.), *Rethinking Third World Politics*, Harlow, Longman, 51–71.

—— 1993. *The State in Africa*, London, Longman.

Beck, U. 1994. 'The Reinvention of Politics: Towards a Theory of Reflexive Modernization', in A. Giddens, S. Lash and U. Beck, *Reflexive Modernization. Politics, Tradition and Aesthetics in the Modern Social Order*, Cambridge, Polity, 1–56.

Beeley, B. 1992. 'Islam as a Global Political Force', in A. McGrew and P. Lewis (eds), *Global Politics. Globalization and the Nation State*, Cambridge, Polity, 293–311.

Beresford, D. 1995. 'Cheery Kaunda Plots his Return', *Guardian*, 10 July.

Berger, M. 1994. 'The End of the Third World', *Third World Quarterly*, 15/2, 257–75.

Bethke Elshtain, J. 1995. 'Exporting Feminism', *Journal of International Affairs*, 48/2, 541–58.

Bill, J., and Springborg, R. 1994. *Politics in the Middle East*, New York, HarperCollins.

'Bite the Ballot'. 1994. *New Statesman and Society*, special supplement, 29 Apr., p. 18.

Black, I. 1995. 'Rich Talk for the Poor', *Guardian*, 4 Mar.

Black, J. K. 1993. 'Elections and Other Trivial Pursuits: Latin America and the New World Order', *Third World Quarterly*, 14/3, 545–54.

Blaustein, A., and Flanz, G. 1993. *Constitutions of the Countries of the World*, Dobbs Ferry, N.Y., Oceana Publications.

Braid, M. 1995. 'How Quality of Life Matches up to Global Sisterhood', *Independent*, 18 Aug.

Bratton, M., and van der Walle, N. 1991. 'Towards Governance in Africa: Popular Demands and State Responses', in G. Hyden and M. Bratton (eds), *Governance and Politics in Africa*, Boulder, Colo., Lynne Rienner, 27–55.

Breyman, S. 1993. 'Knowledge as Power: Ecology Movements and Global Environmental Problems', in R. Lipschutz and K. Conca (eds), *The State and Social Power in Global Environmental Politics*, New York, Columbia University Press, 124–57.

Brittain, V. 1994. 'Victims from Birth', *Observer*, special supplement: 'World on Her Shoulders', 16 Oct., p. 12.

—— 1995a. 'Count the Cost of Women's Work', *Guardian*, 18 Aug.

—— 1995b. 'Riding the Tigress', *Guardian*, 28 Aug.

Bromley, S. 1994. *Rethinking Middle East Politics*, Cambridge, Polity.

Brown, M. B., and Tiffen, P. 1992. *Short Changed: Africa and World Trade*, London, Pluto/TNI.

Brown, P. 1995. 'Was Rio More than a Grand Jamboree?', *Guardian*, 4 Mar.

Bunting, M. 1995. 'Choking the Tiger', *Guardian*, 11 Jan.

Callaghy, T. 1993. 'Vision and Politics in the Transformation of the Global Political Economy: Lessons from the Second and Third Worlds', in R. Slater, B. Schutz and S. Dorr (eds), *Global Transformation and the Third World*, Boulder, Colo., Lynne Rienner, 161–258.

Cammack, P., Pool. D., and Tordoff, W. 1993. *Third World Politics: A Comparative Introduction*, 2nd edn, London, Macmillan.

Carnoy, M. 1984. *The State and Political Theory*, Princeton, NJ, Princeton University Press.

Chazan, N. 1993. 'Between Liberalism and Statism: African Political Cultures and Democracy', in Larry Diamond (ed.), *Political Culture and Democracy in Developing Countries*, Boulder, Colo., Lynne Rienner, 67–105.

Chiriyankandath, J. 1993. 'Human Rights in India: Concepts and Contexts', *Contemporary South Asia*, 2/3, 245–63.

Clapham, C. 1985. *Third World Politics. An Introduction*, London, Routledge.

—— 1994. 'Review Article: The *Longue Durée* of the African State', *African Affairs*, 93/372, 433–9.

Clark, T. N. 1994. 'Clientelism, USA: The Dynamics of Change', in L. Roniger and A. Günes-Ayata (eds), *Democracy, Clientelism, and Civil Society*, Boulder, Colo., Lynne Rienner, 121–44.

Coles, M. 1994. 'Women of Iran "Treated as Sub-Humans" ', *Observer*, 4 Dec.

Cooper, F. 1993. 'Africa and the World Economy', in F. Cooper, F. Mallon, S. Stern, A. Isaacman and W. Roseberry, *Confronting Historical Paradigms. Peasants, Labor, and the Capitalist World System in Africa and Latin America*, Madison, University of Wisconsin Press, 84–205.

Dessouki, A. H. 1982. *Islamic Resurgence in the Arab World*, New York, Praeger.

Diamond, L. 1993a. 'The Globalization of Democracy', in R. Slater, B. Schutz and S. Dorr (eds), *Global Transformation and the Third World*, Boulder, Colo., Lynne Rienner, 91–112.

—— 1993b. 'Introduction: Political Culture and Democracy', in L.

Diamond (ed.), *Political Culture and Democracy in Developing Countries*, Boulder, Colo., Lynne Rienner, 1–33.

Dolan, M. 1993. 'Global Economic Transformation and Less Developed Countries', in R. Slater, B. Schutz and S. Dorr (eds), *Global Transformation and the Third World*, Boulder, Colo., Lynne Rienner, 259–82.

Dorr, S. 1993. 'Democratization in the Middle East', in R. Slater, B. Schutz and S. Dorr (eds), *Global Transformation and the Third World*, Boulder, Colo., Lynne Rienner, 131–57.

Durning, A. 1989. *Action at the Grassroots*, Washington, DC, Worldwatch Institute, Worldwatch Papers no. 88.

Ekins, P. 1992. *A New World Order. Grassroots Movements for Global Change*, London, Routledge.

Emerson, R. 1975. 'The Fate of Human Rights in the Third World', *World Politics*, 27/2, 205–20.

Encarnacion, T., and Tadem, E. 1993. 'Ethnicity and Separatist Movements in South-east Asia', in P. Wignaraja (ed.), *New Social Movements in the South*, London, Zed Books, 149–63.

Engels, D., and Marks, S. (eds), 1994. Contesting Colonial Hegemony. State and Society in Africa and India, London, I. B. Tauris.

Esposito, J., and Piscatori, J. 1991. 'Democratization and Islam', *Middle East Journal*, 45/3, 427–40.

Fairhead, J., and Leach, M. 1994. 'Contested Forests: Modern Conservation and Historical Land Use in Guinea's Ziama Reserve', *African Affairs*, 93/373, 481–512.

Falk, R. 1979. 'Comparative Protection of Human Rights in Capitalist and Socialist Regimes', *Universal Human Rights*, 1/2, 3–29.

Fatton, R. 1992. *Predatory Rule. State and Civil Society in Africa*, Boulder, Colo., Lynne Rienner.

Ferguson, J. A. 1986. 'The Third World', in R. J. Vincent (ed.), *Foreign Policy and Human Rights*, Cambridge, Cambridge University Press, 203–26.

Fisher, J. 1993. *The Road from Rio. Sustainable Development and Non-governmental Movement in the Third World*, Westport, Conn., Praeger.

Foster-Carter, A. 1985. 'The Sociology of Development', in M. Haralambos (ed.), *Sociology: New Directions*, Ormskirk, Causeway, 91–213.

Frank, A. G. 1971. *Capitalism and Underdevelopment in Latin America*, Harmondsworth, Penguin.

—— 1984. *Critique and Anti-critique: Essays on Dependency and Reformism*, Eastbourne, Praeger.

—— 1994. 'Marketing Democracy in an Undemocratic Market', in B. Gills, J. Rocamara and R. Wilson (eds), *Low Intensity Democracy*, London, Pluto, 35–58.

Fukuyama, F. 1992. *The End of History and the Last Man*, London, Penguin.

Furedi, F. 1994. *Colonial Wars and the Politics of Third World Nationalism*, London, I. B. Tauris.

Garreton, M. A. 1991. 'Political Democratisation in Latin America and the Crisis of Paradigms', in J. Manor (ed.), *Rethinking Third World Politics*, Harlow, Longman, 100–17.

George, S. 1993. 'Uses and Abuses of African Debt', in A. Adedeji (ed.), *Africa within the World. Beyond Dispossession and Dependence*, London, Zed Books/ACDESS, 59–72.

Giddens, A. 1990. *The Consequences of Modernity*, Cambridge, Polity.

Gills, B. 1995. 'Feature Review: "Dependency and World Systems" ', *Third World Quarterly*, 16/1, 141–6.

—— , Rocamora, J. and Wilson, R. (eds) 1993. *Low Intensity Democracy*, London, Pluto.

Habermas, J. 1976. *Legitimation Crisis*, London, Heinemann.

Hadjor, K. 1993. *Dictionary of Third World Terms*, London, Penguin.

Hall, M. 1993. 'Zambia: Special Report', *Guardian*, 2 Apr.

Hall, S. 1985. 'Religious Ideologies and Social Movements in Jamaica', in R. Bocock and K. Thompson (eds), *Religion and Ideology*, Manchester, Manchester University Press, 269–96.

Hargreaves, J. 1979. *The End of Colonial Rule in West Africa*, London, Macmillan.

Harrison, P. 1987. *The Greening of Africa: Breaking Through in the Battle for Food and Land*, Harmondsworth, Penguin.

—— 1993. *The Third Revolution. Population, Environment and a Sustainable World*, London, Penguin.

Hawthorn, G. 1991. ' "Waiting for a Text?" Comparing Third World Politics', in J. Manor (ed.), *Rethinking Third World Politics*, Harlow, Longman, 24–50.

—— 1994. 'Liberalization and "Modern Liberty" ', *World Development*, 21/8: 1299–312.

Haynes, J. 1991. 'Human Rights and Democracy: The Record of the Rawlings Regime in Ghana', *African Affairs*, 90/3, 407–25.

—— 1993a. *Religion in Third World Politics*, Buckingham, Open University Press.

—— 1993b. 'The State, Good Governance and Democracy in Sub-Saharan Africa', *Journal of Modern African Studies*, 31/3, 535–9.

—— 1993c. 'Sustainable Democracy in Ghana? Problems and Prospects', *Third World Quarterly*, 14/3, 451–67.

—— 1995a. 'From Dictatorship to Liberalism and Democracy in Africa', in M. Mills and F. King (eds), *The Promise of Liberalism. A Comparative Analysis of Consensus Politics*, Aldershot, Dartmouth, 186–203.

—— 1995b. 'From Personalistic to Democratic Rule in Ghana', in

J. Wiseman (ed.), *Democracy and Political Change in Africa*, London, Routledge, 92–115.

—— 1995c. *Religion, Fundamentalism and Identity: A Global Perspective*, Geneva, United Nations Research Institute for Social Development, Discussion Paper no. 65.

—— 1995d. 'The Renaissance of "Political" Religion in the Third World in the Context of Global Change', paper presented at the conference 'Religion and Global Order', University of Wales, Gregynog Hall, 1–3 Nov.

—— 1996. *Religion and Politics in Africa*, London, Zed Books.

Hettne, B. 1995. *Developmental Theory and the Three Worlds*, Harlow, Longman.

Higley, J., and Burton, M. 1989. 'The Elite Variable in Democratic Transitions and Breakdowns', *American Sociological Review*, 54, 8–28.

Hopkins, A. G. 1973. *An Economic History of West Africa*, London, Longman.

Howard, R. 1986. 'Is there an African Concept of Human Rights?', in R. J. Vincent (ed.), *Foreign Policy and Human Rights*, Cambridge, Cambridge University Press, 11–32.

Human Rights Internet. 1993a. 'Women in Bangladesh', Ottawa, Immigration and Refugee Board.

—— 1993b. 'Women in the Republic of Trinidad and Tobago', Ottawa, Immigration and Refugee Board.

Huntington, S. 1968. *Political Order in Changing Societies*, New Haven, Conn., Yale University Press.

—— 1984. 'Will More Countries Become Democratic?', *Political Science Quarterly*, 99, 193–218.

—— 1991. *The Third Wave. Democratization in the Late Twentieth Century*, Norman, University of Oklahoma Press.

Hutton, W. 1995. 'Myth that Sets the World to Right', *Guardian*, 12 June.

Hyden, G. 1983. *No Shortcuts to Progress. African Development Management in Perspective*, Berkeley, University of California Press.

ILO (International Labour Office). 1989–90. *Yearbook of Labour Statistics*, Geneva, International Labour Office.

—— 1994. *World Labour Report 1994*, Geneva, ILO.

Inoguchi, T. 1995. 'A View from Pacific Asia', in H.-H. Holm and G. Sørensen (eds), *Whose World Order?*, London, Westview, 119–36.

Jackson, R. 1990. *Quasi-states: Sovereignty, International Relations and the Third World*, Cambridge, Cambridge University Press.

Joseph, R. 1993 'The Christian Churches and Democracy in Contemporary Africa', in J. Witte, jr. (ed.), *Christianity and Democracy in Global Context*, Boulder, Colo., Westview, 231–47.

Kamrava, M. 1993. *Politics and Society in the Third World*, London, Routledge.

Kasfir, N. 1976. *The Shrinking Political Arena*, Berkeley, University of California Press.

Kaviraj, S. 1991. 'On State, Society and Discourse in India', in J. Manor (ed.), *Rethinking Third World Politics*, Harlow, Longman, 72–99.

Khan, S. 1988. *The Fifty Percent: Women in Development and Policy in Bangladesh*, Dhaka, Dhaka University Press.

King, A. Y. C. 1993. 'A Nonparadigmatic Search for Democracy in Post-Confucian Culture: The Case of Taiwan, R. O. C.', in L. Diamond (ed.), *Political Culture and Democracy in Developing Countries*, Boulder, Colo., Lynne Rienner, 139–62.

Kothari, R. 1993. 'Masses, Classes and the State', in P. Wignaraja (ed.), *New Social Movements in the South*, London, Zed Books, 59–75.

Lane, J.-E., and Ersson, S. 1994. *Comparative Politics. An Introduction and New Approach*, Cambridge, Polity.

Lemerchand, R. 1992. 'Uncivil States and Civil Societies: How Illusion Became Reality', *Journal of Modern African Studies*, 30/2, 177–91.

Leonard, H. J. et al. 1989. *Environment and the Poor: Development Strategies for a Common Agenda*, New Brunswick, NJ, Transaction Books.

Lewis, P. 1992. 'Political Transition and the Dilemma of Civil Society in Africa', *Journal of International Affairs*, 46/1, 31–54.

Lipset, S. M. 1963. 'Economic Development and Democracy', in S. M. Lipset (ed.), *Political Man*, Garden City, N.Y., Anchor, 27–63.

Magdoff, H. 1986. 'Third World Debt: Past and Present', *Monthly Review*, 38, 1–13.

Mamdani, M., Mkandawire, T., and Wamba-dia-Wamba, E. 1993. 'Social Movements and Democracy in Africa', in P. Wignaraja (ed.), *New Social Movements in the South*, London, Zed Books, 100–19.

Manor, J. 1991. 'introduction' to J. Manor (ed.), *Rethinking Third World Politics*, Harlow, Longman, 1–11.

Marchand, M. 1994. 'Gender and New Regionalism in Latin America', *Third World Quarterly*, 15/1, 63–76.

—— and Parpart, J. (eds) 1995. *Feminism/Postmodernism/Development*, London, Routledge.

Migdal, J. 1988. *Strong Societies and Weak States. State–Society Relations and State Capabilities in the Third World*, Princeton, NJ, Princeton University Press.

Miller, M. 1995. *The Third World in Global Environmental Politics*, Buckingham, Open University Press.

Mitchell, N., and McCormick, J. 1988. 'Economic and Political Explanations of Human Rights Violation', *World Politics*, 40/4, 476–98.

Mitra, S. (ed.) 1990. *The Post-Colonial State in Asia*, Hemel Hempstead, Wheatsheaf.

Mouzelis, N. 1986. *Politics in the Semi-Periphery*, London, Macmillan.

Mullin, J. 1994. 'Trinidad's Islamic Rebel Awaits Final Verdict', *Guardian*, 13 June.

Naanen, B. 1995. 'Oil-Producing Minorities and the Restructuring of Nigerian Federalism: The Case of the Ogoni People', *Journal of Commonwealth and Comparative Politics*, 33/1, 46–78.

Nkrumah, K. 1965. *Neo-colonialism: The Last Stage of Capitalism*, London, Thomas Nelson.

O'Donnell, G. 1973. *Modernization and Bureaucratic Authoritarianism*, Berkeley, Calif., Institute of International Studies.

—— Schmitter, P., and Whitehead, L. (eds) 1986. *Transitions from Authoritarian Rule: Prospects for Democracy*, Baltimore, Johns Hopkins University Press.

Omvedt, G. 1994. 'Peasants, Dalits and Women: Democracy and India's New Social Movements', *Journal of Contemporary Asia*, 24/1, 35–48.

Owen, R. 1992. *State, Power and Politics in the Making of the Modern Middle East*, London, Routledge.

Panikkar, R. 1982. 'Is the Notion of Human Rights a Western Concept?', *Diogenes* 120, 75–102.

Parekh, B. 1993. 'The Cultural Particularity of Liberal Democracy', in D. Held (ed.), *Prospects for Democracy*, Cambridge, Polity, 156–75.

Parpart, J. 1988. 'Women and the State in Africa', in D. Rothchild and N. Chazan (eds), *The Precarious Balance. State and Society in Africa*, Boulder, Colo., Westview, 208–30.

Payne, T. 1988. 'Multi-Party Politics in Jamaica', in V. Randall (ed.), *Political Parties in the Third World*, London, Sage, 135–54.

Peluso, N. L. 1993. 'Coercing Conservation: The Politics of State Resource Control', in R. Lipschutz and K. Conca (eds), *The State and Social Power in Global Environmental Politics*, New York, Columbia University Press, 46–70.

Pendle, G. 1976. *A History of Latin America*, Harmondsworth, Penguin.

Philip, G. 1993. 'The New Economic Liberalism and Democracy in Latin America: Friends or Enemies?', *Third World Quarterly*, 14/3, 555–72.

Pinkney, R. 1993. *Democracy in the Third World*, Buckingham, Open University Press.

Pool, J., and Stamos, S. 1985. 'The Uneasy Calm: Third World Debt – The Case of Mexico', *Monthly Review*, 36, 7–19.

Potter, D. 1993. 'Democratization in Asia', in D. Held (ed.), *Prospects for Democracy*, Cambridge, Polity, 355–79.

Pye, L. 1985. *Asian Power and Politics: The Cultural Dimension of Authority*, Cambridge, Mass., Harvard University Press.

Rai, S. 1994. 'Towards Empowerment of South Asian Women', *Third World Quarterly*, 15/3, 532–4.

Randall, V. (ed.) 1988. *Political Parties in the Third World*, London, Sage.

Randall, V., and Theobald, R. 1985. *Political Change and Underdevelopment. A Critical Introduction to Third World Politics*, London, Macmillan.

Remmer, K. 1993. 'Democratization in Latin America', in R. Slater, B. Schutz and S. Dorr (eds), *Global Transformation and the Third World*, Boulder, Colo., Lynne Rienner, 91–112.

Reuter (News Agency). 1995. 'Women's Conference Attacked', *Guardian*, 23 Aug.

Reveyrand-Coulon, O. 1993. 'Les Enoncés Féminins de l'Islam', in J.-F. Bayart (ed.), *Religion and Modernité Politique en Afrique Noire*, Karthala, Paris, 63–100.

Rich, B. 1990. 'The Emperor's New Clothes: The World Bank and Environmental Reform', *World Policy Journal*, Spring, 305–29.

Rizvi, G. 1995. 'South Asia and the New World Order', in H.-H. Holm and G. Sørensen (eds), *Whose World Order?*, Boulder, Colo., Westview, 69–88.

Robertson, R. 1992. *Globalization: Social Theory and Global Culture*, London, Sage.

Robison, R. 1988. 'Authoritarian States, Capital-Owning Classes, and the Politics of Newly Industrialising Countries: The Case of Indonesia', *World Politics*, 26, 52–74.

Rodney, W. 1972. *How Europe Underdeveloped Africa*, London, Bogle l'Ouverture.

Roniger, L., and Günes-Ayata, A. (eds) 1994. *Democracy, Clientelism, and Civil Society*, Boulder, Colo., Lynne Rienner.

Rostow, W. 1959. *The Stages of Economic Growth. A Non-Communist Manifesto*, Cambridge, Cambridge University Press.

Rudolph, S. 1987. 'State Formation in Asia – Prolegemon to a Comparative Study', *Journal of Asian Studies*, 46/4, 731–46.

Rueschemeyer, D., Stephens, E., and Stephens, J. 1992. *Capitalist Development and Democracy*, Cambridge, Polity.

Sabbagh, R. 1994. 'Jordanian Women Pay the Violent Price of Traditional Male "Honour" ', *Guardian*, 28 Dec.

Safa, H. 1990. 'Women and Social Movements in Latin America', *Gender and Society*, 14/4, 354–69.

Sahliyeh, E. (ed.) 1990. 'introduction' to E. Sahliyeh (ed.), *Religious Resurgence and Politics in the Contemporary World*, Albany, State University of New York Press, 1–20.

Saif, W. 1994. 'Human Rights and Islamic Revivalism', *Islam and Christian–Muslim Relations*, 5/1, 57–66.

Sanneh, L. 1991. 'Religion and Politics: Third World Perspectives on a Comparative Theme', *Daedalus*, 120/3, 203–18.

Scott, N. 1995a. 'Argentines Strike against Job Cuts', *Guardian*, 11 Aug.

—— 1995b. 'Mexico Blazes Path to Ruin', *Guardian*, 14 Jan.

Sethi, H. 1993. 'Survival and Democracy: Ecological Struggles in India', in

P. Wignaraja (ed.), *New Social Movements in the South*, London, Zed Books, 122–48.

Shenon, P. 1995. ' "Islamic bombers" Linked to Philippines Raid', *Guardian*, 10 Apr.

Shepherd, G. 1981. 'Transnational Development of Human Rights: The Third World Crucible', in V. Nanda, J. Scaritt and G. Shepherd (eds), *Global Human Rights: Public Policies, Comparative Measures and NGO Strategies*, Boulder, Colo., Westview, 213–18.

Shin, D. C. 1994. 'On the Third Wave of Democratization. A Synthesis and Evaluation of Recent Theory and Research', *World Politics*, 47/3, 135–70.

Sigmund, P. 1993. 'Christian Democracy, Liberation Theology, and Political Culture in Latin America', in L. Diamond (ed.), *Political Culture and Democracy in Developing Countries*, Boulder, Colo., Lynne Rienner, 329–46.

Sikkink, K. 1993. 'Human Rights, Principled Issue Networks and Sovereignty in Latin America', *International Organization*, 47/3, 411–41.

Sisson, R. 1993. 'Culture and Democratization in India', in L. Diamond (ed.), *Political Culture and Democracy in Developing Countries*, Boulder, Colo., Lynne Rienner, 37–66.

Skocpol, T. 1985. 'Bringing the State Back In: Strategies of Analysis in Current Research', in P. Evans, D. Rueschemeyer and T. Skocpol (eds), *Bringing the State Back In*, Cambridge, Cambridge University Press, 3–37.

Smith, T. 1985. 'Requiem or New Agenda for Third World Studies?', *World Politics*, 37, 532–61.

So, A. 1990. *Social Change and Development*, London, Sage.

Sparr, P. 1994. 'Feminist Critiques of Structural Adjustment', in P. Sparr (ed.), *Mortgaging Women's Lives*, London, United Nations/Zed Books, 20–35.

Spybey, T. 1992. *Social Change, Development and Dependency*, Cambridge, Polity.

Stiefel, M., and Wolfe, M. 1994. *A Voice for the Excluded*, London, Zed Books.

Sweezy, P., and Magdoff, H. 1984. 'The Two Faces of Third World Debt: A Fragile Financial Environment and Debt Enslavement', *Monthly Review*, 35, 1–10.

Thomas, A. et al. 1994. *Third World Atlas*, 2nd edn, Buckingham, Open University Press.

Thompson, M. 1993. 'The Limits of Democratisation in ASEAN', *Third World Quarterly*, 14/3, 469–84.

Timberlake, L. 1985. *Africa in Crisis*, London, Earthscan.

Tomasevski, K. 1988. *Foreign Aid and Humna Rights: Case Studies of Bangladesh and Kenya*, Copenhagen, Danish Centre of Human Rights.

Tran, M. 1994. 'World Bank Sees Nepal Project as Test of Credibility', *Guardian*, 17 Nov.

UNDP (United Nations Development Programme). 1994. Human Development Report 1994, Oxford, Oxford University Press for the UNDP.

UNRISD (United Nations Research Institute for Social Development). 1995. *States of Disarray*, Geneva, UNRISD.

Vidal, J. 1995. 'Nepalese Hail Move to Scrap Huge Dam', *Guardian*, 5 Aug.

Vincent, R. J. 1986. *Human Rights and International Relations*, Cambridge, Cambridge University Press.

Vogler, J. 1992. 'Regimes and the Global Commons: Space, Atmosphere and Oceans', in A. McGrew and P. Lewis et al., *Global Politics*, Cambridge, Polity, 118–37.

von der Mehden, F. 1989a. 'The Philippines', in S. Mews (ed.), *Religion in Politics*, Harlow, Longman, 215–18.

—— 1989b. 'Thailand', in S. Mews (ed.), *Religion in Politics*, Harlow, Longman, 265.

Wade, L. L., and Kim, B. S. 1978. *Economic Development of South Korea*, London, Praeger.

Walker, M. 1995. 'How the Existing Consensus on Foreign Policy Goals is Collapsing', *Guardian*, 21 Feb.

Waylen, G. 1993. 'Women's Movements and Democratisation in Latin America', *Third World Quarterly*, 14/3, 573–87.

White, G., Murray, R., and White, C. 1983. *Revolutionary Socialist Development in the Third World*, Brighton, Wheatsheaf.

Whitehead, L. 1993. 'The Alternatives to "Liberal Democracy": A Latin American Perspective', in D. Held (ed.), *Prospects for Democracy*, Cambridge, Polity, 312–29.

Wiebe, V. 1989. 'Jamaica', in S. Mews (ed.), *Religion in Politics*, Harlow, Longman, 141.

Wignaraja, P. 1993. 'Rethinking Development and Democracy', in P. Wignaraja (ed.), *New Social Movements in the South*, London, Zed Books, 4–35.

Witte, J. jr. 1993. 'introduction' to J. Witte, jr. (ed), *Christianity and Democracy in Global Context*, Boulder, Colo., Westview, 1–20.

Woollacott, M. 1994. 'A Mad World of Rambos', *Guardian*, 15 Nov.

World Bank. 1990. *Bangladesh: Strategies for Enhancing the Role of Women in Economic Development*, Washington, DC, World Bank.

—— 1991. *World Development Report 1991*, New York, Oxford University Press.

—— 1995. *World Development Report 1995*, Oxford, Oxford University Press.

Index

Note: page references in *italic* locate information in the notes, references in **bold** are to information in tables.